The Gothic World of Anne Rice

DATE DUE

GAYLORD   PRINTED IN U.S.A.

The Gothic World of Anne Rice

edited by

Gary Hoppenstand and Ray B. Browne

Bowling Green State University Popular Press
Bowling Green, OH 43403

Library of Congress Cataloging-in-Publication Data
The Gothic world of Anne Rice / edited by Gary Hoppenstand and Ray
  B. Browne.
        p.   cm.
        Includes bibliographical references.
        ISBN 0-87972-707-1. -- ISBN 0-87972-708-X (pbk.)
        1. Rice, Anne, 1941-   --Criticism and interpretation. 2. Women
and literature--United States--History--20th century. 3. Fantastic fiction,
American--History and criticism. 4. Horror tales, American--History
and criticism. 5. Gothic revival (Literature)--United States. 6. Witch-
craft in literature. 7. Vampires in literature. 8. Mummies in literature.
I. Hoppenstand, Gary. II. Browne, Ray Broadus.
PS3568.I265Z68 1996
813'.54--dc20   96-20467
                                                                      CIP

Contents

Introduction

Vampires, Witches, Mummies, and Other Charismatic Personalities: Exploring the Anne Rice Phenomenon

Gary Hoppenstand and Ray B. Browne

Anne Rice's immensely popular horror fiction attracts both the academic reader and the general reader with equal ease. During the past several years, for example, no other writer of popular horror fiction has drawn as much academic attention at the national Popular Culture Association conference meetings as has Anne Rice. Typically, at least one entire panel of scholarly essays is offered annually on Rice's gothic fiction, and these presentations are always well attended. In fact, a number of the articles appearing in this collection originated as papers delivered at one of these PCA conference panels. Such scholarly interest indicates that her best-selling gothic novels draw the highly educated, the academically oriented, or those who recognize in her fiction evidence of sophisticated characterization and intricate plotting. These readers also identify in her gothic fiction numerous allusions to other great works of literature, ranging from Horace Walpole's seminal gothic tale *The Castle of Otranto* (1764), to Ann Radcliffe's massive gothic romances such as *The Mysteries of Udolpho* (1794), to, of course, Bram Stoker's masterpiece, *Dracula* (1897). As are the finest contemporary authors of popular horror fiction—such as Clive Barker, Robert R. McCammon, and Stephen King—Rice is faithful to the gothic tradition and honors that tradition in her own work. The erudite reader, well versed in bookish knowledge, appreciates and, as evidenced by the academic participation at the national Popular Culture Association conference, obviously responds enthusiastically to Rice's skilled incorporation of traditional literary themes in her best-selling gothic novels.

But Rice is not just the darling of the ivory-tower intelligentsia. Her fiction is not mere slavish imitation of the efforts of past masters of the gothic form. Her most popular novels, such as *Interview with the Vampire* (1976) and *The Witching Hour* (1990), though situated within the gothic narrative tradition, go far beyond the conventions of the formula and explore important contemporary social issues. Her other major audience, the "mainstream" reader, is perhaps best represented by the gathering at an Anne Rice book-signing engagement held in the Lansing, Michigan, area. What quickly became evident to anyone witnessing this event was how untypical the typical Rice aficionado is. There was in attendance at this signing that unique assembly of young people—clothed entirely in black and sporting "alternative" hairstyles and jewelry—who had apparently adopted Rice's *Vampire Chronicles* series as a fashion statement. But interspersed among this group were baby boomers, conservatively clad, as well as a considerable number of older readers. The immediate conclusion to be drawn from the assemblage of this otherwise disparate congregation is that Rice enjoys a tremendously wide appeal, one that transcends the traditional appeal of the horror genre. Rice seems to attract those readers who perhaps otherwise don't read horror fiction. In this sense, her allure is like Stephen King's—both authors entice numerous mainstream readers, enough to push each newly published novel to the top of the best-seller lists. The question, then, to be asked regarding the Anne Rice phenomenon is, What is there in Rice's gothic fiction that makes her novels so immensely popular?

An answer to this question can be found in the horror genre's recent past. Since the publication of Ira Levin's *Rosemary's Baby* (1967), contemporary best-selling horror fiction has incorporated domestic issues (such social factors as child abuse and marital violence) as part of its narrative focus. In his introduction to a recent edition of *Rosemary's Baby*, Levin states, "I'm not a believer—in witchcraft or any other religion. *Rosemary's Baby* isn't really about witchcraft at all, as its editor, the late great Lee Wright used to say—it's about motherhood" (i). Two of Levin's more commercially successful contemporaries, Thomas Tryon and William Peter Blatty, also deal with the theme of children-as-victims in their most popular horror novels, *The Other* (1971) and *The Exorcist* (1971) respectively. What makes Stephen King's finest horror novels, such as *The Shining* (1977), so effectively horrifying is his portrayal of unrelenting or menacing violence directed against children and women. For King, the supernatural pyrotechnics in his fiction are mere window-dressing, more or less; the representation of *true* evil, as King well knows, is the battered child or the victimized wife. Other best-selling horror fiction authors, such as John Saul and V.C. Andrews, have based their entire literary careers on the use of domestic themes in their work.

Part of Rice's own great success, then, might be explained by her expert combination of the prosaic with the fantastic in her horror novels. At first glance, Rice's gothic fiction holds the same attraction for us as does television soap opera. Such an observation is certainly not meant to denigrate Rice's artistic skills. Quite the contrary, it is instead intended to illustrate Rice's ability to craft stories featuring characters who, on the one hand, are very similar to us, but who, on the other hand, are decidedly unlike us. These characters are, simultaneously, better than we are and worse than we are. Rice's elegant monsters, such as the vampire Lestat or the immortal Ramses, are appealing because they embody such strikingly contrasting personality traits.

Ramses, for example, the protagonist featured in *The Mummy, or Ramses the Damned* (1989), is handsome, charming, and intelligent. He possesses an animal-like attraction for the opposite sex (all of those qualities that can be found in the standard television soap-opera idol). And if these attributes aren't enough, Ramses is also immortal. He has lived for thousands of years, and no naturally occurring disease or human-directed violence can destroy him. He is a type of "reverse" vampire who, instead of being destroyed by sunlight, gains his strength and vitality from exposure to the sun. He is god-like, nearly all-powerful. Yet Ramses the Great is also called Ramses the Damned. His gift of immortality brings with it a terrible responsibility. Ramses's dark curse is to forever guard his knowledge of the elixir that gave him eternal life. If this knowledge were to be stolen from him, the chaos resulting from a world inhabited by immortals would be apocalyptic. Ramses is more powerful than we mortals, Rice suggests to us in her novel, but his is a power that brings with it severe limitations. In addition, Ramses's ardent fascination with Queen Cleopatra (who is one of the real monsters of Rice's story) reveals a flawed personality trait. Despite his ageless knowledge, Ramses's reviving of Cleopatra's corpse is a blatantly stupid mistake. His passion, which is his one great weakness, overcomes his reason. His pursuit of this notorious *femme fatale* directly leads to other people's deaths. Rice makes it abundantly clear in *The Mummy* that even though Ramses is in many ways superior to us both physically and intellectually, his fatal error in judgment (i.e., his all-too-human blunder) is designed to make us feel superior to him.

Rice herself argues the point that her supernatural characters are intended to represent the human (rather than the inhuman) condition. In a brief introduction entitled "A Message from Anne Rice" featured in the recent video release of the 1994 blockbuster film, *Interview with the Vampire*, Rice provides an unqualified endorsement of the film. The reason for this endorsement stems, for the most part, from Rice's highly publicized criticism of the producers' selection of Tom Cruise to play the role of the vampire Lestat. Rice's vocal criticism early during the film's production, and her subsequent public recanting of that criticism after she viewed the film, actually increased the flame of publicity already surrounding the movie (as the truism states, "there is no such thing in Hollywood as bad publicity"). Indeed, the initial controversy between Rice and the film's producers, in retrospect, is really nothing more than an interesting production footnote to an otherwise commercially successful horror film.

What is of more interest in Rice's endorsement, especially to those of us intrigued with the philosophy behind her work, is her statement that the supernatural vampire characters portrayed in the film are, in actuality, very much like us. Rice proclaims this in her interview not once but twice. This particular revelation, a point that Rice herself insists we understand about her work, provides an important key to our approaching Rice's artistic design in her popular horror fiction. Lestat himself echoes this sentiment in the prologue to *Memnoch the Devil* (1995) by stating, "We have souls, you and I. We want to know things; we share the same earth, rich and verdant and fraught with perils. We don't—either of us—know what it means to die, no matter what we might say to the contrary" (4). Rice wants her stories to be not an escape from reality but a venture into reality. Her gothic tales featuring charismatic vampires, witches, and mummies are intentionally constructed as a mirror displaying our own prosaic life. Rice intends her writing to be an imaginative fictional metaphor representing our everyday reality. The vampire Louis's quest for a deeper meaning to his macabre existence in *Interview with the Vampire*, Rice would like us to understand, is but a reflection of our own sometimes fruitless quest for life's meaning. Rowan Mayfair's search for her personal identity in *The Witching Hour* is but a reflection of our own need for a connection to our family heritage that defines who we are. Ramses's desire for love and respect in *The Mummy* is but a reflection of our own desire for these indispensable, yet often elusive, human requirements.

If Rice's gothic fiction reveals to us stories about our own lives clothed in sophisticated allusion, symbolism, and metaphor, it also then suggests a larger social function, a more fundamental plan. Obviously, popular horror fiction should be most concerned with entertainment; that is its purpose. But a handful of contemporary authors working in the horror genre—like Anne Rice—perceive in its otherwise predictable narrative structures a means by which a larger, more interesting cultural mythology can be developed. Indeed, with the appearance of each new novel, Rice is creating, refining, and embellishing her invented mythology. For her, the process of mythmaking—of inventing a literary universe that postulates a new way of examining reality—better expresses those things she finds important to discuss in her writings. These areas include the mystical relationship in our lives between life and death and the larger moral definitions of good and evil.

Yet, Rice's writing is also a deeply intimate personal expression. It is even cathartic. In "Interview with the 'Vampire' Author," published in the October 22, 1994 *TV Guide,* Rice explains to her interviewer Merle Ginsberg:

I know my dark periods, and, as a writer, I've learned to ride them out. Darkness never really goes away once you've seen it. You learn to see the light in the darkness. In fact, once you've seen the darkness, the light is brighter. Writing is my way of working it. It's what dancing is to a dancer. (26)

Anne Rice has recently published her sixteenth book, *Memnoch the Devil,* which quickly climbed to the number one spot on the national best-seller lists. In this, her most recent work, Rice returns to *The Vampire Chronicles* that brought her national recognition with the appearance in 1976 of her first novel, *Interview with the Vampire.* Nearly twenty years separate the publications of these two books, the first novel and the fifth novel in the series respectively, a period that witnessed two significant events: the emergence of the horror story as a best-selling genre and Anne Rice's rise to national prominence as one of the most commercially successful authors of popular horror fiction.

Memnoch the Devil will, no doubt, become an important milestone in Rice's ongoing development as a serious (and popular) novelist. Interestingly, her book's initial critical reception, however, has been mixed. A number of reviewers have attacked Rice's novel because, for the most part, it is unlike her earlier vampire fiction. One newspaper reviewer (who echoed the sentiments of many other reviewers) proclaimed that the beginning of *Memnoch the Devil* was the only redeeming feature to be found in Rice's story. The reviewer liked the part of the narrative where Lestat stalks and kills the urbane art collector/drug dealer named Roger, no doubt because these early chapters read like traditional horror fiction. This specific example illustrates a larger problem with Rice's horror fiction. When Rice's story meets the critics' formulaic expectations, they enjoy what they see, but when she moves her plot away from conventional expectations into a different, more abstract philosophical area, they find fault with her efforts. This mixed critical reception has failed to harm the novel's enormous popularity with the readers. However, it reveals both the artistic limitations of the horror novel in the eyes of the critics and the difficulty Rice faces in her attempt to transform horror formula into mythology, an attempt that has won approval from her readers as demonstrated by the book's fantastic commercial success.

Memnoch the Devil is the culmination of Rice's movement in her fiction toward myth making. Employing the narrative frame of the gothic horror story, she departs from genre conventions early in the novel and develops what essentially amounts to a theological dialogue between the vampire Lestat and that notorious fallen angel who has been called a variety of names during the course of human history (including Satan, meaning "accuser") but who prefers to be known as Memnoch. Memnoch attempts to involve Lestat in his quest and his curse: the salvation of human souls trapped in Sheol. Lestat's journeys to Heaven and to Hell, guided by Memnoch, literally allow Rice to reconstruct Judaism/Christianity, which she does in an amazingly complex and sophisticated fashion. Her visions of God, the Devil, and a morally evolving humanity are strikingly as well as meticulously described. Her grand achievement in *Memnoch the Devil* is the writing of a modern-day *Divine Comedy*. Interestingly, however, her most hostile critics don't recognize in her novel this marvelous accomplishment. (We have not read one review thus far in the popular press that has identified this important literary connection.) After all, as every critic-in-good-standing for *Entertainment Weekly* or *People* knows, popular horror fiction is only done well if it provides a cheap thrill, a visceral rush. If anything other than a "quick fix" of fear appears in Rice's gothic writing, some of her reviewers yammer that something has gone dreadfully wrong with her story. Rice has lost her "edge," these reviewers proclaim. Her latest vampire novel is disappointing, they argue, and, because of their own ignorance of the important history of genre, they miss entirely her point in her novel.

For Rice, in *Memnoch the Devil* horror elements are secondary to the novel's unusual theology. This is a book about religion, salvation, and personal confession. Rice shows us that God's compassion for humanity has been forced by the iconoclastic archangel, Memnoch, and that compassion itself, as a virtue, is something that has to be achieved. Regarding Memnoch's ongoing debate with God about mercy, Rice's novel also echoes John Milton's religious epic *Paradise Lost*, paralleling Milton's poetic dramatization of the origins of good and evil in a Christian world. Rice understands that the world's best horror stories are the most venerable, such as Dante's *Inferno*. Despite attacks by reviewers, readers have connected with Rice's story and have made *Memnoch the Devil* a national best-seller.

Memnoch the Devil is the fulfillment of Rice's revision of classic horror literature themes. She states in Teresa Simmons's interview, "The Queen of the Chroniclers," appearing in *The Vampire Companion*:

I think *The Body Thief* [the fourth novel in *The Vampire Chronicles*] is attempting something a little more difficult, a little finer perhaps—a truthful statement about honesty and art in the entire Chronicles which needed to be said. *The Body Thief* tries to come to terms with the lies in the Chronicles. Evil is, after all, evil. It is not beautiful, really. In sum, I feel the new book is more like *Interview with the Vampire*—a deep dark debate on salvation and damnation, on truth and personal ruthlessness—how far each of us is willing to go to be happy, to achieve excitement, to feel alive. And surely it is a window into a character's dark and tormented and very human soul. (4)

   Much in Rice's popular horror fiction, in fact, harkens back to its ancient gothic lineage. Rice's sometimes controversial use of sex and violence in her stories has several distant literary ancestors. The same gothic horror formula Rice uses so effectively in her novels *Interview with the Vampire* and *The Witching Hour* can be traced to Horace Walpole's *The Castle of Otranto*, the short novel that basically invented the gothic story and that remained the dominant type of horror fiction for over fifty years, reaching its apex in Matthew Gregory Lewis's *The Monk: A Romance* (1796) and in Charles Robert Maturin's *Melmoth the Wanderer* (1820). In the typical gothic story from this period, human will is subverted by Fate (with a capital F). The castle is the genre's dominant symbol, its hidden passages and dark chambers often embodying repressed, irrational emotions or perverse sexual urges. Irrationality, in fact, in the gothic story subsumes the individual's rational will. The supernatural controls and subverts the world of nature. Personified evil (both psychological and supernatural) exists side by side with mere mortals and influences the mortal sphere. Nightmares reside in the real world, possessing substance and vitality, and they portend disaster when social or sexual taboos are violated. Rice's own gothic efforts are certainly defined—in part, at least—by this literary heritage.

   The traditional gothic narrative has always been a subversive literature, shocking its audience by attacking established social conventions, and Rice continues this practice in her own work. Pornographic images function as a subtext in much of her gothic fiction. In her Sleeping Beauty series, the pornography intent is overt. Yet, Rice's use of sexuality to challenge middle-class values was also a motif found in Walpole's and Lewis's "scandalous" gothic novels. In her best work, Rice does what Clive Barker does in writing horror fiction: blending what has worked successfully in the past as formula with a very personal, contemporary voice that engages important modern-day issues.

   Rice also has borrowed from two additional thematic traditions that originated in the gothic tale. The publication of several important early gothic novels not only split the horror genre into other formula categories but also established totally new genres in the process. The first of these gothic novels, *Vathek* (published in an English version in 1786) by William Beckford, reads like a pastiche of an Arabian fairy tale, mimicking and emphasizing exotic and grotesque elements found in Middle Eastern folk legends. Indeed, Beckford's short novel may be considered one of the first examples of modern fantasy. Rice's own gothic fiction (such as *The Mummy* and *Memnoch the Devil*), like Beckford's, is more fantasy than horror. Traditional horror motifs in these two novels generally are not to be found: there are relatively few killings, and suspense is emphasized in these stories in place of what Stephen King would call the "gross-out."

The second important novel to divert from Walpole's original gothic model was Ann Radcliffe's *The Mysteries of Udolpho*. Basically, Radcliffe retained Walpole's gothic setting featuring the castle or mansion in her variant of the gothic narrative. She also retained the victimized gothic heroine character, but she eliminated the overtly supernatural narrative elements found in Walpole's novel, replacing these with suspense. Radcliffe seduced her reader into thinking that the supernatural might intrude at any moment into her plot, but it never actually did. What appeared to be supernatural instead had a rational explanation. Radcliffe replaced Walpole's use of supernatural horror in the gothic with romantic suspense, and thus she was the founder of both the gothic romance formula in the horror genre and the new, separate genre of romance fiction. In addition, Radcliffe expanded the length of the gothic narrative. She helped to make fashionable the "triple-decker" novel (that is, the lengthy novel published in several volumes). Romance is also an important element in Rice's gothic fiction, as perhaps best illustrated in *The Witching Hour*, and it frequently dominates the action in a number of her stories.

Rice's updating of the Ann Radcliffe gothic variant, however, possesses a decidedly contemporary twist in novels such as *Interview with the Vampire* and *The Vampire Lestat* through her use of homosexual eroticism. Rice's vampires are, in a sense, symbolic of an open-minded attitude about sexual mores. Regarding her view of sexuality as a type of social expression in her fiction, Rice says in Kenneth W. Holditch's interview in the October 1989 issue of *Lear's,* "Pornography is literature intended to sexually arouse the reader and I think it's completely legitimate to write it. It's sad that good writers have not explored this side of the imagination. I don't see anything wrong with literature devoted to sex, anymore than cookbooks are bad because they're devoted to food" (89). "We can found a code of morality on ethics," Rice continues later in the same interview, "rather than outmoded religious concepts. We can base our sexual mores on ethics rather than on religious beliefs" (155). Just as Rice's supernatural characters are not bound by mortal definitions of rationality or science, they are also not bound by mortal definitions of proscribed sexual conduct. Lestat, for example, is powerful because he is a supernatural "creature of the night" (to borrow a cliché from Hollywood) and because his masculinity is not limited by conventional gender-role expectations. "I really see the vampires as transcending gender," Rice states in a March 1993 *Playboy* interview conducted by Digby Diehl: "If you make them [vampires] absolutely straight or gay, you limit the material. They can be either one. They have a polymorphous sexuality. They see everything as beautiful" (60).

As the following collection of essays will demonstrate, the appeal of Anne Rice's gothic fiction is as wide as is the breadth of her singular achievement as a popular novelist. Along with Stephen King, Dean Koontz, and Clive Barker, she is among a small number of horror authors whose stories have successfully crossed media boundaries. Her tales of vampires, witches, and mummies have demonstrated commercial mastery of a diverse collection of media, including not only print best-sellers but also comic book and film adaptations. In a genre dominated in recent years by male writers, Rice has proved herself a force to be reckoned with. Although infrequently granting interviews, she has nonetheless made herself accessible to her legion of fans by her numerous book-signing engagements and has thus made herself a public figure to those whom she considers most important—her readers. Rice, in fact, has become an icon of the horror genre. Like Stephen King, her work has achieved a type of "brand name" status that continues to flourish with the release of each new novel. Indeed, the current Anne Rice phenomenon is not only alive and thriving, but the prospect for its continuing prosperity appears strong as well.

In this insightful collection of studies of Rice's works, Katherine Ramsland begins by tracing the circuitous route of a troubled person who always considers herself an outsider trying to work her way toward the inside accepted body of society. But Rice is simply too large for one body, one person. Consequently, she has taken her troubled personality and tried to use it to explore the limits of human truth. She likes best to be clothed in words. In this guise she has searched through all kinds of novels and is still the seeker. Rice thinks that perhaps, as Ramsland says, as long as she is searching for philosophical truth, for meaning, "she believes she can express the ideas and themes that are meaningful to her in whatever framework she chooses." To her millions of fans the most effective framework is the exotic erotic.

Rice's search for truth parallels that of anthropologists in their seeking to understand the influence on people and society of both nature and nurture. She questions both but especially challenges the artificiality of cultural construction. At her best she becomes the anthropologist, who, as Frank A. Salamone says in his study "The Anthropological Vision of Anne Rice," understands "the ambiguity of 'reality,' the relativity of good and evil, the role of perspective in understanding and interpretation, the interaction of nature and nurture, and the conflict and dependence of humanism and science." And she does all this in a way that teaches her many readers. Such accomplishments are rewarding to both author and audience.

To Garyn G. Roberts in his study "Gothicism, Vampirism, and Seduction: Anne Rice's 'The Master of Rampling Gate'" another evidence of Rice's creative genius is her ability to turn from the rich creative voluptuousness of her powerful long novels to the ordinary commonplace in her short stories, and in them, to craft masterpieces. In fact, though it may be difficult to theorize convincingly, many authors recognize that the short story, because of its constraints and limitations, is more difficult to write than the more expansive novel. Rice does each well. According to Roberts, her "The Master of Rampling Gate" is "a classic of modern fiction."

In "Development of the Byronic Vampire: Byron, Stoker, Rice" Kathryn McGinley reminds those of us who wonder why the vampire's attraction is so overwhelming that such dead-living bloodsuckers seem to have existed from the beginning of the human race. The attraction is in the DNA. Yet the two outstanding authors of such literature—as far as Rice has been concerned—are Byron and Bram Stoker (and now for us, Anne Rice). Each created vampires that reflected and served their societies. Vampires, though immortal, are not unchanging, as Rice's creations demonstrate. Hers are creatures of her imagination and our needs. The needs seem eternal, and the vampire story therefore seems immortal.

The full complexity of Rice's gothic novels is demonstrated by Edward J. Ingebretsen in "Anne Rice: Raising Holy Hell, Harlequin Style." He suggests the novel idea, if we may pause to pun, that Rice's novels are in fact deeply enriched Harlequin romances and they are "imitators of domestic [American] gothic." In so demonstrating, Ingebretsen adds new complexity to our understanding of both the Harlequin romance and Rice's works.

Rice's relentless search for these resolutions is dramatized, as Terri R. Liberman tells us in the next essay, "Eroticism as Moral Fulcrum in Rice's *Vampire Chronicles*," by opposites—life-death, good-evil, love-hate, heterosexuality-homosexuality, innocence–erotic titillation. The tension between these opposites and its release create the impact of Rice's adventures beyond the normal and traditional and take the stories into new fields of exploration for us.

We all know how jealously, and at times blindly, creators of works of art fear having their thoughts adapted to another medium, especially the movie. Rice's fear of what might happen when *Interview with the Vampire* was made into a motion picture was especially acute, particularly in the choice of Tom Cruise for the role of Lestat. But, as Diana C. Reep, Joseph F. Ceccio, and William A. Francis explain in their account of the transformation from novel to film, Rice's fears were premature and proved to be groundless. Contrary to the self-serving saw of most authors, it is possible to make a successful film from a successful novel.

Rice's perceived difficulty with casting Lestat is perhaps clarified in Aileen Chris Shafer's "Let Us Prey: Religious Codes and Rituals in *The Vampire Lestat.*" Rice's interest in Lestat's motivation and actions regarding the metaphysical question of good and evil places readers' sympathy with Lestat instead of his victims as he searches for identity and for meaning in his life. Since his motivations and actions are bisexual instead of heterosexual, Lestat's story poses a new question about gender roles. As a mutant, his sexual, psychological, and philosophical mutation probes new areas of concern for people of our time.

Like most writers, Rice demonstrates that she is serious and wants to be recognized as an author of "literature." And she demonstrates a knowledge and understanding of much more than most critics will allow the successful popular writer. Just how deeply and skillfully she uses the works of other authors—especially H.P. Lovecraft and Robert Bloch—is demonstrated by Joseph F. Ceccio in his essay "Anne Rice's *The Tale of the Body Thief* and the Astral Projection Literary Tradition."

In the next two essays, the authors discuss *Lives of the Mayfair Witches* and several, but not all, of the themes developed there. Ann Larabee turns to one aspect of the heroic—the scientific—and shows how Rice uses it in order to develop her heroic characters and their probings into the meaning of life. In Ellen M. Tsagaris's "'He's not one of them': Michael Curry and the Interpellation of the Self in Anne Rice's *The Witching Hour*" we see how all of Rice's individual developments bend toward her ultimate goal: her sense of belonging and of community, where good triumphs over evil.

That Rice wears several hats in her fiction is detailed by Bette B. Roberts in her essay "The Historical Novels of Anne Rice." But under the different hats the same head and body direct Rice's intentions. In her historical novels, not surprisingly, she duplicates her larger accomplishment. As Roberts says: "The persistent darkness and violence of these fictional worlds challenge the resilience of the human spirit and affirm its capacity for survival."

Rice's works have been influenced not only by writers of vampire and supernatural literature but also by authors such as William Faulkner, Eudora Welty, Flannery O'Connor, Carson McCullers, and others in the Southern gothic tradition. "Characteristic of this style," say Marte Kinlaw and Cynthia Kasee in "Degrees of Darkness: *Gens de Couleur Libre* Ethnic Identity in *The Feast of All Saints*," "is a sense of decay and dissolution, a tension caused by unrevealed secrets and taboos broken, as well as a sense of topicality." One evidence of this interest is Rice's concern with free people of color, especially in *The Feast of All Saints*. Though this work was not well received, in it she opened up a subject of growing interest in society.

With Rice's works saturating the conscious and unconscious public and literary mind, it is little wonder that her influence would extend to TV horror shows, especially *Forever Knight*, a successful CBS cult show. How this influence has resonated is historically outlined by James F. Iaccino in "The World of *Forever Knight:* A Television Tribute to Anne Rice's New Age Vampire," the final essay in this collection.

With this collection of essays the wheel of Anne Rice's creations has turned analytically and revealingly before your psyche. It is a full and complicated wheel, well worthy of our examination. We editors and authors wish full enlightenment and pleasure in the perusal of its revolutions both day and night.

Works Cited

Diehl, Digby. "Playboy Interview: Anne Rice." *Playboy* Mar. 1993: 53-64.

Ginsberg, Merle. "Interview with the 'Vampire' Author." *TV Guide* 22 Oct. 1994: 24-27.

Holditch, W. Kenneth. "Interview with Anne Rice." *Lear's* Oct. 1989: 86+.

Levin, Ira. *Rosemary's Baby*. New York: Armchair Detective Library, 1991.

Rice, Anne. *Memnoch the Devil: The Vampire Chronicles*. New York: Knopf, 1995.

Simmons, Teresa. "The Queen of the Chroniclers." *The Vampire Companion* 1.3 (1992): 3-6.

The Lived World of Anne Rice's Novels

Katherine Ramsland

Her father named her Howard Allen O'Brien. When she was old enough to assert herself, she changed her name several times, calling herself variously Francis, Barbara, Gracie, and Anne. It was the latter that took, and upon her marriage to Stan Rice, she became Anne Rice. It was not the last time she would use a different name. Under two pseudonyms, she has authored five novels, but her greatest fame rides on the two series of books known as *The Vampire Chronicles* and *Lives of the Mayfair Witches,* penned under her own name.

Anne Rice made her publishing debut in 1976 with her first novel, *Interview with the Vampire.* She was thirty-four. Born in New Orleans on October 4, 1941, she lived in this exotic city until she was fifteen. Her father, Howard (yes, he gave her his own name because, as he put it, he didn't like it and thought it better fit for a girl), worked for the post office while Katherine, Anne's mother, set out to raise four daughters as geniuses. Being well-educated for a woman in those times, Katherine aspired to great things. She wanted her children to be brilliant and talented and she instilled in them her belief that they could do anything they set their minds to. This made a strong impression on Anne. "She gave me so many wonderful things," she says about her mother, "but above all, she gave me the belief in myself that I could do great things, that I could do anything I wanted to do. She gave me a sense of limitless power."[1]

Anne was the second of the four girls (she later gained a half sister with her father's second marriage), and Katherine allowed them a great deal of freedom in the household. Her idea of encouraging genius was to allow her children to follow their whims, and through that to discover and support their strengths. If Alice wanted to dance, all the furniture was moved back to see what she could do, or if they wanted to draw, they could draw on the walls. Unfortunately, the family could not afford lessons, so the children often found their ambitions stymied. Thus, they learned to use their imaginations.

Part of Katherine's influence on Anne was her ability to tell detailed stories. She memorized movies and novels word for word and told them to her children. She read poetry to them on a regular basis, introduced

13

them to Dickens (Anne's favorite author), and told them ghost stories. Young Anne often walked past the large deteriorating mansions of New Orleans, peering inside to catch sight of the female ghost with the flaming hair or the Devil himself—said to keep residence there. She wrote about these childhood fantasies in her first published short story, "October 4, 1948."

Along with ghosts, Anne liked the stories of vampires she heard, particularly one that provided the vampire's perspective. Called "Dress of White Silk," by Richard Matheson, it was about a child vampire who fascinated Anne. "I never forgot that story," she says. "I wanted to get into the vampire. I wanted to know what is was like to be the interesting one—the point of view of the person right in the center of it all." Later she saw the movie *Dracula's Daughter* with Gloria Holden and admired the tragic sensuality. Such supernatural images left a deep impression on her and inspired much of her later work. "Writing supernatural fiction feels authentic to me," she affirms. "I don't think there's any moral, psychological, or aesthetic limit to supernatural fiction."

At Katherine's encouragement, Anne and her older sister Alice developed a complex fantasy life for their mutual entertainment. They used plots from Shakespeare that their parents related to them and acted out the various parts. Later, Anne wrote plays in which her other sisters participated, including one called "The Mummy Ghost." She also lost herself in complicated daydreams that often lasted many years. One fantasy involved a contemporary world in which characters developed according to her own interests and grew older as she did. Another daydream was sexual, set in a slave market in ancient Greece. (See Elliott Slater's private fantasy in *Exit to Eden* for details.) Although Anne claims that her dream worlds have little overlap with her books, this early employment of her imagination immersed her in a form of activity that influenced how elaborate her novels later became.

Another aspect of Anne's childhood that impressed itself on her imagination was her healthy sense of the physical world. She liked to be touched and she noticed the finest details in her surroundings. In the humid and colorful city, she exercised her strong sensitivities on the abundance of fragrant flowers, architectural styles, and interesting personalities that she encountered on her long walks to and from school. She also found stimulation in the daily ceremonies of her parochial education.

Raised Catholic, she learned early to envision union with God through the sacrifice of Christ: "You sit there and you imagine what Christ felt as he walked down the street carrying the cross," she recalls, "what the thorns felt like going into his forehead and the nails into his hands. All this meant using your imagination—trying to make the leap into something else. It was natural to come out of that writing the kind of fiction I do. It was filled with sensuality."

She also heard stories about the suffering and transports of the saints, and she favored St. Francis, St. Rose de Lima, St. Teresa of Avila, and St. Therese of the Little Flower. In them she saw the rich spiritual payoff for self-sacrifice and personal agony. "The lives of the saints were very sadomasochistic," she says. "They drove themselves into a state of ecstasy that was erotic." In her own private oratory, made from an unused bathroom in the back of her home on St. Charles Avenue, Anne prayed fervently for the stigmata, the bloody imprint that marked unusual devotion. She wanted to be special in the eyes of God. "Anne's temperament was such," her father said, "that when she embraced something, she had to exercise real restraint not to become a fanatic."

During this period, she decided that she would become a nun. To her mind, the religious experience offered a way to become extraordinary, which was her single-minded goal: "I want to excel at one thing." She later used her memories of this religious fervency to provide thoughts and feelings for the nun, Gretchen, in her fourth vampire novel, *The Tale of the Body Thief*. "[Gretchen] had been deeply religious, reading the lives of the saints and dreaming of being a saint . . . to find a life of all-consuming and heroic work. She'd built a little oratory behind her house when she was a girl, and there she would kneel for hours before the crucifix, hoping that the wounds of Christ would open in her hands and feet" (242-43).

Secretly, Anne was also experiencing strong erotic feelings. Told this was a sin, she wondered if her desires were like those of other children. She felt ashamed over what she later described as masochistic fantasies, and as an author she used this experience to deepen the moral/sexual conflict suffered by her character Lisa in *Exit to Eden*. "I had dark, strange sexual feelings when I was very little," Lisa admits. "I wanted to be touched and I made up fantasies" (193).

Anne simply felt different, set apart from her peers, "more physically *there*." She wanted to fit in but her individuality "was almost irrepressible." To make matters worse, her mother's encouragement to view herself as having unlimited potential came up hard against the expectations of the church. As much as she wished to abide by church standards of goodness and obedience, she resisted what she soon discovered. As a maturing young woman, Anne learned that girls did not receive the same status and privileges as boys, and that to be in a relationship with a boy was to lose some of one's own power. Socially, girls were scorned for the same sexual desires that were tolerated in boys.

Awareness of such gender inequities made her view adolescence as a treacherous period. She had lost something simply because she was female, and as a young woman she was no longer a free spirit. Anne began to grow restless with a faith that stipulated behavior that felt repressive to her. Her confusion and anger from this period flowed into her second novel, *The Feast of All Saints*. Although it is set in antebellum times, the central characters are adolescents whose development into young adults plays havoc with their lives and relationships. For example, the young Marie cannot understand why kissing bears the same mortal penalty as real crimes, and the shame she feels over her arousal erodes her sense of self. Unfortunately for Anne, when she most needed her mother's reassurance during this time, Katherine was deep into addiction.

When Howard's three-year hitch in the navy in 1942 had left her alone with young Alice and Anne, Katherine drank to stave off loneliness and fear. Yet even after Howard had returned, she was never able to get her drinking under control. Katherine's vision of what life should be had outdistanced her economic means. She had wanted so much more, artistically and socially, and her thwarted ambitions depressed her, so she buffered her disappointments with alcohol. As Anne neared the age of fifteen, Katherine died after a long binge. Despite its inevitability, the loss devastated Anne. She had to learn to take care of herself.

In search of a better life, Howard remarried and moved his daughters to Richardson, Texas, near Dallas. For the first time, Anne found herself in a secular school. She no longer had to wear uniforms, walk quietly in the halls, or attend to other aspects of strict Catholic etiquette. She discovered the freedom to think, and she read books that had been forbidden throughout her childhood, planting the seeds for giving up her faith altogether when she reached college. She read existential philosophy and writers like Ernest Hemingway and Virginia Woolf, and thrilled to the new worlds opening up. Although she and her father argued over her intellectual curiosity, she continued to explore. It was in this school where she also fell in love.

One day a boy named Stan Rice sat next to her in class and she found herself instantly under his spell. She thought, with his wildly creative air, he looked like James Dean. They dated briefly and even went together to New Orleans once, but Stan showed no real interest in her so Anne decided to make a future for herself. She wanted to get educated and have a career.

After spending a year at Texas Woman's University, Anne moved to San Francisco. She and her college roommate, Ginny, had dreamed of going to a big city and finally decided to make it happen. (She would later give the same yearning and adventure to Lestat and Nicolas in *The Vampire Lestat*.) Anne and Ginny set up house together in the low-rent Haight-Ashbury district, and when Anne got a job as a claims processor for an insurance company, she experienced the freedom of truly being on her own.

In the meantime, Stan Rice was beginning to wonder where Anne O'Brien was. He remembered her as a girl with real intensity and he wanted badly to see her again. When he discovered she had gone to California, he was stunned. "It was a staggering shock," he says. "My heart just stopped." He found out where she was and wrote her a letter. Anne was delighted to hear from Stan and she wrote back, starting up a torrid romance by correspondence. They saw each other briefly a couple of times and then Stan proposed by mail. Anne accepted and they got married shortly after her twentieth birthday in 1961. When Stan finished his semester at North Texas State, they packed up everything they owned and went to make their home in the liberal city of San Francisco. There they both worked and went to school while Stan began to make a name for himself as a poet.

Although Anne knew she wanted to write, she majored in political science at San Francisco State College (later University). She took literature courses as well and wrote stories for a select group of friends. Stan exposed her to contemporary poetry, broadening her appreciation for the pliability and richness of language, and she eventually published a short story and the first chapter of a novella in the school's literary journal. Attracted to erotic writing but unsatisfied with what was then available (with the exception of Nabokov's *Lolita*), Anne decided to try her hand at this genre. She wrote several pieces on the theme of consensual dominance/submission and seemed particularly taken with the image of a beautiful and precocious young boy named Jean who was sexually exploited by older men. He became the main protagonist of her novella "Nicolas and Jean," then later of "Katherine and Jean," her master's thesis in creative writing.

Anne soon grew aware of how attuned she was to the aesthetic of gay men and she began to think of herself as a gay man in a woman's body: She was attracted to men in the way she understood gay men to be, with deep appreciation for their physical beauty, but she had been told many times that women did not have such feelings. She felt as if she did not fit the ideas about her own gender and she identified with what she understood about gay culture, so she developed her fantasies in that direction. She was an outsider like them. To make her descriptions authentic, she put questions to gay acquaintances. One friend, Michael

Riley, recalls this period: "She showed an absolute fascination with everything that had to do with being gay. I think Anne identified with it, that in some way she felt her own passionate nature put her on the outside."

During the late 1960s, Anne set herself the task of writing one short story per day to develop her skills. Many involved memories of New Orleans or examined offbeat relationships, but one of those stories from 1968 was about a vampire telling a reporter what it was like to live as one of the undead. Anne put the story aside, taking it out to revise only after one of the most pivotal and tragic events of her life.

In 1966, Anne and Stan had a daughter whom they named Michele. Blond and precocious, she became the center of their lives. Stan was teaching in the creative writing department at San Francisco State University while Anne signed up for graduate courses and stayed home to raise their child. She took Michele on outings to the library, where she could explore subjects for potential novels, study for her courses, or just read great literature. Michele was only four when she complained one day of a strange fatigue. A trip to the doctor brought a shocking diagnosis. The child had acute granuleucytic leukemia and her prognosis was poor.

Anne and Stan both threw themselves into exploring every possibility for a cure, from vitamin C to experimental drugs, but over the next two years Michele's health declined. Finally, she was hospitalized, and friends and family assisted in around-the-clock care for the ailing child. She had grown wise beyond her years and seemed to know the end was near. "She had an otherworldly quality about her," Stan recalls. "There was something in her eyes. She knew stuff that adults didn't know because they hadn't been through compulsory medical tests." Early one morning, just a few weeks before her sixth birthday, she slipped away. Her parents were in the room and, after efforts to revive her failed, they looked at each other in shock and despair. Their sweet daughter was gone.

They then entered the darkest period of their lives. Nothing made sense. There seemed to be no meaning that could accommodate such a tragic and brutal loss. "There were no rules for me after that," says Stan. They drank to numb their grief, staying drunk from one day to the next to stave off despair. For Anne, losing a mother and a daughter made her feel vulnerable and terribly alone. She wanted to die as well. There seemed to be no point in going on. For many months, she could not get through the day without several six-packs of beer, and she seemed destined for the road her mother had taken, but she did not care.

Eventually, however, Anne decided to try to do something with her life. She believed her only real talent was writing. She was torn between quitting her job as a copy editor for a law book company and going all out or just trying to write part-time while she worked. Stan encouraged her to quit. She grabbed the opportunity and looked over some of her earlier work for possibilities. She had her novellas, "Katherine and Jean" and "Nicolas and Jean," which she felt were not ready to send to publishers, and some erotica. The story that caught her eye, however, was the one called "Interview with the Vampire." She decided to revise it to submit to a writing contest.

In the story, the vampire had no name but Anne referred to his maker as Lestat, an unadventurous vampire who owned a plantation. Lengthening the tale, Anne described the vampire's experience with his unusual form of existence, including an encounter with a member of the Mafia, who invites him to use his indestructible body to become a hit man. He refuses and kills the man. By the time the vampire tells his story to a reporter, he is biding his time in San Francisco, sometimes killing, sometimes just taking a drink from victims that are easily seduced. (This story can be read in its entirety in the revised edition of *The Vampire Companion: A Guide to Anne Rice's* The Vampire Chronicles.)

Anne sent this story with several others to the contest, but a reader eliminated her collection early from the competition. Yet at the urging of friends, she continued to work on her vampire tale. She named the narrator Louis and delved further into his background as a mortal. When she came to the part where his brother dies, she tapped into her own grief over Michele and her mother and started to write with great emotional fervor. She knew intimately the loss and regret. Transferring herself from the perspective of the interviewer to that of the vampire, she probed his inner darkness.

"I wrote about vampires on a whim," Anne explains. "I was sitting at the typewriter wondering what it would be like to be a vampire. I wanted to see through his eyes and ask the questions I thought were inevitable for a vampire to ask who'd once been human. I was just following my imagination and my instinct. Seeing through Louis's eyes allowed me to write about life in a way I hadn't been able to do in a contemporary novel. I couldn't make my life believable in that form. I didn't know how to use it. When I abandoned that struggle and wrote *Interview with the Vampire*, it all came together for me. I was able to describe reality through fantasy."

In five short weeks, working mostly at night, she finished the novel and knew that with this book she would see publication. "I dream, hope, imagine that this will be my first published work," she wrote in her diary. "I feel ashamed of nothing in it—not even what I know to be flaws. I feel solidly behind it as though Louis's voice were my voice and I do not run the risk of being misunderstood." Despite several rejections, she soon found an agent who sold her novel to Knopf, and she was on her way.

Interview with the Vampire found a phenomenal reception, earning within the first year nearly $1 million from hardcover, paperback, and movie deals. It is about a twenty-five-year-old plantation owner from Louisiana who, during a period of deep mourning, elects to become a vampire. He is drawn to an enigmatic, mesmeric vampire named Lestat, who promises escape from his unhappy existence. Although with his conversion Louis experiences a heightened sensory state, he soon regrets his decision and spends two centuries grieving over what he views as his state of eternal damnation. The story intimately captures the loneliness and guilt he experiences as he travels the world in search of meaning and redemption.

With its lush language and existential questing, this novel hit a nerve with the 1970s culture and found a large, appreciative audience. Young people seeking alternatives to traditional religion or craving unique, deeply subjective ways to view human experience found resonance with Louis's spiritual lament. As one reader remarked: "Rice goes into the darkness and illuminates it for us."

"I think the vampire represents someone who's transcended time and transformed himself into an immortal and has become a dark saint," Anne explains, "a being with all the powers that transcend the corruptible. He represents the longing for immortality and freedom, while our culture tells us to be practical and to face the fact that nothing lasts forever."

The story connected with another social current as well, which Anne gradually realized with the emergence of a large gay following: She was writing about people who did not belong and who suffered over it. "I see the vampires as outsiders," she says, "creatures outside of the human sphere who can therefore speak about it the way Mephistopheles could speak about it to Faust. I gave them conscience and intelligence and wisdom so they could see things humans aren't able to see. They are tragic heroes and heroines who suffer. The are not pure evil. They have hearts and souls. They have a conscience; they suffer loneliness. They know what they're doing but they're trapped by their nature."

Many readers noted the erotic qualities of Anne's writing, as well as recognizing the way the vampire itself portrayed a perverse sexuality. Anne affirmed this perception. "Vampire fiction is erotic because the vampire is an erotic image," says Anne. "Religions have long used sensuous gods and goddesses, but they're gone now and what lingers in our imagination is the vampire. He demands a sacrifice from us, but in that sacrifice is great rapture, and we respond subconsciously."

One of the most poignant aspects of this novel was the child vampire, Claudia, whom Louis and Lestat made from a five-year-old child. Clearly there was some connection between this character and Anne's deceased daughter, although Anne insisted she had been unaware of it as she wrote *Interview with the Vampire*: "I never consciously thought about the death of my daughter when I was writing it. I wasn't conscious of working anything out. When I wrote it, it was like dreaming. The book had a life unto itself. The child vampire Claudia was physically inspired by Michele but she ultimately became something else—a woman trapped in a child's body, robbed of power, never knowing what it's like to really be a woman and to make love. She became a metaphor for a raging mind trapped in a powerless body. That's really how I see her."

Interview with the Vampire became a cult favorite, gaining in momentum until millions of copies had sold. Yet it took nearly twenty years before this novel reached the silver screen. When it came out in November 1994, with a script by Anne, she was overcome by how well Neil Jordan's treatment captured her intent. "The entire look of the film was perfection. You walk out exhilarated." Despite her initial reticence over the casting of Tom Cruise for Lestat, she praised his work. "From the moment he appeared Tom was Lestat for me. He has the immense physical and moral presence; he was defiant and yet never without conscience." She was particularly pleased with the performance of Kirsten Dunst, the actress who played Claudia. The scene in which Claudia was destroyed moved Anne to tears. "Claudia is all children," she comments, "when they reach the understanding that they will die, they want to know why they were ever brought into this world for that." Over all, she felt a great sense of satisfaction and completion. "It's about us as well as about vampires. It's about those who feel deeply, who have lost faith in a meaningful universe and find an immoral or amoral existence impossible."

After her success with the first novel, Anne resisted pressure to write a sequel and turned instead to historical novels that satisfied her appreciation for the richness of earlier, more romantic eras. She had already done a great deal of research on Louisiana so she decided to pursue a novel about the *gens de couleur libre*, the class of the free people of color in her hometown of New Orleans. *The Feast of All Saints* is about adolescents from this class finding their way in a confusing world of racial and sexual issues, and Anne drew her main character, Marcel, closer to a sense of personal freedom and power than she had allowed Louis. With Marcel's sister, Marie, Anne also addressed the fear experienced by young women over having strong sexual feelings and conflicts with the expectations of the Catholic church. She used one character, Dolly Rose, to affirm female sexuality and power, even as the women around her in the San Francisco area were reaching for liberation and respect as equals in the workplace and bedroom.

While Anne was at work on this novel, she became pregnant again. In 1978, six years after losing Michele, she had a son, Christopher. Deciding that he was not going to grow up with parents who drank all the time, she and Stan decided together to simply stop. It gave Anne a sense of power over her life that would show up in later novels.

Even greater steps were taken with the theme of self-actualization against all odds in *Cry to Heaven*. Set in Italy, where Anne had explored Rome and Venice, this tale featured the celebrated castrated opera singers of the eighteenth century. One such singer, Tonio, has been forced into this neither-male-nor-female existence and he struggles with issues of gender, self-expression, art, and power before he finally embraces his identity.

Neither of these novels saw the strong success that *Interview with the Vampire* had generated, so Anne decided against another story in the historical milieu. She had planned one set during the time of Oscar Wilde, but opted instead to return to the type of erotic writing she had explored in the 1960s. Although friends warned her against such a career move, she insisted on writing authentically and wanted to give voice to what was pressing for expression. "The idea was to create a book where you didn't have to mark the hot pages," she says, "where every page would be hot. I was trying to get right to the heart of that fantasy—to reach the moment of pounding intensity and to take away everything extraneous, as much as could be done in a narrative. To do that, you have to be absolutely alive to what you're writing."

To gain maximum freedom, Anne elected to write under a pseudonym. She chose the name A.N. Roquelaure, from the French word for cloak. Basing this novel loosely on the fairy tale of Sleeping Beauty, Anne created erotic adventures for a young princess and her prince. *The Claiming of Sleeping Beauty* begins with Beauty's awakening from her hundred years' sleep into a fantasy land of S&M scenarios. The prince who revives her becomes her master and takes her to his mother's castle, where she is trained as a love slave. "I just wanted to take those fantasies," says Anne, "and put them into some form that could be written down, being true to what they were and making the least possible concession to literary form."

Then came the second novel in this series, *Beauty's Punishment,* which exposed Beauty to even more extreme punishments and transports (within safe parameters). She finally surrenders to the truth about herself, that she craves the experience of being mastered. She also meets masochistic young men—all princes—whose personal stories of submission to pain and humiliation teach her even more about the benefits of severe discipline. In the third and last novel, *Beauty's Release,* Beauty and her friends find even greater enhancement in a sultan's palace, but Anne eventually tired of the repetition inherent in such books and decided to end the series. Beauty returns home and finds love with a prince who understands her needs and knows how to meet them.

Although these novels were written during the mid-1980s, when a conservative backlash from many feminists denounced pornography, Anne insisted that women should have the freedom to read, think, and write whatever they pleased. For her, the books were a political statement. "I'm proud of the Beauty books," Anne declares, "and happy with them. But they're over. I did what I wanted to do." Although Anne had set out to explore female sexuality in this series, her most fully developed character is male. His name is Prince Laurent and he is the only one able and willing to play the roles of both slave and master, hero and victim, and who truly understands the fullness and complexity of human experience. His story takes precedence in the third novel as Beauty's recedes, and in him Anne found a resonant male voice. He gave her a way to deepen another character about whom she was writing simultaneously under yet another pseudonym.

While writing the Roquelaure novels, she adopted the name Anne Rampling for the erotic novel *Exit to Eden.* The story is told from two alternating points of view: that of Lisa, a dominatrix who runs a pleasure club on a private island and that of Elliott, a bisexual man who signs up to become a pleasure slave for the wealthy patrons. "My intention was to write a pornographic novel," Anne recalls, "but the characters of Elliott and Lisa came alive for me. I fell in love with them right away. When I finished, I felt that something terrific had happened in that book." Elliott and Lisa explore the psychology of S&M as a safe discharge of innate violence and they fall in love and opt for marriage.

With Lisa, Anne felt she actually made the breakthrough she had desired in her Roquelaure series by presenting a developed female perspective. Looking back, she realized that she had hidden behind the guise of a gay man to write and now she wanted to change that. She reached for authentic feeling and gave Lisa her own beliefs about sexual outlaws, transgender experiences, and the inability to view sexual play between consenting adults as deviant or wrong. She felt that *Exit to Eden* was a bold novel and she was proud to have it published in hardcover in America. In addition, while creating Elliott, she found the voice that took her back to her vampires.

Nine years after *Interview with the Vampire,* in 1985, Anne published the long-awaited sequel, *The Vampire Lestat.* Having experienced trouble with writing it, she had at last developed the protagonist she had envisioned. No longer in deep mourning, she wished to avoid echoing Louis's despair. Now she had a hero, a man of adventure, and her exploration of the psychology of males who were both dominant and submissive had made that possible. Reading the fast-paced American detective fiction of James M. Cain and Raymond Chandler, Anne deepened her sense of how Lestat should tell his story.

"Lestat grew as a character almost beyond my control," Anne admits. "He spontaneously appeared in the corner of my eye when I was writing *Interview with the Vampire,* and then he took on great strength and had experiences that went into the second novel. I had been focusing so totally on Louis and Claudia [in *Interview with the Vampire*] that I didn't realize Lestat was developing such coherence."

Having been abandoned by Louis and gone into a deep trance, Lestat awakens in the late twentieth century and decides to become a rock star. Adventurous and feisty, he exhibits a greater range of sensuality and bisexual capacity than Louis, while being more decidedly assertive. He quickly became Anne's favorite character. "If I were a vampire, I would certainly want to be Lestat," she says. "My idea with him was that he was a comic and tragic character combined, that he would be unkillable and always triumph in the comic sense. Yet he was also tragic in that he had a great capacity to understand evil and suffering. What fascinates me about him is that he knows right from wrong and he still does what he has to do. His strength, his penchant for action, his lack of regret, his lack of paralysis, his ability to win over and over again, his absolute refusal to lose—I love to write from that point of view. Lestat is the dream of the male I would love to be."

In his autobiography, Lestat explains how he became a vampire and how he pursued a much older vampire, Marius, to learn the story of the vampire origins. Marius tells Lestat about their progenitors, Akasha and Enkil, who were possessed by an immense spirit during early Egyptian times that had fused with their hearts and created an unbearable blood thirst. To diffuse the spirit's craving, they made more vampires, and as they aged, they experienced less need for blood. Nevertheless, their many "children" killed to survive and made even more of their own kind. Lestat is their descendant.

After listening to Marius's tale, Lestat turns all that he learns into rock videos, identifying himself with the Greek god Dionysus and using his rock music to wake Queen Akasha from her centuries-long trance. By this brash act, he ushers into both the mortal and vampire worlds a menace that nearly changes the face of human destiny.

This story concludes in the third vampire novel, *The Queen of the Damned*. Akasha wants to kill ninety-nine percent of the male population in order to set up a new Eden where feminine perception would transform the world into a peaceful place. She forces Lestat to help, but after much slaughter he turns against her and joins other vampires who resist Akasha's tampering with human evolution. They risk their lives to defy her, but in destroying Akasha, they discover an effective new way to preserve the spirit that animates them.

This novel was one of Anne's most abstract, relying on philosophy rather than her experience or fantasies to carry the plot. She has expressed a mixed reaction to it, from feeling it was her most accomplished work to date, to viewing it as the only one of her novels that she dislikes. Yet she had wanted to develop the theme of how an idea that sounds good can be evil, and that not all evil is found in dark stereotypes like Satan or Hitler. To her mind, writing about pure abstractions like the traditional notions of good and evil hindered real understanding. "What interests me," she explains, "is the mixture of those opposed elements— the transcendence of dramatic extremes. I don't usually create pure opposites who interact as such. The tension between opposites as I see it is not a violent clash of objects so much as a mixing in each individual character. To me, what's fascinating in art is to get inside evil and see the good inside it. I don't think you can understand evil until you do that. That doesn't for a moment mean that one excuses evil or sympathizes with it. I just want to understand what it's about and so I go into the complexity of it."

Both *The Vampire Lestat* and *The Queen of the Damned* brought Anne the success she had known with her first vampire novel, and even surpassed it.

Between these two novels, Anne published *Belinda* in 1986 under her Rampling pseudonym. Set in her own house in San Francisco's Castro District, she wrote about an artist in his forties who falls in love with a sixteen-year-old runaway. The girl, Belinda, had grown up with an alcoholic mother who needed her own child to take care of her, similar to the way Anne's mother depended on her and her sisters. When Anne wrote this novel, she was the same age as the artist, Jeremy

Walker, and was reaching for the same artistic freedom that he craved. He wished to stop writing the children's books that had earned him much success and do something wild and unusual, just as Anne wanted to explore unusual fictional subjects that might scandalize others. The parallels between Jeremy and Anne indicate how her forays into erotica brought her the kind of success for which she had hoped and none of the problems. "*Belinda* is a symbol of the pornography," Anne admits, "and of the way it meant breaking down barriers and opening up doors." Jeremy, too, gets to transcend his previous work. Despite warnings of disgrace and demise as he unveils his nude paintings of Belinda, he actually triumphs.

Yet with *Belinda*, the experiment with pseudonyms came to an end. Anne felt it did not work, and since she had been revealed as the author of both the Rampling and Roquelaure novels, she saw no reason for hiding behind another name. She decided to write all future books under her own name.

Her next novel was *The Mummy*. Intended as a plot for a television miniseries, she turned it into a novel when disagreements with producers disillusioned her. Viewing it as a "romp," in the tradition of the B-grade horror movies, Anne created a tale about a beautiful immortal man who comes to life in Edwardian England and falls in love. "It was fun evoking that atmosphere and doing outrageous things that I wouldn't do in other books," she insists. This paperback best-seller was a runaway success, and plans are now in place to make it into a movie.

Anne followed this novel with *The Witching Hour*, her saga about thirteen generations of a family of witches who end up living in New Orleans. She was still in San Francisco when she started it, so in 1988 she decided to return to New Orleans to reestablish connection with the sights, sounds, smells, and accents of this Euro-Caribbean city that would make the details in her novel authentic. "It was very important for me to come back to New Orleans," she says. "The older I got, the more bitter—almost panic-stricken—I became about not being here. I couldn't establish any kind of rooted feeling in California. I needed to be near the landscape and the incidents of my childhood. Now that I'm back here, my fears about death, old age, and the passage of time are much less because I'm where I want to be. I'm home."

Anne wandered her old neighborhoods to collect background detail for her character Michael Curry, who grew up in the Irish Channel where her father's family had settled. "I discovered hundreds upon hundreds of buried memories," she recalls, "triggered by things I saw and heard." Michael's life story borrowed much from Anne's. "He's more like me than any other character," she admitted when the novel was published in

1990, "except that I didn't have his father and I didn't grow up in the Irish Channel. Everything in these novels comes from my life, and there's more of it in Michael than in anything I've written so far." Michael shares with Rice a love of Dickens and architecture, the same Catholic and secular education, an alcoholic mother, an aversion to the liberal hypocrisies of the 1970s, a desire to learn, and the ability to teach himself. He also has many of her same aspirations.

It was exciting for Anne to come so close to her inner experience through a character she admired. Through him she expressed what she had felt upon returning to New Orleans and walking along streets and into churches that had been so central to her youth. She also talked about her agnosticism (and when she began to regain her sense of God, she gave this experience to Michael as well). When Michael and Rowan decide to renovate their home, Anne used details from her own renovations, and when they throw a large family party, the food, music, and decorations came from Anne's own family reunion. More significantly, the house in which they make their home was Anne's own. She had spotted it for sale one day as she wandered in the Garden District.

New Orleans's Garden District was settled by Americans in the mid-1800s between the French Quarter and the uptown area. They built magnificent mansions inspired by Greek Revival and Italianate architectural styles. The quiet streets are shaded by massive live oaks, crepe myrtles and magnolias. As a child, Rice had walked on these streets as she went to school and back home to her house on St. Charles Avenue. Being just outside this wealthy area, she had cut the teeth of her ambitions on what she had witnessed there of elderly ladies riding in black limousines and having servants and gardeners. As she describes through Michael Curry, she desperately longed to own one of those mansions. So she bought the one she saw on First Street. "It called to me," she insists. Little did she realize how central this house would become to a whole series of novels or how she herself would become like the Garden District residents that she had so longed to be.

Setting *The Witching Hour* in her new home, she went from room to room, or out to the pool or "Deirdre's Oak" to experience scenes that she was describing: Deirdre's bed was one she owned; Lasher was "born" in her parlor; Michael nearly drowned in her pool; and Stuart's ghost appeared on the impressive twenty-seven step staircase. The real settings added powerful sensual detail, and haunting her own house with her witches, ghosts, and malevolent characters fueled her momentum. This house "belonged" to the many generations of the Mayfair family who had occupied it as part of the "legacy" of wealth settled on designated Mayfair females—always witches. The incubus spirit that haunted it had influenced its design in anticipation of the day he would be born into flesh via the thirteenth and most powerful witch, Rowan Mayfair. His symbol was the Egyptian keyhole doorway—a genuine architectural feature of the First Street house that Anne eagerly incorporated into the plot. Through it, Lasher finally entered the physical realm.

One of the primary themes that inspired *The Witching Hour* and its sequels was the theme of kinship. As a child, Anne had taken a strong interest in the members of her extended family. "I don't remember a time when I didn't care about family," she admits. "I cared about who they were. I was hungry to have a family and I was envious of kids who had large families." However, there were many members of her family that she knew little about and when she returned to New Orleans, she set about rectifying the situation. She invited two hundred aunts, uncles, and cousins to get reacquainted with one another. Simultaneously, she expanded the character and relationships in her novels: As Anne learned more about her own kin, the Mayfair family swelled in size and history. She listened to dialects, dug up family stories, and studied character traits even as she reveled, like Rowan, in the feeling of being connected to so many people. For example, the story of Uncle Mickey's eye that Dora relates in *Memnoch the Devil* is based on an actual incident in the family involving her mother's brother Mickey. Anne made a point of having more such parties.

The Witching Hour was her longest novel to date and, although she believed it was finished with Lasher's birth and Rowan's defection, she soon thought up a sequel.

Before that, however, another vampire novel demanded to be written. While on a book tour, Anne had imagined various scenes and was particularly taken with the seamy milieu of Miami, so that was the city in which she started Lestat's new adventure in *The Tale of the Body Thief*. She had stayed in the Park Central Hotel on South Beach, where she gave Lestat permanent quarters.

As he opens the story, he is in the process of tracking serial killers for his "meals," while an unusual type of vampire hunter is simultaneously tracking him. His name is Raglan James and he offers Lestat a temporary body exchange. Intrigued with the idea of experiencing a mortal existence again, Lestat agrees to switch, then gets duped as James makes off with his powerful vampire body. With the help of his friend, David Talbot, Lestat retrieves it, but continues to be plagued by the idea that he is Mephistopheles to David's Faust: He tempts his morally upright friend to join him in immortality. David refuses but Lestat does not give up. Given the choice, Lestat recognizes that he prefers to be a vampire despite the evil it entails, and so he acts on his unredeemable nature by making David into a vampire against his will.

As Anne wrote this novel she entered a dark period. Life seemed especially fragile and she felt terribly fatigued. "It was an awful time," she admits, "a black, black period. I don't know how the novel got written. I just did it."

A few months later, she had another family party to celebrate her fiftieth birthday. Her father attended, although his health was deteriorating, and that night he had a bad fall that put him in the hospital. Anne wondered if the spell of depression she had experienced earlier that year had been a dark foreboding. A similar portent had preceded her daughter's fatal illness. Organizing continuous care for her father, Anne spent long hours in the hospital with him, musing over how Lestat had worried over the fragility of his mortal friend David Talbot—the same age as her father. Shortly after Thanksgiving in 1991, her father died as she held his hand. "I felt grateful to fate that I was there at the moment he died," she says. The experience reaffirmed for her the importance of family and of staying connected.

When she went back to look at her novel, she was amazed by the prescience it seemed to express: "Anyone reading this book," says Anne, "would think it had been written after my father's death. It was almost as if it had been written in a state of premonition. It was about what was happening to him." It was also clear that the same urge to rescue her mother from death that had motivated Lestat to make his mother, Gabrielle, into a vampire had also motivated him to bring David Talbot into immortality.

Anne thought that *The Tale of the Body Thief* might be the last of the vampire series. It seemed to answer many of the questions raised in *Interview with the Vampire*, and she felt she had thoroughly explored the metaphysical implications of the vampire figure. She turned her attention back to the Mayfairs.

Lasher was Anne's first venture into science fiction terrain. She proposed a DNA basis for the sort of creature that Lasher turned out to be—a Taltos—and gave him a story to explain his presence in the Mayfair history. He had once been alive, the offspring of Anne Boleyn and a member of the clan of Donnelaith that carried the "giant helix"—a gene that made possible the birth of a nonhuman creature called a Taltos. Although he was simple and loving, Lasher suffered from ignorant prejudices that condemned him to a brutal death. For a century he hovered over Donnelaith in spiritual form until Suzanne Mayfair called him forth. From that moment, his destiny was linked to the Mayfair witches as he manipulated them to regain his physical form.

At the same time, Anne developed more characters among the Mayfairs and within the Talamasca, her secret organization of psychic investigators. Her favorite was Mona Mayfair, a precocious, sexually charged thirteen-year-old genius who embodied the adventurous spirit that Anne wished for herself. Anne received criticism in her local paper for allowing Mona to be so promiscuous and for promoting incest in her novels, but Anne defended her right to fictional expression. She also insisted that mature young women be allowed to make their own sexual choices. To her mind, American culture turned a blind eye to the needs of such people, insisting that they remain children when they have the appetites of adults. "We must come to recognize that sexual maturity comes much earlier than it did in ages past," she claims, "and we must stand up for the rights of young people." She used her writing to bring attention to this issue, creating in Mona, and later in the nineteen-year-old character Mary Jane Mayfair, a bold attitude of taking from life what one can get. These characters continued the train of thought about the liminal mode of adolescence that had begun even with Claudia, an adult mind trapped in a child's body.

Mary Jane shows up in *Taltos*, the novel that followed *Lasher* in 1994. One thread of the plot depicts the adventures of Mary Jane and Mona as they assert their right to make decisions for themselves despite their youth, and includes Mona's giving birth to a child. The other thread presents the full story of Lasher's nearly extinct race, the Taltos. Told by Ashlar, the oldest living Taltos, the tale begins well before human history and details events from British prehistory, including the making of Stonehenge. Identifying the Taltos with a Scottish tribe known as the Picts, Ashlar explains how his own conversion to Christianity brought about the annihilation of most of the other Taltos. He is aware that the Mayfair family carries a gene that makes possible the revival of his race, but he has declined to follow up on this opportunity. Yet when Mona delivers a Taltos via the right pairing of Mayfair genes, Ashlar is quick to embrace his mate—a union that has potentially devastating implications for the human race.

Anne wanted to follow this novel with yet another in the same series. She plotted *Morrigan*, named after Mona's Taltos offspring, but was unable to sustain the effort to bring it to fruition. She set it aside and returned once more to Lestat, her vampire hero.

The fifth vampire novel, *Memnoch the Devil*, takes Lestat on his ultimate adventure. Stalked by a creature he believes to be the Devil himself, Lestat fears for his soul. After an encounter with the ghost of one of his victims and with a female televangelist who believes in the supernatural, Lestat learns that the Devil wants to enlist his aid in the struggle against world suffering. Lestat agrees to accompany the Devil, whose name is Memnoch, to Heaven and Hell to hear the story of creation and the origin of evil. Lestat meets God and witnesses Christ's crucifixion, then enters Hell. There he discovers what it means to grapple with the full experience of redemption—to confront one's victims—and the horrors of what he sees impel him to flee the Devil's grasp and return to his existence on Earth. He decides that he can never really know whether his experience was truth or illusion or whether he played into the Devil's hands, and he believes he will never again feel safe.

Anne used this novel to include research on church history, iconography, and illuminated manuscripts that she had left out of *Taltos*. She presents these subjects through Roger, a collector of religious relics, and his televangelist daughter, Dora. Anne had originally intended to make one or the other of these characters the central protagonist (she saw herself as Dora) and to use the format of a ghost story, but after several false starts she changed her mind and gave the story to Lestat. She thought it worked well through him. The tale that Roger tells of a medieval saint of sensuality, Wynken de Wilde, held special fascination for Anne and she pondered writing a book that expanded it.

Anne wrote *Memnoch the Devil* in a month. She felt drained by the effort and could barely communicate with anyone. It haunted her. Nearly a year later, when she read the page proofs, she had the experience that Lestat had gone out of her life. What they had done together was finished. She felt that, as he walked down St. Charles on the last page of the book, he looked into the window of an abandoned Mercedes dealer and disappeared from her imagination. "He left me. He just left me. He said, 'Anne, no more for now.' And off he went." (Of course, she could find him again in the future.)

Taking a break from sequels, Anne wrote a Jewish ghost story, *Servant of the Bones*, for publication in 1996. She then explored the Romantic era for another ghost story unrelated to the first, but calling on her sense of history, music, and dark excess.

For each book, Anne adopts the point of view of her main character, male or female, and through the character she expresses her own beliefs. As Louis, she felt hopeless; as Marcel, confused but hopeful; as Lestat, assertive and ready for anything. "I just get into their skin," she insists, "and everything happens. It's not hard for me to create these various characters because they all represent longings and aspirations in myself."

Although Rice has used numerous settings for her novels—Egypt, Manhattan, Venice, San Francisco, London—she brings her characters over and over again to her hometown of New Orleans. She likes to describe things close by. In *Exit to Eden* and *Belinda*, she took her characters on long walks all over the city, which felt liberating to her. Having used her Garden District home for *The Witching Hour*, she has continued in this tradition for novels that followed.

Although Lasher flees New Orleans after his birth into mortal form, many events in *Lasher* and *Taltos* take place in the First Street house. Rowan nearly dies and thirteen-year-old Mona Mayfair inherits the house and all of its ghosts, one of which is her great-grandfather, Julien Mayfair. He wants to stop Lasher so he materializes on the third floor and tells his story to Michael. Much of New Orleans plays a part in his story, including the historical red-light district known as Storyville. He also describes a house on the corner of St. Charles Avenue and Amelia Street that Anne bought. She gave this house to another branch of the Mayfair family and when she finished the novel in which it figured, she sold it.

In the meantime, she had purchased her most exotic piece of New Orleans real estate to date: a 47,000-square-foot building that had once been a Catholic orphanage. Known as St. Elizabeth's, it needed restoration, so Rice took on the five-year project. "It was an empty, benignly haunted building when I bought it." Not one to miss the wealth of literary detail to be gleaned from such a place, she made Dora, one of her characters in *Memnoch the Devil*, its owner. When Lestat returns from his adventure with Memnoch, he brings an icon that makes Dora give up all claim to her property in New Orleans and she deeds St. Elizabeth's to Lestat. Anne viewed this as a way of giving him one last gift.

Yet another home on St. Charles will figure into a future novel. When Anne was a teenager, she had lived for a year in a former rectory on St. Charles Avenue. The priests wanted someone to take care of it, so they made the rent reasonable for a large family of limited economic means. Howard moved his daughters and his ailing wife into this house, and it was the last home in which Anne had her mother's company, for Katherine died that year. When the house came up for sale, Anne purchased it. As the day of closing approached, she had mixed feelings. Her memories of the house were among the best and worst of her youth and she thought about her mother's needless illness and how much she wanted Katherine to be alive to see how she had come full circle: She could now buy this house for herself. She set about reclaiming it and recording the details.

It is likely that New Orleans will continue to inspire settings and characters for future works.

As Anne looks over her authorship, she notes that the novels draw together along similar themes. All of them are about the rich existence of people considered outsiders by normal social standards, and all emphasize the wisdom of experience over abstract ideas. "The books are always talking about truth being in the flesh," she explains. "They say that what the flesh desires is not necessarily bad, but requires exploration, attention." Aware that readers want complex plots and characters, she advocates that quality writers take imaginative fiction more seriously. "We've lost faith in imaginative fiction and many of our finer writers have turned away from it," she insists. "Deeply embedded in our culture is the idea that truth lies in the familiar, the ordinary. But I refuse to believe that fantasy cannot be enormous in scope and profoundly valid and meaningful."

Anne constantly evolves and renews herself with her writing. The way she develops her plots and characters reveals much about the person behind the authorship. She believes that serious subjects can be addressed in speculative and supernatural formats and she hopes to continue to work along these lines. As long as she takes care to make the feelings authentic, she believes she can express the ideas and themes that are meaningful to her in whatever framework she chooses.

Note

1. All quotes not attributed to one of Rice's novels come from my interviews with her in preparation for my books on her and her work: *Prism of the Night: A Biography of Anne Rice* (1991, revised 1992, 1994); *The Vampire Companion: The Official Guide to Anne Rice's* The Vampire Chronicles (1993, revised, 1995); *The Witches' Companion: The Official Guide to Anne Rice's* Lives of the Mayfair Witches (1994); *The Anne Rice Trivia Book* (1994); *The Roquelaure Reader: A Companion to Anne Rice's Erotica* (1996); and *The Anne Rice Reader* (1997).

The Anthropological Vision of Anne Rice

Frank A. Salamone

Literature, especially those genres loosely bound together as science fiction, has frequently employed anthropologists such as Mr. Spock to draw attention to the humanity of alternate realities. I consider novelists often to be most successful in capturing the essence of the construction and use of symbols in maintaining group identity and distinguishing insiders from outsiders, self from others. John Marquand's *Point of No Return*, for example, was a successful attempt on his part to demonstrate to his friend, the anthropologist William Lloyd Warner, that he could write a more interesting and accurate fictional ethnography of Newburyport, Massachusetts, than Warner had written in *Yankee City*.

Specifically, there is a pressing need in anthropology and fiction to tease out and confront the implications of the fact that identities, even those that appear most ascriptive, are largely achieved. In fact, we need to grapple with the fact that which identity or set of identities individual social actors choose to use depends on the situation. Moreover, these identities are never fixed. Rather, social actors continually redefine them through their actions and transactions. An integral factor in the negotiation of these identities is the choice and use of salient symbols in defining identities and delineating the boundaries of those identities.

Those whose actions are not in conformity with negotiated identities, that is, are "ungrammatical" in some way, provoke hostile responses *simply because* they threaten the prevailing negotiated social order. Their very existence forces people to consider that what is apparently fixed is in reality in flux and, furthermore, that what is perceived as "natural" is in truth "artificial."

In a passage of significance to Anne Rice's work, Henry Louis Gates, Jr., cites Immanuel Wallerstein's definition of ethnic group (295). Wallerstein emphasizes that such groups are interest groups who assume an identity grounded within a system of relationships. Such groups frequently go into and out of existence depending on socially and culturally mediated circumstances. Gates logically attacks the notion of tradition as a long-lasting and constant cultural heritage. Groups draw boundaries around selected symbols that serve as identity markers in order to emphasize their contrast with other similar group/categories and mask differences among their own members. They do so to present a united front so that they gain political advantages not otherwise perceived as attainable. E.J. Hobswam and T.O. Ranger remind us that cultural "tradition" is whatever a group says it is. People invent traditions to suit occasions and conform with relevant identities.

Giles Gunn discusses effects that the "problematization of the concept of culture" and the related post-colonial critique have had in liberating thinking regarding the relationship of culture and context and in directing our attention to the arbitrary nature of boundaries and their use in relationships of power (254). Identities are never merely givens. They also are texts not works, processes not products.

The study of culture as text has led to the study of the cultural milieux revealed in fictional texts. Rice's best fiction shares with Jane Austen's what Richard Handler and Joel Segal recognize as a denaturing of social reality through drawing attention to its artificial, that is, cultural construction (10). They put it quite succinctly:

Because Austen's texts generate voices that question apparently unquestioned (and unquestionable) cultural rules, she teaches us that such rules are not determinative but fictive, not natural objects but creations made and remade by people. (11)

This questioning of cultural rules is an integral quality of Rice's work. Her retelling of significant segments of her story within and between the various books in the Mayfair trilogy is not done out of a mere desire to pad the work or to allow the reader to catch up on missing portions. Rather, each time a portion of the tale is reiterated it is done so either by a different character or in a different setting. There is always a different shading and at least a subtle contrast in the meaning of the narrative. It is a technique Pirandello used to perfection and of which postmodernists have made us newly aware. This focus on the ambiguity of reality and meaning is central to both good fiction and good anthropology.[1]

At this point we can determine that as various anthropologists become aware of the rhetorical nature of ethnographic writing, they increasingly turn to literature, literary criticism, and even fictionalizing their own ethnographies in order to impart the subjective nature and psychological ambiguity of their field experiences. In turn, as Culler indicates, ethnography and anthropological theory in general provide significant sources for what is now called "literary theory." Studies such as Handler's and Segal's concerning Jane Austen's "fiction of culture" and this present study on Anne Rice form a promising subgenre of the emerging but still nameless field of work stemming from the *rapprochement* between literary studies and anthropology.

Focus on writers such as Rice who evidence a grasp of basic anthropological principles: the ambiguity of "reality," the relativity of good and evil, the role of perspective in understanding and interpretation, the interaction of nature and nurture, and the conflict and dependence of humanism and science, further advances that *rapprochement*. Rice's obsession with these themes and the manner in which she works them out evoke a sympathy and understanding in many anthropologists. There is a certain envy as well, for she presents our themes in a far more attractive package than most of us are able to do, for anthropology has sought a deeper sense of renewal and more reflexive ethnographic depiction in an engagement with literature and literary theory.

Anthropologists, above all, seek to distill meaning from an empirical body of data. At times, that body of data may seem overwhelmingly detailed and hopelessly dense. Often only through seeking and employing patterns can any meaning be teased from the data. Frequently, only after years of painstaking research do any significant patterns emerge at all. Nonetheless, there is an unshakable faith that there must be patterns and meaning in even the most seemingly trivial actions and symbols. There is an equally unshakeable belief that in the final analysis nothing is "unnatural" and inexplicable. If something appears to be beyond the natural and beyond human explanation, anthropologists chalk it up to our limited experience and undeveloped theories or to hidden ethnocentricism that prevents us from grasping the point of view of the other and understanding his or her reality. As an anthropologist, I am fascinated with the manner in which identity is constructed and the symbols intrinsic to that process.

Anne Rice appears to share this anthropological temperament. Moreover, she exercises that temperament in each of the major areas that have come to mark American anthropology: ethnography and ethnology, linguistics, archeology, and biological (physical) anthropology. Rice's grasp of these areas is not a mere surface familiarity. It extends, remarkably, to their basic principles and applications. Although this anthropological temperament reveals itself in one form or another in all her books, it is most fully realized in the Mayfair witches trilogy: *The Witching Hour, Lasher,* and *Taltos.*

The Saga of the Mayfair Witches

Rice states that she wrote the books that comprise the Mayfair trilogy at optimistic times in her life as opposed to the dark periods in which she wrote the vampire novels. Her very anthropological theme for the Mayfair witches' series is stated most clearly in Rice's own words.

The Mayfair trilogy works as a whole. It is about the Mayfair family struggling through time to survive. The Mayfairs represent an ideal for me of a clan that stays together. These books contain very heartfelt ideas of mine about how we struggle for survival, how we fear other races, and how the more aggressive tribes wipe out the gentler ones. The question of earthbound souls and ancestor ghosts are central to my drama of birth, death, and rebirth. (qtd. in Ramsland, *Witches'* xii)

Given Rice's stated theme, that of the struggle of a clan to survive under inconceivable trials and of its ties with a gentler race that has all but failed to survive because of the aggression of human beings, the story progresses in a logical if rather wondrous manner.

The first book in the trilogy, *The Witching Hour* (1990), sets the main outlines in which the series unfolds. It was supposed to be complete in itself. However, just as its central ghost, Lasher, was supposed to appear briefly in one of the Vampire tales, *The Queen of the Damned*, only to outgrow the confines of a cameo appearance so, too, did *The Witching Hour* fail to be confined to a single volume.

The story is a sprawling one, covering three centuries of the Mayfair family history while documenting the paranormal powers of its thirteen major witches. Rice sets a major portion of the significant action in her own home on First Street in New Orleans. She has further personalized the story through lending Michael Curry, Rowan Mayfair's husband, her own background. This personal element lends emotional depth as well as realism to Rice's literally fabulous tale.

The story begins with Suzanne, the first of the Mayfair witches, accidentally calling up Lasher, a wandering spirit, to her aid. Suzanne is rather an innocent in the ways of the supernatural. We later learn that Lasher is really named Ashler after the legendary folk saint, Ashlar. Like his namesake, Lasher is a Taltos, a member of a species parallel with humans but with its own biochemical makeup and cultural history.

Although Lasher is unable to save Suzanne from dying at the stake, he destroys those who sentence her to death or acquiesce in it, including the Laird of Donnelaith, who had fathered her daughter. Moreover, he attaches himself to the females of her family, choosing one in each generation to be his chosen witch. In return, he gains an increase in consciousness and power through them. In some manner, he learns to wrap himself in matter so that he can have sexual intercourse with these women and thus grow in feeling like a man, his principal goal for three centuries.

Almost at the same time as Lasher enters the Mayfair history, so does the Talamasca, an order of quasi-religious nature, that studies the paranormal. In the seventeenth century, it was involved in trying to save the lives of those sentenced to death for witchcraft. Petyr van Abel, the son of a prominent physician-scientist, who was raised by the order after his father's death, saves Suzanne's daughter, Deborah, and takes her to Amsterdam to live with the Talamasca. However, after Lasher's appearance to her, she leaves the Talamasca. Soon Lasher has given her the emerald necklace she had admired in a shop window. The necklace becomes the sign of Lasher's favor and passes to the witch who inherited the Mayfair legacy.

Under Lasher's guidance, Deborah begins to prosper and founds the Mayfair fortune. She seduces Petyr and gives birth to their daughter, Charlotte. In turn, Charlotte seduces her father when he tracks the family to Haiti. Lasher, ever-jealous of his witches, causes Petyr's death. The remainder of the history to the setting of the major action in the 1980s involves repetitions of the basic patterns of incest and the strengthening of Lasher's consciousness and the witches' power. The witches move from Haiti to a Louisiana plantation and then finally into the city of New Orleans. There are many branches and segments of the Mayfairs but the family keeps in contact with one another even though very few know the full family history.

In Julien, Rice creates a fascinating character who is a mixture of good and evil but whose allegiance to the family is never in doubt. Julien, born in the late nineteenth century, is the first powerful male witch. He inherits Lasher's favor when his sister Katherine rejects Lasher and witchcraft. Their sexual union results in the birth of Mary Beth, the most powerful witch up to that time. Julien mates with Mary Beth but their daughter, Stella, and her daughter, Antha, die young under mysterious circumstances. Carlotta, Antha's sister, has vowed to end the witch line, although she herself has powerful paranormal capacity. Toward that end, she uses drugs and electroshock therapy to keep Antha's daughter, Deirdre, virtually perpetually comatose.

Carlotta sends Deirdre's daughter, Rowan, to live with relatives in San Francisco. These adoptive parents keep secret from Rowan her family history. She becomes a major surgeon who has the ability to alter matter, including genetic coding. Rowan realizes she has paranormal power but, after inadvertently killing people, she vows to use that power in a healing fashion, combining her heritage from the van Abel's with that of the Mayfairs.

When Deirdre dies, Carlotta calls to tell Rowan's adoptive parents the news. However, Rowan's adoptive parents have also died and Carlotta tells Rowan of her mother's death. Filled with a desire to know her history, she goes to New Orleans to attend her mother's funeral.

Rowan is the thirteenth witch, the "doorway" for which Lasher has been preparing. Since Rowan also is a neurosurgeon with a knowledge of genetic structure and an ability to mutate matter, Lasher has chosen her to bring him into the world and later to mate with him to begin the revival of the Taltos. Since she is a powerful witch with the extra chromosomes that mark witches, Lasher believes that their mating will be successful.

When Rowan comes to New Orleans, however, she had left behind in San Francisco the man with whom she had fallen in love, Michael Curry. Curry is originally from New Orleans, and as we later discover also a Mayfair. Curry had been a successful architect in San Francisco. Rowan had rescued him from drowning. While drowning, he saw a vision of Katherine, Julien, and the other Mayfair witches. Although he awakens from his vision with paranormal powers, he is unable to remember his vision. He believes that if he can meet the woman who saved him, he will be able to recover that vision and fulfill its directives.

He meets with Rowan. They fall in love and eventually marry. First, however, he goes to New Orleans and meets with Aaron Lightner who has been investigating the history of the Mayfairs for the Talamasca. Lightner is one of Rice's more charming creations. He is in his seventies, a cultured, gentle Englishman, with his own paranormal powers, basically the ability to read minds and move matter mentally. Lightner gives Michael the file on the Mayfair witches. Michael eventually shares the file with Rowan.

Despite her resolutions to resist Lasher, Rowan submits to his enticements on her wedding night. When Michael goes to San Francisco on business, Rowan's sexual activities with Lasher become tempestuous. Julien appears to Michael and has him return to New Orleans. On Christmas Eve, Lasher fuses with Michael's and Rowan's unborn child while Rowan mutates its cells so that Lasher can be born. When Michael awakens from Rowan's drugging, he attacks Lasher, who, as is the nature of the Taltos, grows rapidly to adulthood. Lasher with Rowan's aid survives Michael's attacks and then attempts to drown him. Rowan, then, in turn saves Michael by setting off the house's alarms.

Michael's vision returns but he suffers a heart attack. Although he recovers from the attack, he says that he has replaced Lasher in haunting the First Street house. Lasher and Rowan have escaped from New Orleans, and the book ends at this point. It is obvious that the book required a sequel to fill in the missing gaps and to finish the story. *Lasher* fills in many of the gaps and continues, but does not completely finish the story.

Lasher opens with the story of Rowan's adventures with Lasher. They have traveled to New York and then Europe, visiting Donnelaith along the way. Rowan, who has become increasingly apprehensive in her captivity to Lasher, has had two miscarriages and is pregnant with Emaleth, whom Lasher has named after his half-sister, a witch herself. Because of her apprehension, Rowan has sent tissue samples from Lasher to a laboratory in San Francisco. The Mayfair family, also becoming apprehensive, has sent birth tissue to a laboratory in Paris and New York.

Michael, although recovering from his heart attack, has become deeply depressed. Mona, a powerful thirteen-year-old witch and computer wizard from the Amelia Street branch of the family, and a "twenty-fold Mayfair," has taken it into her head to seduce Michael. She believes Rowan to be dead. With Julien's help she succeeds and becomes pregnant.

Meanwhile, Lasher has been seeking other Mayfair women to impregnate. Unfortunately, they all die almost immediately through miscarrying. The Mayfair family is in a panic and seeks to protect the family through hiring security agents. To compound their problems, members of the Talamasca have become involved in seeking to save Lasher and have him mate with a female Taltos they have found. These rogue Talamasca steal and kill in their attempts to get a Taltos. Aaron Lightner and his friend, Yuri Stefano, leave the Talamasca in protest against their actions while seeking Rowan on their own initiative.

Julien once again appears to Michael, filling him in on the family history and his own role in it. He repeats a poem in which he states that a "too-good man" will kill Lasher with a "crude weapon," thus saving the Mayfair family.

Rowan gives birth to Emaleth after escaping from Lasher. Emaleth goes to New Orleans in search of Michael. Rowan is found but remains in a coma. Mona is named the designee of the legacy since Rowan is unable to have any more children. Michael sits by Rowan's bed, comforting and protecting her.

Lasher, accompanied by two Talamasca, comes to the First Street house dressed as the Catholic priest he had been in his earlier incarnation. He insists on telling Michael his story and Michael agrees to listen to it. Lasher states that he first lived as the son of Douglas of Donnelaith and Anne Boleyn. He was named Ashlar in honor of St. Ashlar, an early Taltos leader, priest, and holy man. He was later killed after being forced to mate with the little people for the amusement of the people who killed the resulting Taltos in a Christmas sacrifice.

Although moved by Lasher's story, Michael remembers how Lasher killed his own child by taking its mutated body for his own. He kills the

Talamasca who seek to stop him from reaching Lasher. He then kills Lasher with a hammer and throws him from the attic window. Lasher's body is buried under an oak tree by Aaron and Mona.

Emaleth saves her mother's life through breast feeding her. Rowan, seeking to save the human species from what she perceives to be the danger of the Taltos, shoots and kills her daughter. She buries her under the oak with Lasher.

The final book in the trilogy, *Taltos*, is named after a Hungarian sect of sorcerers who appear in Carlo Ginsburg's book *Ecstasies: Deciphering the Witches' Sabbath*. These sorcerers claimed to be created by God to combat witches. As Rice states,

I was inspired in many ways by my creation of the species. There are numerous legends of tall, blond-haired, 'superior' people in Britain. There are legends that say King Arthur was seven feet tall. I let my imagination delve deeply into all the folklore, myth, and history I could get my hands on. (qtd. in Ramsland, *Witches'* 434)

In this work, Rice invents the origin, culture, and mythology of a species of people, the Taltos. The story is dominated by Ashlar, the oldest surviving Taltos who is thousands of years old. Ashlar is currently an inventor, entrepreneur, and philanthropist, who has taken to specializing in dolls and whose dream is to make the best dolls available to even the poorest children. This fascination with dolls is compatible with the child-like nature of the Taltos. It is the source of their charm as well as their weakness in the face of human attacks.

Along with the Taltos, Rice gives us the "little people," especially in the character of Samuel who has rescued Yuri Stefano from an assassination attempt by the renegade group within the Talamasca. This same group has killed Aaron Lightner.

The remainder of the story involves Ashlar's rescue of the Talamasca and its restoration to its original purpose. Ashlar had a hand in founding the original order. Ashlar meets with Michael and Rowan and tells them his fascinating tale of the Taltos, their meeting with humans, their retreat to Donnelaith, their mating with humans and its result, their conversion to Christianity, its tragic results, and his own history as St. Ashlar and after. He desires to be friends with both Rowan and Michael and, therefore, resists the strong mutual desire he shares with Rowan.

The Talamasca's female, Tessa, is too old to mate and Ashlar treats her with a great gentility, dancing with her sweetly. Mona's child, however, is another matter. Mona and her cousin, Mary Jane, a delightfully off-center character, contrive to have Morrigan born in Mary Jane's sinking house. Mary Jane's grandmother assists at the birth, knowing exactly what a Taltos is and adding to the girls' knowledge as well.

The scent of Ashlar on the returning Michael and Rowan, however, threatens to upset Mona's plans to pass on the Mayfair legacy to Morrigan. Michael and Rowan have had their fill of killing. They promise not to kill Morrigan. In return, they seek her promise to wait to mate with Ashlar until they have had a chance to educate her in their ways. Although Morrigan agrees, she cannot control herself when Ashlar, lonely for Michael and Rowan, comes to New Orleans just to get a glimpse of his friends, who have not returned his attempts to maintain friendly ties.

Morrigan catches Ashlar's scent and rushes past the gathered Mayfair family, who have assembled to decide what to do about Morrigan. Ashlar and Morrigan depart, agreeing to delay their mating with its immediate birth of a Taltos until they reach the sacred circle at Donnelaith.[2]

Rice's Reflections on the Nature and Causes of Colonialism

In discussing the relationship between Taltos and humans, Rice is really addressing one of the key issues in anthropology, indeed in all of social science, namely that of the relationship between heredity and environment. She approaches this discussion from a number of angles in order to build her picture from diverse perspectives. Thus, she discusses genetic evidence taken from the members of the Mayfair family; she resents analyses of the Taltos's DNA results. Moreover, she considers the "nature" of the Taltos from many different perspectives. However, she is at her most convincing in using the life history technique, presented in classic form by L.L. Langness (1965) and modernized by Vincent Crepanzano (1980).

She uses this technique to illustrate the interaction between heredity and environment, that is, between innate tendencies and the environmental shaping of those tendencies. It touches on the area that Margaret Mead termed the "plasticity" of human nature. (See Margaret Mead *Coming of Age; Growing Up; Sex and Temperament;* and *Continuities,* for example, for discussions of the concept.) Rice presents this truth of the plasticity of development through contrasting the lives of Lasher and Ashlar, the major representatives of the Taltos presented in the trilogy.

Rice's creation of the Taltos, alone, would ensure her a place among novelists with anthropological understanding. Briefly, the Taltos are a nonhuman hominid species who have similarities with humans but also important differences. Among those differences are their virtual immunity from disease and their ability to procreate instantaneously upon coupling. They also have twice the number of human chromosomes and other biochemical divergences.

Although both Lasher and Ashlar share the hereditary nature of the Taltos and their basic characteristics, their individual differences with one another are also clear. Rice masterfully depicts the role of environment, or experience, in shaping their contrasting characters. On a fundamental level, unless the Taltos drinks of its mother's milk immediately after birth it does not develop at all. Moreover, although a Taltos is born "knowing," much of what it knows is dependent upon what its mother knows and what it hears while developing in the womb. Additionally, although a Taltos has a childlike nature, loving rhyme, music, and games, outside social and cultural forces can distort and pervert these characteristics. As Lasher's witch sister, Emaleth, says to him:

. . . you are a good follower of St. Francis, a mendicant and a saint, because you are a simpleton, a fool. That's all St. Francis ever was—God's idiot, walking about barefoot preaching goodness, not knowing a word of theology really, and having his followers give away all they possessed. It was the perfect place to send you—the Italy of the Franciscans. You have the addled brain of the Taltos, who would play and sing and dance the livelong day and breed others for playing and singing and dancing. (*Taltos* 541)

Both Lasher and Ashlar have had tragic lives. Lasher, who is the son of the witch and queen Anne Boleyn and the heir of Donnelaith in Scotland, is a Taltos. This sixteenth century reincarnation of an all but extinct species is born at the time of great religious wars. His father views him as the return of St. Ashlar, an earlier Taltos chieftain converted to Catholicism by St. Columba of Ireland. He believes that Ashlar's purpose in returning is to lead the Catholic highland Scots to victory over the Protestant forces of John Knox and Elizabeth, Lasher's half-sister.

Lasher's return to Scotland from Italy and his discovery of his "true nature" and human interpretation of it is, perhaps, the most poignant moment in the book. It reveals another anthropological concern, the relationship of colonized peoples and their colonizers. It touches on the meaning of human power and its corrupting influence. The Taltos throughout the history of their contact with humans, as related in *Lasher* and *Taltos,* have been exploited peoples.

This theme is more fully developed in the history of Ashlar. Although still alive in twentieth-century New York as the successful philanthropist-businessman, Ashlar was once the Taltos's great chieftain. His memory stretches to a time before he knew humans, perhaps, two thousand years ago. He was born on an island of perpetual warmth, a kind of Garden of Eden where life went on in innocence and crimes were rare. Sexuality, like other simple pleasures, was enjoyed without remorse and guilt.

But like other Edens, this one also ended. There was a great cataclysm, probably an earthquake or a volcanic eruption. The Taltos were forced from their islands. They came to Britain and broke up into a number of tribes. In her description of this event, Rice displays skills an ethnographer would envy. For example, she describes the process through which the Taltos of the "Lost Land" adapt their initial cultural practices to the changed circumstances of a land with four distinct seasons. Moreover, she notes the manner in which a hunting and gathering subsistence forces the Taltos to punish those who threaten the community, albeit reluctantly. A process of fission, noted by anthropologists as a characteristic of hunters and gatherers, is described for the Taltos. Their disdain for, and indifferent (not cruel) treatment of, humans is also noted.

Eventually, invaded by humans more technologically developed than those whom they had known, they moved to the Scottish highlands, settling at Donnelaith. Ashlar's description of these human invaders points to their basic differences and to the manner in which social and cultural influences worked on the basic nature of the Taltos:

They stole our women and raped them until they died of the bleeding. They stole our men and sought to enslave them, and laughed at them and ridiculed them, and in some instances drove them mad. . . . Often we fought them off. We were not by nature as fierce as they, by any means, but we could defend ourselves, and great circles were convened to discuss their metal weapons and how we might make our own. Indeed, we imprisoned a number of human beings, invaders all, to try to pry the knowledge from them. . . . And the men had a deep, inveterate hatred of our softness. They called us "the fools of the circle," or "the simple people of the stones." (*Taltos* 344)

Ashlar continues his story and describes the slaughter of his people while they were celebrating a great religious festival. On their flight to escape the humans, they find it necessary to resort to slaughter to rescue their fellow Taltos or to protect themselves. Although they understand that their only hope of survival lies in killing every human being, as a group they cannot do so. Some of them, Ashlar notes, could do so, but not enough. He draws the parallel with other tribes throughout history who underestimated the blood lust of their conquerors and so lost out to them although in many other ways they were their superiors. Specifically, he mentions the Spanish and the Incas as an exemplar case. Earlier, he had noted in a passage that resonates with intimations of other colonial instances, "I have spent my life proving to myself that I am as good as humans. Remember. To Pope Gregory himself I once made the case that we had souls" (*Taltos* 297).

In spite of Rice's obvious affection for the Taltos, she does not fall into the trap of regarding them as noble savages. Ashlar notes that he would have killed Lasher himself for his offenses. He notes, also, in several places that there were "bad" Taltos and that disputes arose among Taltos. There were Taltos who had become bloodthirsty and even before their contact with technologically advanced humans with a blood lust, there were murders among the Taltos, rare as these might be (*Taltos* 296, 333, 336, 343-46).

The role of Christianity as a corrupting influence is a topic requiring far more attention than I can give it in this chapter. Rice's choice of William Blake's "The Garden of Love" as her tone-setter speaks volumes in itself. Ashlar notes that human sacrifice and blood lust are at the root of human religion (*Taltos* 348). Even as Ashlar is attracted to the teaching of the gentle Christ through St. Columba, he notes that even these teachings stressing Christ's gentleness lose their meaning, as they become the basis for even greater slaughter. The virtual annihilation of the Taltos results from their division into Christian and "pagan" groups. Ashlar himself is forced to watch the burning of his own wife who refuses to abandon the old ways.

As with many colonized peoples, Ashlar spends the remainder of his life as a marginalized person, seeking to prove in various ways that he indeed "has a soul." He is both repelled and attracted to his colonizers, unable to condemn all the members of the imperial group because he knows too many whom he loves among them but unable to accept them totally because of their numerous barbarities. Moreover, he has been educated among them and knows their high culture far better than most of their members. This ambiguity is echoed in the works of many Third World intellectuals (Achebe, Somé, Soyinka, and many others).

Certainly, it is clear that humans have exploited the Taltos. A mere listing of their atrocities is sufficient to make the point. Rice lists, at one time or other ritual slaughter, rape, infanticide, various tortures, and other physical violations. In addition, there are the usual psychological abuses: perpetuation of stereotypes, denigration of their physical and cultural traits, attribution of brutal traits, and various other means for devaluing their lives.

In turn, the Taltos incorporate and internalize this derogatory image. They view themselves as "different" and in need of proving themselves endowed with a soul. Often, they accept the fact that they have but two choices in life: either to "save" humans or to be a personification of evil for them, a "choice" often found thrust upon colonized peoples as Joyce Cary, for example, made clear in *Mr. Johnson* (1961) or as Dorothy Hammond and Alta Jablow (1992) show in their study of the image of Africa in British literature.

Rice symbolizes the horror of this psychological degradation and its corrupting influence of even "good" humans in Michael's murder of Lasher and Rowan's murder of their Taltos daughter, Emaleth. Rowan Mayfair is a surgeon/scientist and also the designee of the Mayfair witches' legacy. The spirit Lasher has watched over the Mayfair witches since the seventeenth century when Suzanne, a simple Scots "cunning woman" (a woman with power to cure) accidentally called him from his wandering. He has done so to work toward his return to the flesh. In Rowan and her husband, Michael Curry, also a Mayfair although he does not discover this until late in the trilogy, he has found the witches whose mating will allow him to return to the incarnate world.

Despite Michael's pity for Lasher after Lasher relates his tragic story, Michael kills him. In spite of her love for Emaleth, her Taltos daughter who saves her life through breast-feeding her, Rowan shoots her to save humans from the danger the Taltos present to their existence. Although Ashlar, Rice's most sympathetic and sophisticated character in the series, deepens their understanding of the Taltos and appears to change their views of them, these "good" people showed them no mercy even after first knowing their story, imitating the "good" imperialists who reluctantly killed Africans or Native Americans even after trying to understand and defend them.

The Family

Anthropological studies on the family stretch back to the discipline's earliest beginnings. Certainly, Lewis Henry Morgan's 1871 masterpiece helped set the tone for the profession. It noted the many various ways humans have interpreted marriage and the family and by so doing gave equal weight to these human inventions. That marriage in various places was seen as somehow equal to marriage in Europe and America was an important battle in the war for human compassion and the principle of cultural relativity.

Therefore, Rice's focus on the family is of particular interest to the anthropologically inclined, for her Mayfair clan is not a "typical" western family although it clings tenaciously to its Catholicism and includes members of the clergy among its members. It is a strongly matrilineal, almost matriarchal, clan. The female name, Mayfair, is taken and kept by its female and male members. Its legacy passes on to a designated witch and she is generally chosen by the holder of the legacy.

This Mayfair family of witches also has the protection of Lasher, the ghost whom Suzanne, the first of the line, accidently called up. This Taltos phantom protects the family and gathers strength and understanding from it, appearing to them and advising them. He is jealous of them and kills any who either injure them or whom he perceives as dangerous to his overall plan.

This plan involves a return to life in the flesh, a literal joining of his family with theirs. Since he is a Taltos, this merger is also a merger of species. A Taltos can only be born of a union of Taltos or of a union of a Taltos and a witch. There is a third manner in which they can be born, a union of a Taltos or a witch with "the little people." The little people often result from mixed unions.

This merger of species and subspecies provides Rice ample room for reflection on the manner in which racial and ethnic groups form and interact with one another, the explicit theme of *The Feast of All Saints* and some of her other works. In the Mayfair trilogy, she is able to treat the issue at a step or two removed and more metaphorically. She can bring in the language and paraphernalia of science, discussing genome, DNA distribution, the Darwinian theory, laws of heritability, inbreeding and its effects, and various forms of physical and cultural adaptation.

She can also reflect on the manner in which Lasher's relationship with the Mayfairs parallels some of the effects of the South's "peculiar institution." There is a good deal of reference to black and white relationships and "black Mayfairs" and "mixed blood." These discussions echo in the reader's mind as Rice draws out the history of the Taltos and one Taltos's particular interest in the Mayfairs.

Lasher's knowledge of the family, in fact, enables him through selective breeding to produce just the perfect combination of witches to father his own rebirth. Rice's insistence that even the supernatural must be understand in natural terms makes the return of Lasher even more eerie. Her attitude is amazingly like that of humanistic anthropologists who seek to understand phenomena in their natural contexts from the perspective of the people involved with these phenomena (Boddy).

Rice delights in tracing out the abstruse family connections, finding unexpected ties along the way. Unlikely people are seen to be related. In fact, the key relationship between Michael Curry and Rowan Mayfair is not revealed until well into the last book of the series, *Taltos*. The connection between science and witchcraft in the Dutch scientist who is an early founder of the family is revealed later in the series. Indeed, Rice's treatment of witchcraft as an innate tendency bound with physiological characteristics, in her telling genetic, bears a close relationship to anthropological treatments of the subject (Salamone).

Rice's treatment of a matrilineal/matrilateral descent system is also carefully handled. The descent of witchcraft through the mother's line, again found in most African witchcraft, is reinforced through incest of various kinds. This incest, undertaken under Lasher's influence but clearly working on people's predispositions as well, further serves to strengthen and focus the witch's power. Indeed, the stronger witches in the family are aware of this strengthening and see it focused through Oncle Julien, a male witch who finally proves to be Lasher's undoing.

It is Oncle Julien's fierce family loyalty that first leads him to cooperate with Lasher and then has him stay as a ghost to counter his power. The incarnate Lasher, certainly, is terrified of Julien, and it is Julien's appearance to him that forces Lasher into his fatal mistake.

In the last analysis, family prevails. Much of the chronicle stresses the overemphasis on family throughout the Mayfairs' history. Attempts to weaken the family, as on the part of the fanatical Carlotta, fail. Carlotta had killed one of the witches and kept another drugged to the point of catatonia. She had planned to burn the family center in the Garden District of New Orleans. Julien, however, valued family above all else, even his own redemption, and at the last prevails. Goodwin (43-44) is correct when she notes that in the final analysis Rice is writing a family saga.

The Anthropologist in the Mayfair Trilogy

In one sense or another, there are a number of anthropologists in the Mayfair trilogy. I wish to concentrate briefly, however, on the Talamasca, Ashlar, and Rowan Mayfair. These three provide sufficient examples to establish Rice's anthropological sensibility.

The Talamasca is a secular organization based on the structure of religious institutions. It is composed of scholars who observe and wait. The organization is an old one, stretching back to the early Middle Ages. Ashlar, in fact, had deep contact with them after his disillusionment with organized Christianity.

Their ostensible purpose is to understand religious, supernatural and occult matters. They worked to rescue witches from the fires of the sixteenth- and seventeenth-centuries' religious madness. They have saved many people abandoned by circumstances and have sought out those with psychic powers of all kinds.

However, their mysterious elders have kept a hidden agenda from the rank and file of their members, namely the search for the Taltos. In many ways, this search parallels that of those physical anthropologists who hunt fossils seeking for human ancestors and relatives. At times, they remind me of the scientists in the movie *Ice Man* whose work was, indeed, opposed by the humanistic anthropologist in the film.

Here that role is partially taken by Aaron Lightner, an elderly, gentle Englishman. Lightner is ambivalent about Lasher. His elders kept him in the dark about the Taltos, keeping the Talamasca's files from him. Their disregard for his ability leads to many deaths and near-deaths. They are willing to sacrifice almost anything for "pure science."

Lightner is not so sure. He is in the field and more involved with the "messiness" of reality. Life is more ambiguous "on the ground." He understands both his elders' theories and the pull of his family ties to the Mayfairs. By marrying Beatrice, an attractive elderly Mayfair, Aaron has become "involved" and lost his objectivity. The dilemma is a familiar one to most field anthropologists (Salamone and Grindal).

The battle between more humanistic and scientific anthropologist rages within Rowan Mayfair herself. She realizes the danger that her relationship with Lasher presents. Yet she cannot forego the experiment of continuing her relationship with him. She allows him to make love to her, a relationship he has enjoyed with his special witches. She communicates with him even as she knows that doing so strengthens him. She even allows him to be born in place of the child she carries in her womb. Finally, she protects him when Michael first attempts to kill him. Paul West is correct in noting that for the Mayfair witches "witchcraft is their science" (38).

However, she becomes appalled by his cruelty, by his disregard for others. She attempts to understand Lasher scientifically but inadvertently causes the death of the medical personnel who investigate the death. Rowan has attempted to use her power to preserve life, failing now and then to her deepest regret. The failure of her "experiment" with Lasher and her murder of her Taltos daughter virtually paralyze her. A position that some see as that of modern anthropology's, torn between the desire to be scientific and to express more humanistic concerns.

Finally, Ashlar provides a more fundamental and straightforward model for anthropology. He has been studying his people and humans for centuries. He has participated in many major movements, learning from each of them what is good and what is not. He has compiled a history and ethnography of the Taltos in what appears to be a sympathetic and objective fashion. He does not romanticize them. Rather, he seeks to understand his people. He does not, on the other hand, demonize humans. These people, too, he seeks to understand.

Ashlar seeks to understand a reality below the surface reality presented to the senses. In that, he shares a desire dominant in anthropology. Surface reality often blinds the investigator to what is really happening, as Ashlar demonstrates throughout *Taltos*. The human misunderstood the Taltos, seeing them as childish and incapable of serious thought. The Taltos thought humans to be like monkeys, incapable of further development. Neither group went beyond what presented itself to their immediate senses.

Moreover, it is only Oncle Julien and Ashlar who understand the true nature of Lasher and his innate evil. Evil, true, is always ambiguous and the overly softhearted are seduced by its ambiguity. But Ashlar is able to tolerate and understand ambiguity. He was able to pity Lasher but to point out to others how insidious his evil was.

This ability and desire to pierce the ambiguity of meaning, this contextualization of reality, is a basic prerequisite for the humanistic anthropologist. It is not surprising that Ashlar seeks out the evil that has corrupted the Talamasca, an organization he has helped and kept in touch with over the centuries. He moves directly to kill those responsible for unnecessary deaths and to set the Talamasca back on its scholarly road.

The Talamasca, Rowan Mayfair, and Ashlar provide some insight into the manner in which people and their organizations are studied to elicit meaning. The interpretation of actions, finally, becomes central to the understanding of those actions. The arguments that rage in the anthropological profession are interestingly reflected in the pages of the Mayfair trilogy.

Reflecting on Roland Barthes's musing on the significance of his shift from studying "works" to text (73-74), Giles Gunn notes the subversive nature of interdisciplinary studies (244-45). These broader studies upset critics, as do any studies that blur borders that once were distinct and apparently eternal. In a similar manner, Clifford Geertz refers to interdisciplinary studies leading to "blurred genres" and the hostility these blurred genres engender (165-79). Rice herself has crossed numerous boundaries in her writing. In so doing she has provided a model for the anthropologist who also seeks hidden meaning beneath the surface of the obvious. In her, anthropology has found a kindred spirit for its own studies of the ambiguity of human life.

Notes

1. Katherine Ramsland notes, "One of Rice's motifs is to begin a tale, then deepen it with a more ancient point of view: she did this in her vampire chronicles with Louis, then Lestat, then Marius, and finally Maharet. This brings her

closer to an intelligence that embodies the concept of continuous consciousness" (*The Witches' Companion* 435).

Rice notes that "I've always found the concept of a continuous awareness
to be very seductive. . . . There's a great promise of recognition of order and
justice and harmony; of all the suffering, pain and confusion being redeemed in
a moment of great illumination and understanding" (qtd. in Ramsland, *Witches'*
435).

2. I have leaned heavily for this summary and other interpretation on Ramsland's *The Witches' Companion,* which she wrote in cooperation with Anne
Rice. The specific pages in which her summaries are found are 207-09, 435-40,
and 474-79. Anyone seeking an in-depth understanding of the Mayfair trilogy
should start with Ramsland's book.

Works Cited

Achebe, Chinua. *Things Fall Apart.* New York: Astor-Honor, 1959.

Rev. of *Anne Rice,* by Bette Roberts, *Choice* 32 (1995): 938.

Barthes, Roland. *Mythologies.* Trans. Annette Lavers. New York: Hill, 1972.

Boddy, Janice. "Spirit Possession Revisited: Beyond Instrumentality." *Annual
    Review of Anthropology* 23 (1994): 407-34.

Cary, Joyce. *Mr. Johnson.* New York: Berkley, 1961.

Crepanzano, Vincent. *Tuhami: Portrait of a Moroccan.* Chicago: U of Chicago
    P, 1980.

Culler, Jonathan. *Literary Theory. Introduction to Scholarship.* Ed. Joseph
    Gibaldi. New York: Modern Language Association of America, 1992.
    201-35.

Ferraro, Susan. "Novels You Can Sink Your Teeth Into." *New York Times Mag-
    azine* 14 Oct. 1990: 27+.

Gates, Henry Louis, Jr. "'Ethnic and Minority' Studies." *Introduction to Schol-
    arship.* Ed. Joseph Gibaldi. New York: Modern Language Association of
    America, 1992. 288-302.

Geertz, Clifford. "Blurred Genres: The Refiguration of Social Thought." *Ameri-
    can Scholar* 50 (1980): 165-79.

Ginsburg, Carlo. *Ecstasies: Deciphering the Witches' Sabbath.* New York: Pen-
    guin, 1989.

Goodwin, Joanne. "Return of the Repressed." *New Statesman* 26 Nov. 1993:
    43-44.

Gunn, Giles. "Interdisciplinary Studies." *Introduction to Scholarship.* Ed.
    Joseph Gibaldi. New York: Modern Language Association of America,
    1992. 239-61.

Hammond, Dorothy, and Alta Jablow. *The Africa that Never Was: Four Centuries of British Writing about Africa.* Prospect Heights, IL: Waveland, 1992.

Handler, Richard, and Joel Segal. *Jane Austen and the Fiction of Culture.* Tucson: U of Arizona P, 1990.

Hobswam, E.J. and T.O. Ranger, eds. *The Invention of Tradition.* Cambridge: Cambridge UP, 1983.

Langness, L.L. *The Life History in Anthropological Science.* New York: Holt, 1965.

Mead, Margaret. *Coming of Age in Samoa.* New York: Morrow, 1928.

——. *Continuities in Cultural Evolution.* New Haven: Yale UP, 1964.

——. *Growing Up in New Guinea.* New York: Morrow, 1930.

——. *Sex and Temperament in Three Primitive Societies.* New York: Mentor, 1950.

Morgan, Lewis Henry. *Systems of Consanguinity and Affinity of the Human Family.* Washington, D.C.: Smithsonian Institution, 1871.

Ramsland, Katherine. *Prism of the Night: A Biography of Anne Rice.* New York: Dutton, 1991.

——. *The Witches' Companion: The Official Guide to Anne Rice's* Lives of the Mayfair Witches. New York: Ballantine, 1994.

Rice, Anne. *The Feast of All Saints.* New York: Simon and Schuster, 1979.

——. *Lasher.* New York: Ballantine, 1994.

——. *Taltos.* New York: Knopf, 1994.

——. *The Witching Hour.* New York: Ballantine, 1993.

Salamone, Frank A. "Gbagyi Witchcraft: A Reconsideration of S.F. Nadel's Theory of African Witchcraft." *Afrika und Ubersee* 68 (1982): 1-20.

——, and Bruce Grindal, eds. *Bridges to Humanity.* Prospect Heights, IL: Waveland, 1995.

Somé, Malidoma Patrick. *Of Water and the Spirit: Ritual, Magic, and Initiation in the Life of an African Shaman.* New York: Putnam, 1994.

West, Paul. "Witchcraft Is Their Science." *New York Times Book Review* 24 Oct. 1993: 38.

Gothicism, Vampirism, and Seduction: Anne Rice's "The Master of Rampling Gate"

Garyn G. Roberts

"Nevertheless, in this mansion of gloom I now proposed to myself a sojourn of some weeks. . . . Perhaps the eye of a scrutinising observer might have discovered a barely perceptible fissure, which, extending from the roof of the building in front, made its way down the wall in a zigzag direction, until it became lost in the sullen waters of the tarn."

—Edgar Allan Poe, "The Fall of the House of Usher,"
Burton's Gentleman's Magazine September 1839

Anne Rice is best known for lengthy novels, and her single most popular and famous of these is *Interview with the Vampire*, a genre favorite that came early in her career (1976); the short story is not her usual literary forum. The critical, cult, and mass-market successes of *Interview with the Vampire*, as is the case with several of the author's later works like those comprising *The Vampire Chronicles*—*Interview with the Vampire, The Vampire Lestat* (1985), *The Queen of the Damned* (1988), *The Tale of the Body Thief* (1992), and *Memnoch the Devil* (1995)—and *The Lives of the Mayfair Witches*—*The Witching Hour* (1990), *Lasher* (1993), and *Taltos* (1994)—are due largely to elaborately drawn and detailed settings, atmospheres, character types, images, metaphors, and allegories. It is obvious, then, that the short story does not afford Rice the opportunity to delineate such settings, atmospheres, character types, and the like; for Anne Rice particularly, the short story is a beast of another color—it requires a technique different than that used in her novels. Hence, the incorporation of very recognizable, even arche-typal conventions like very rich, easily recognizable character types, set-tings, rituals, and iconography accounts for the critical acclaim for her short story, "The Master of Rampling Gate," first published in the Febru-ary 1984 issue of *Redbook*.[1] The powerful, universal conventions of this short story replace the exquisitely delineated passages of Rice's novels. Subsequently, "The Master of Rampling Gate" is an important counter-point to Anne Rice's career, and is at the same time a logical component of that career. This story is firsthand proof of the dexterity of the Big Easy's most famous contemporary wordsmith. Because the story is very short (compared to the rest of the canon of Rice's prose), it is the story most often reprinted in anthologies that seek to feature a sampling of Anne Rice. Because of its typical and atypical qualities, "The Master of Rampling Gate" is a perfect choice for such anthologies. In essence, Anne Rice's "The Master of Rampling Gate" is so conventional, so invested with literary and cultural archetype and literary and cultural heritage at every turn, that it is inventional. This short story is a paradox; its weakness—strict reliance on very old conventions—is its very strength.

Right from the opening lines of the tale, the gothic imagery and setting are elaborately established. It is spring 1888—the Victorian era with all its trappings and connotations. We suspect that "Red Jack" (a.k.a. Jack the Ripper) and those of his ilk are close at hand. Rampling Gate, the gothic structure from which the story claims its title, is described as "rising like a fairy-tale castle out of its own dark wood. A wilderness of gables and chimneys between those two immense towers, gray stone walls mantled in ivy, mullioned windows reflecting the drifting clouds." The structure, the estate, is four hundred years old and is situated in the town of Rampling. The reader aware of world literary history is immediately reminded of classic stories such as Horace Walpole's *The Castle of Otranto* (1765), Ann Radcliffe's *The Mysteries of Udolpho* (1794), Matthew Gregory Lewis's *The Monk* (1796), Mary Shelley's *Frankenstein* (1818), Edgar Allan Poe's "The Fall of the House of Usher" (1839), Nathaniel Hawthorne's *The House of the Seven Gables* (1851), Bram Stoker's *Dracula* (1897), and an array of many other tales that feature castles and old houses, and the goings on in their deep, dark, moldy and dank interiors, as the initial imagery unfolds.

In London, a train's trip from Rampling Gate, the narrator and her brother, Richard, listen to the last request from their father, who lies on his deathbed. Their father asks that they tear down Rampling Gate— something that he should have done, but could not bring himself to do, a long time ago. The story jumps ahead. Two months after their father's death, the narrator and her brother arrive at Rampling Gate. We learn that the narrator is a writer, so she is equipped, as was Jonathan Harker (from Stoker's *Dracula*) before her, to relate events as they transpire. The narrator/writer goes to Rampling Gate not so much with the intention of destroying the "castle," but in quest of a potential story to write. This, as we immediately suspect and learn for sure later, is a ruse—she is motivated to make the trip because of her fascination with, and excitement for, the lore of the place. Already, in the first short paragraphs of

the narrative, there is a compacting and fusing of major literary conventions and plot motifs including setting, character types, situation, and
complication.

The father's last request reminds the narrator of a time in her youth
when her father flew into a rage at the sight of a particular young man
who, in the narrator's recollection, was "remarkably handsome, with a
head of lustrous brown hair, his large black eyes regarding Father with
the saddest expression as Father drew back." Mysteries surrounding the
young man, the reader suspects, will be steadily unraveled as the story
progresses. The repeated appearances of this figure in the early stages of
the story serve as a motif that contributes to the suspense of the evolving
tale. Rice further develops the character in the narrator's memory. The
narrator recalls, "I saw in my mind's eye that pale young man again,
with his black greatcoat and red woolen cravat. Like bone china, his
complexion had been." Already, the man is assigned sensual, even erotic
qualities. He is provided a mystique that both attracts and horrifies the
protagonist and reader alike, much like the allure of, and horror assigned
to, eighteenth- and nineteenth-century highwaymen and rogues like the
title character in Stoker's classic, *Dracula*.

Numerous other story conventions abound, and their respective
appearances are additional plot motifs for "The Master of Rampling
Gate." Included early in the story are "the old trap" which carries the
narrator and her brother to Rampling Gate, the "sky [at Rampling Gate
which] had paled to a deep rose hue beyond a bank of softly gilded
clouds, and the last rays of sun," the people of Rampling—villagers such
as those that populate Shelley's *Frankenstein* and Hawthorne's tales of
colonial New England—and Mrs. Blessington—the blind housekeeper
of Rampling Gate. Mrs. Blessington is the stereotypic, all-knowing servant who has spent many years at her post observing and protecting the
family for whom she labors.

Rampling Gate is a complex of conventions itself, replete with
towers, a massive front door, garden paths, and stone corridors, "bed
chambers well aired, with snow-white linen on the beds and fires blazing
cozily on the hearths," and "small, diamond-paned windows [which
open] on a glorious view of the lake and the oaks that enclosed it and the
few scattered lights that marked the village beyond." The reader gets the
feeling that should the true horror of Rampling Gate be unmasked for all
to see, the residents of the village of Rampling, these villagers, might
easily be persuaded to take up torches, pitchforks, and other implements
of destruction and storm the massive building in the dead of night.
During the early sequences of the story, Rice's narrator and protagonist
for the story ponders, "What was the house really? A place or merely a

state of mind? What was it doing to my soul?" Again, Poe's "The Fall of the House of Usher" comes to mind. The mystique of the building is central to the story. Obviously there is more to the gothic edifice than simply its physical structure. This is a powerful metaphor indeed. But there are many more such story conventions and plot motifs in "The Master of Rampling Gate."

Two story conventions that pervade the entire story are the moral dilemma and confusion in which the characters find themselves, and the oft-repeated phrase that becomes a story motif, "Unspeakable Horror!" The narrator and her brother, Richard, are faced with the responsibility of fulfilling their father's dying wish—for Richard this is no problem since he agrees with his father's desire to destroy the old gothic structure known as Rampling Gate, but for the narrator, there is a powerful romance of the place and its legacy that only increases for her as she becomes more and more a part of its history. For the narrator of the story, the moral dilemma and confusion become epic struggles within her, fueled by passion for the physical structure, its setting, and the young man who resides there. When the story concludes, the moral dilemma and confusion are resolved. In other words, the narrator chooses to either comply with her father's wishes or deny them. Such emotional, psychological, moral turmoil is, of course, a hallmark of tales of gothicism, vampirism, and seduction. Do we follow the mind or heart? The struggle is intense.

The phrase "Unspeakable Horror!" means implied, larger-than-life and incapable-of-human-description horror. The reader's imagination is to take over, and the assumption is that this type of horror supersedes mere gore and human agony and arrives at a supernatural, after-life damning and/or denying plateau that is so horrendous, so profound that it defies human language. There is a degree of intended and unintended art and cleanliness in this level of horror fiction, a subgenre of horror fiction as a whole, that is associated with the ghost story and writers such as Sheridan Le Fanu (1814-1873), M.R. James (1862-1936), H.P. Lovecraft (1890-1937) and others. In a sense, this type of horror is a horror based in fear of the unknown and the inconceivable. The "Unspeakable Horror!" motif in Anne Rice's "The Master of Rampling Gate" should be subsequently considered a very powerful, long-lived convention of the tradition in which Rice writes, just as the ongoing, intensifying moral dilemma is standard, archetypal fare.

Having arrived at Rampling Gate with her brother, the narrator begins to explore the world around her. The allure of the structure and its surroundings intensifies for the narrator, and the task before the brother and sister looms even larger, even more oppressive. Already, the narrator feels a sympathy for, and affinity with, the place, and the conflicts with her brother's conviction to tear down the structure, and within herself, escalate. Then, early one morning, a pivotal event leads the narrator to a point of no return. Here, Anne Rice pulls out the stops on the conventions. It is during this part of the story also that we learn that the narrator's name is Julie. In terms of the story's development, this sequence that begins for Julie one morning at 3:00 A.M. also begins the second quarter of the saga. Roughly one fourth of the story's text has been completed. (In total, in its original *Redbook* appearance, "The Master of Rampling Gate" is 166 paragraphs long, many of which are single-line pieces of dialogue.)

The plot thickens. After "some vague and relentless agitation, some sense of emptiness and need," Julie rises from her bed, dons a woolen wrapper and slippers, and walks out into the hallway. Julie recounts, "The moonlight fell full on the oak stairway and the vestibule far below." "The great hall gaped before me, the moonlight here and there touching upon a pair of crossed swords or a mounted shield. But far below, in the alcove just outside the library, I saw the uneven glow of the fire." The words and iconography speak for themselves; here, Anne Rice has made formula storytelling art. At first, Julie believes that the figure she sees is her brother, Richard. But, it is not. She comes face to face with the young man whose very mention caused her late father to recoil in terror. The young man is poring over a collection of loose pages in his hands; he is seated in a leather chair. His hair is "thick and lustrous and only carelessly combed as it hung to the collar of his black coat, and those dark eyes" look up suddenly. Julie recalls, "My heart stopped." " 'Julie!' he whispered."

The young man is the very conventional, but still dramatic, compelling, horrifying, and even attractive individual we have seen countless places before. When he first speaks Julie's name, we the readers first learn the narrator's name. The papers he holds in his hands are pages from her story and letters written by Richard that discuss the proposed razing of Rampling Gate. The encounter between Julie and the young man is fraught with complication and conflicting emotion, and it is Julie's curiosity about, and fascination with, the figure in the library area that tells us that the relationship between the two will not come to an abrupt end but is in fact just beginning. In this sequence, the conventions of the young man's description, Julie's troubled sleep and ensuing curiosity, the descriptions of the atmosphere and related iconography (e.g., the great hall, crossed swords, the mounted shield, the alcove, library doors, and the long supper table) in and about the library, and the deception that the man sitting by the fire is Richard, stand out. The blazing fire and the golden light the fire renders accent the scene. There is no doubt of the literary and popular media heritages that have fueled Rice's imagination and hence this sequence of events in "The Master of Rampling Gate." Among other things, readers may be reminded of images and sequences and events from English horror movies (such as those of Hammer Studios and starring Peter Cushing and Christopher Lee), and those based on tales by dark fantasist Robert Bloch (especially stories like "The Feast in the Abbey" [1935] and *American Gothic* [1974]). Of course, in the midst of Julie's encounter with the young man (itself invested with dream-like qualities), there appears the convention of conventions—Julie screams.

The next day, Richard rationalizes the previous night's events, and naturally, Julie disagrees with her brother's analysis. Yet another conventional conflict emerges, a conflict between reality and unreality, between belief and disbelief. In terms of conflicts, still more complications emerge. Julie further sees the paradoxes of the young man. Here is an individual of gentleness and innocence, it would seem, and mystery. She feels both revulsion for, and attraction to, him, and these feelings are becoming increasingly troublesome for her. Richard summarizes the situation when he states, "Julie, you have created an impossible situation. . . . You insist we reassure this apparition that the house will not be destroyed, when in fact you verify the existence of the very creature that drove our father to say what he did." Julie responds that she cannot go on living without knowing. The need to know is a powerful motivating factor in this tradition of literature. It is what leads story characters to forget where their best interests lie, and proceed foolishly into imminent danger.

There are yet more icons and motifs. Included among these are the grandfather clock in the great hall, the staircase, beds and bedrooms, and repeated references to the heart. Julie's heart stops, was beating too fast, becomes audible to Julie, and is eventually broken by the young man. And there is a revelation. Julie tells us, "There was a tingling pain in my throat where his lips had touched me that was almost pleasurable, a delicious throbbing that would not stop. I knew what he was! . . . 'Vampire'! I gasped." This revelation confirms what the reader previously suspected, based on hundreds of years of gothic and vampire fiction, and proves for Julie a source of ecstasy, delight, and trepidation. For a moment, Julie resists, but only for a moment. The pair begin an ascent up the stairs of the north tower.

With each step upward in the tower, the passion flares and burns brighter. Ultimately, the procession upward leads to a climax and kaleidoscope of images and emotions. The topmost chamber of the tower is flush with iconography and additional story conventions. The young man opens the topmost chamber with an iron key. The chamber itself is spacious and replete with high, narrow windows that contain no panes of glass. Here also are found a writing table, a great shelf of books, soft leather chairs, scores of maps and framed pictures, candles, sketches, and Julie's poems—covered in wax. Given the imagery throughout "The Master of Rampling Gate" in general and in this sequence in particular, one can sense a milieu of sensuality and even eroticism within the objects and atmosphere depicted. The list of conventional icons and standard props continues. There are a black silk top hat, a walking stick, a bouquet of withered flowers, daguerreotypes and tintypes in little velvet cases, London newspapers, and opened books.

There is something else, though apparent other places in the story, that stands out in this episode of "The Master of Rampling Gate." This topmost chamber of the north tower is filled with many varied sources of writing and illustration. Such libraries have been, of course, a story convention for this literary genre for generations. To extend the significance of this convention, Rice tells us that the young man has used Julie's poems and sketches to learn about her. But, this may be more than a meaningful, carefully drawn narrative element. Anne Rice, like her fictional character Julie, is a lover of books and poems and all manifestations of writing. We know that like most popular writers, Rice has an extensive personal library. Certainly there is a fantasy element here that extends beyond the fictional Julie, and beyond the author, to a universal level. Words and stories are seductive, they provide credibility and make human life significant, and they offer a sort of permanent record, a sort of immortality. Likewise, the sequence with Julie and the young man in the tower has such qualities of seduction. The vampire offers Julie self-fulfillment, significance, and immortality. The combination of the mysterious library and the mysteries of passion and love is most effective here.

At this point in the tale, we are better than halfway through the telling. And Anne Rice is about to launch into the most mystical, fantastic, and ethereal section of "The Master of Rampling Gate." The passion and romance between Julie and the vampire continue to grow, and the young man begins to ritually light the candles around them. He takes Julie to the window and presents her with a vision that is deep, dark, and complicated. Julie states, "I was afraid suddenly, as if I were slipping into a maelstrom of visions from which I could never, of my own will, return." The vision begins with the pair riding horseback through the forest. (Think of how many stories, including most notably Poe's "The Fall of the House of Usher," that begin with a horseback ride through a wooded glen or forest.) They come to a magical village Julie senses is named "Knorwood." Knorwood is a netherworld of the dead and undead.

Upon arrival at Knorwood, Julie encounters unbearable stench, the "most terrible of all stenches, the stench of death." And, in a most disturbing sequence of events, Julie follows the young man through one door after another. At last, they come "to a hot, reeking place where a child screamed on the floor. Mother and father lay dead in the bed. And the sleek fat cat of the household, unharmed, played with the screaming infant, whose eyes bulged in its tiny, sunken face." The true horror of this imagery and situation is that, as Julie's companion tells her, this is just the beginning. He has no power to change or stop events in this world. There is found death in all the houses of Knorwood, in the cloister, and death in the open fields—Knorwood is a village of the living dead and damned. Apocalypse—the judgment of God—is unrelenting.

Ultimately, the vampire tells Julie that he is the master of Rampling Gate, that he took the "Dark Gift" to save himself from the plague, and we learn also that "all through the walls of Rampling Gate were the stones of that old castle, the stones of the forgotten monastery, the stones of that forgotten church." It is apparent then that the complexity of this gothic structure goes even further. The vampire and Julie return to the tower at Rampling Gate—the vampire's sanctuary. At this point in the story, Julie begins to give herself, to relinquish herself, in full. There is romance and passion, and the life and world of the vampire is delineated in sensual, erotic, impassioned, troubled images. Julie is now fully part of this exquisitely painful world, and she now has the "thirst," and "the promise of satiation measured only by the intensity of the thirst." Her soul has been violated. The motif of "Unspeakable Horror!" reaches fruition—Julie realizes its full importance and impact. And as in "The Fall of the House of Usher," the people—Julie and her vampire lover/the young man/the Master of Rampling Gate—become one with the house/the castle/the physical gothic edifice.

In the final paragraphs of the story, we learn that Richard has signed over Rampling Gate to Julie; there is now nothing he can do to obey his father's dying wish. Richard stays at Rampling Gate, and Julie returns to Mayfair. Unbeknownst to Richard, Julie is accompanied by her new lover, the young man who again eludes the unbeliever's eyes. The vampire lovers plan to "hunt the London streets," and then plan to return "home" when Richard tires of Rampling Gate. In the most ingenious plot twist of the story, Anne Rice suggests to the reader that Julie and her lover's "hunt" in London at this time (circa 1888) is the explanation for the "Red Jack"/"Jack the Ripper" phenomenon of the period. The ending of the story is satisfying and unrelenting in its use of classic story traditions and conventions. Again we see that the strength of "The Master of Rampling Gate" is its very weakness; the invention is the creative, exacting use of age-old convention. And there are additional conventions and traditions yet to consider in the story.

Some of the most subtle conventions of Anne Rice's "The Master of Rampling Gate" are again age-old and are hallmarks, essential elements, and themes of Poe's "The Fall of the House of Usher" and all the rest. These elements and themes are related to issues of human sexuality in a range of expressions. Hence, in "The Master of Rampling Gate," there are found eroticism and sensuality of various sorts, homoeroticism, and incest. Remember all the connotations and meanings and puzzles of the physical House of Usher—its representation of the individual and social psyche and so much more? (At least that is what many literary historians, analysts and scholars have told us, and they seem to be quite credible in most of their discussions.) Remember also what was the single greatest sin of the Usher family—what led to the downfall of the family and the structure in which it had resided for generations? The answer to the second question, of course, is incest, what sociologists tell us is one of the very few and one of the most powerful taboos of virtually all world cultures. In "The Master of Rampling Gate," as in Anne Rice's novels, themes and images related to human sexuality are found, and there are indeed specific images and themes regarding aspects of this sexuality. Of course, the ongoing, developing, intensifying relationship between Julie and her newly found vampire lover is full of such things. In addition to and beyond this relationship there are more subtle, even implied, images and themes that contribute to an atmosphere, a literary tradition, and a sensuality that provide the story with yet another facet, yet another complexity.

Examples of such sensual and erotic images and themes in "The Master of Rampling Gate" include the following. There is the seemingly innocuous, but yet again maybe not so innocent, incident when the narrator recalls, "Richard [her brother] gave me the smallest kiss on the cheek." Some of the most dramatic, intense, and even disturbing images are found late in the story when Julie (the narrator) is taken by her new companion to Knorwood—a place of terrors and delights reached through a vision provided by the young man. In a sequence from that vision, Julie tells of the young man's encounter with the lord of the ethereal world to which Julie has been escorted. Julie recalls, "And my companion, my innocent young man, stepped forward into the lord's arms. I saw the kiss. I saw the young man grow pale and struggle and turn away, and the lord retreated with the wisest, saddest smile." Shortly thereafter, the kiss is repeated and elaborated upon, but this time, the horrible yet exhilarating consequences of the kiss are better detailed. Rice writes, "The kiss again, the lethal kiss, the blood drawn out of his dying body, and then the lord lifting the heavy head of the young man so the youth could take the blood back again from the body of the lord himself." The imagery here is disturbing, even brutal. There has been a terrible compromise, a sacrifice of soul. The two kisses frame the story within a story within a story: the story of the lord and the young man; the story of the vision/Knorwood; the story of Rampling Gate. As "The Master of Rampling Gate" further unfolds and nears conclusion, there is one more highly suggestive, erotic scene. Now a vampire herself, Julie needs victims, sources of life-sustaining blood and nourishment. Soon, she is presented with an array of erotically posed female subjects. In this story sequence, Julie comes upon "bedrooms papered in red damask, where the loveliest women reclined on brass beds, and the aroma was so strong now that [she] could not bear it." Elements of sensuality, eroticism, and sexuality are hence overtly and covertly incorporated into Rice's short story. And again, these are mainstay conventions of the literary tradition in which Anne Rice is working in this story.

In November 1991, Katherine Ramsland published *Prism of the Night: A Biography of Anne Rice*. With this publication, and her subsequent books, *The Vampire Companion: The Official Guide to Anne Rice's* The Vampire Chronicles (1993) and *The Witches' Companion: The Official Guide to Anne Rice's* Lives of the Mayfair Witches (1994), Ramsland has established herself as the foremost authority on the life and works of Anne Rice.[2] Ramsland's scholarship on Rice in these books, and in other places, is thorough, insightful, and well informed. In *Prism of the Night*, Ramsland provides a brief discussion of Rice's "The Master of Rampling Gate." What she says is revealing. Ramsland writes, "The story opens inauspiciously with the date of spring 1888, the year of Jack the Ripper, although no mention is made of the notorious killer."[3] What Ramsland probably means to say is that no direct reference is made to the Ripper at this early stage of the story. Indirectly, of course, the alert reader understands the convention of a setting established as spring 1888 in London. At a minimum, most readers—even if they do not associate the world's most famous serial killer with this setting—understand that this a time in world history near the height and end of the Victorian era. (Queen Victoria reigned in England for the better part of the nineteenth century.) Ramsland does mention some four paragraphs later in her analysis that, at the end of "The Master of Rampling Gate," "Julie becomes a vampire and talks Richard [her brother] into giving Rampling Gate to her. She and her vampire companion go to London to hunt for victims, presumably to set off the outrage and fear that took the form of a maniac called Red Jack."[4] So, Ramsland's analysis of this plot twist in the story is precisely accurate. In other words, Anne Rice only indirectly references Jack the Ripper at the beginning of the story via a reference to the specific era and geographic location of the setting. At the story's end, Rice brings the tale full circle by identifying the vampiric Julie and her companion as the explanation for the Jack the Ripper phenomenon. Remember, the true identify of the Ripper has never been revealed, although some, such as the notorious Aleister Crowley (1875-1947), claimed to have known the villain's identity.

From Ramsland's analysis, we can derive and verify two key points. First, and once again, a true source for invention in Anne Rice's formulaic "The Master of Rampling Gate" is the use of very carefully drawn, archetypal conventions like her reliance on a specific historical setting. Second, the ending, which uses the story's protagonists (indeed Julie and her newly found companion are the protagonists much as vampires are the protagonists of Rice's vampire novels) and their quests to satisfy their life-sustaining thirsts for blood as an explanation for Jack the Ripper, is a plot twist—an invention—which further proves the narrative a work of a clever, creative mind.

Katherine Ramsland observes something else in "The Master of Rampling Gate." She discusses the phrase in the story that becomes a significant motif—"Unspeakable Horror!" Ramsland finds the first time the phrase is used particularly revealing. She writes concerning the beginning of the tale, "One day Julie sees a pale man with black eyes who embodies for her the ideal of masculine beauty. The man glances out the window of a train, and her father cries out, 'Unspeakable Horror!' The scene demonstrates Anne's talent for creating impressionable images from fleeting images and dark hints."[5] In addition, Ramsland sees the sequence in the story when the vampire provides Julie with a vision of his world as important. Ramsland writes,

She [Julie] watches as time devours a village and expresses the sentiment that Anne calls up over and over: "And it seemed the horror beyond all horrors that no one should know anymore of those who had lived and died in that small and insignificant village." The mark of disloyalty to a loved one is to forget them when they are gone. It haunted Anne in its implications—that she was not immortal and would one day die and be forgotten. Julie's horror is the instinctive revulsion Anne felt over how human indifference can diminish a life.[6]

Ramsland's idea that Rice has a "talent for creating impressionable images from fleeting images and dark hints" reinforces the primary thesis of this essay. The impressionable images Ramsland identifies and references in "The Master of Rampling Gate" are the archetypes, the conventions upon which Rice draws from literary and cultural tradition. These images and metaphors are the substitutes for the extended images, metaphors, and allegories that Rice delineates with great detail in her famous novels. When Katherine Ramsland writes that "Julie's horror is instinctive revulsion Anne felt over how human indifference can diminish a life," she is reminding us that the most embraced storytellers—the most popular—like Anne Rice, strike a responsive chord of social thought and even morality, to which the reader responds. There is a great deal of sensitivity, passion, and compassion in Rice's writings—in this famous short story and her best-selling novels alike.

In her final analysis of "The Master of Rampling Gate" and its place in Anne Rice's literary career, Katherine Ramsland writes, "The story was a simple, romantic vampire tale, carried by the wealth of detail and voluptuous writing for which Anne was becoming famous, but without the complexity of imagery and metaphor."[7] Ramsland continues, "The published version cut out a few plot twists that Anne developed, and soon she made a decision to avoid writing short stories. The extended form of the novel seemed more fitting to her imagination."[8] This seems logical. Again, the reader comes to understand that elaborately detailed discussions cannot be provided within the parameters of the short story; there are some rather obvious constraints inherent in this prose form. But, Anne Rice does an amazing job in substituting for such complexity when she evokes centuries-old archetypes and conventions replete with very strongly implied images, metaphors, and allegories established and celebrated in genre and nongenre classics of days gone by. What reader is not stirred, having read and while reading "The Master of Rampling Gate," by personal remembrances of, and cultural references to, Mary Shelley, Nathaniel Hawthorne, Bram Stoker, and numerous others? The heritage is here. In 1991, Innovation Books, a comic book publisher, restored the excised material in its graphic novel adaptation of Rice's short story.

The debut of Anne Rice's "The Master of Rampling Gate" in *Redbook* is significant. In 1984, *Redbook* had a broadly based, primarily female audience. Women with a range of social backgrounds, professions, personal experiences, and philosophies were targeted in the pages of this, one of the most popular magazines of the 1980s, a decade after John Jakes had first introduced his best-selling historical romances commemorating the Bicentennial, first entitled *The American Bicentennial Series* and later retitled *The Kent Family Chronicles*. Larger-than-life, sweeping, international epics of love, romance, and intrigue were very popular—they had been in the 1970s (as with Jakes's *American Bicentennial Series*), they had been since the advent of serial magazine epics and dime novels in the mid-nineteenth century. And one cannot but see significant elements of these things in Rice's story. "The Master of Rampling Gate" combines historical romance, social melodrama, love, eroticism, gothicism, and classical literary tradition; subsequently, it has an appeal to a broadly based readership. For decades, *Redbook* has been synonymous with tales of allure, of forbidden love and fantasy that are both passionate and restrained in their presentation of story elements. "The Master of Rampling Gate," in 1984, fit this story form perfectly.

Two anthologies that have reprinted Anne Rice's "The Master of Rampling Gate" are Richard Dalby's *Vampire Stories* and Byron Preiss's *The Ultimate Dracula*.[9] Dalby's book reprints the *Redbook* version of the story word-for-word. Preiss's does not. So then, there exist at least four versions of the story that we know about; three of which are generally accessible to the public. The first version, Anne Rice's manuscript, is not accessible. The second version is the *Redbook* story that cut some story elements; the third is the further edited and revised rendition in *The Ultimate Dracula;* the fourth is the graphic art/comic art telling that restores material previously unique to the author's manuscript. Preiss's edited collection lists the copyright by Rice as 1985, not 1984 (the year of the *Redbook* publication). In this version of the story, Richard and Mrs. Blessington have much larger roles. Here also, there are far fewer elements of romance and eroticism, many fewer archetypal conventions. The story is smoother, but less artistic. (Maybe more mainstreamed—targeted at a less informed audience.) The blind housekeeper Mrs. Blessington has a much more significant, extended role, as do the memoirs of Richard and Julie's Uncle Baxter. There is no historic reference to set the time of the story at the beginning of the telling (no opening "Spring 1888"), though later in this version there is a reference to the death of Uncle Baxter some fifty years before in 1838. And, there is no apparent or obvious connection or reference to Red Jack. In general, it is also apparent that the story conventions so carefully detailed in *Redbook* are less frequent in appearance and muted in significance in the version of the story that appears in *The Ultimate Dracula*.

Innovation Books's comic book adaptation of Anne Rice's "The Master of Rampling Gate" provides the following explanation on its inside cover: "Adapted from the original manuscript by Anne Rice. An abbreviated version was published in short story form by *Redbook*."[10] In essence, the graphic novel (comic book) adaptation of Rice's short story is good, clean, and succinct. Several conventions from the *Redbook* story are preserved in the word balloons that accompany the illustrations. (The illustrations feature rich pastels and stark blacks.) Some of the conventions are captured in the illustrations. Still others are lost. Detail and imagery are often compromised in this presentation of the story. Mrs. Blessington is a significant player in the graphic novel, as are Uncle Baxter's writings. The graphic novel does not emphasize the Knorwood sequence of the tale as much as does the *Redbook* printing, but the comic book does keep the extended homoerotic episodes between the young man and the Lord of the Castle intact, dedicating several pages of illustration to the depiction of these episodes. There are other noticeable differences. Katherine Ramsland writes,

> Rice's original version of this story had a twist that *Redbook* cut, but was then restored when Innovation Corporation made it into a graphic novel. There is a blind housekeeper [Mrs. Blessington] who is aware of the vampire, and her long tenure at the mansion is a metaphor of endurance that parallels the vampire's existence. When Richard finds ominous diary entries his dying uncle [Uncle Baxter] wrote describing the presence in the house of a demon, he mentions tearing down the house, and the housekeeper warns him not to do it. (11)

Innovation's graphic novel adaptation of "The Master of Rampling Gate," owing to its restored storyline and illustrative contributions to the story, is an essential piece to the Anne Rice canon—for the completist fan and the scholar alike. This adaptation literally illustrates the reasons for the popularity of Anne Rice's prose. And the reasons for Anne Rice's popularity are many and profound.

Consider for a moment some of this century's most popular storytellers, authors such as Stephen King, Clive Barker, and Anne Rice, and motion picture directors such as Steven Spielberg and George Lucas. Each of these weavers of fiction makes millions of dollars per year because each is able to hit, exploit, or strike a responsive chord in American and world society. The genius of each of these artisans of the narrative is not in their new ideas, their groundbreaking, earth-shattering insights. Rather, it is in their abilities to reintroduce, recontextualize very old, archetypal, conventional storylines for modern day audiences. When analyzing the life and career of internationally acclaimed fantasist Clive Barker in *Clive Barker's Short Stories* (1994), Gary Hoppenstand suggests that these stories are "essential stories." He quotes Barker as saying, "It is not that the old stories are necessarily the *best* stories; rather that the old stories are the only stories. There are no new tales, only new ways to tell."[12] Stephen King has resurrected vampires, gothic mansions, plagues, werewolves, and outer space invaders in tales like *'Salem's Lot* (1975), *The Shining* (1977), "The Mist" (1980), *Cujo*

(1981), *Cycle of the Werewolf* (1983), and *The Tommyknockers* (1987) respectively. Clive Barker has done the same, with an even older, even more traditional, European-based literary mythology in his *Books of Blood* (1984-85) and his novels from *The Damnation Game* (1985) forward. Michael Crichton's and Steven Spielberg's *Jurassic Park* (1993) is a fun, imaginative twist on tales like Sir Arthur Conan Doyle's *The Lost World* (1912) and an array of early twentieth-century fantasies by Edgar Rice Burroughs (1875-1950). In his *Star Wars* movies—*Star Wars* (1977), *The Empire Strikes Back* (1980), and *Return of the Jedi* (1983)— George Lucas has recontextualized both the nineteenth-century American frontier-based western and 1930s pulp magazine "space opera." Lucas's Indiana Jones movies—*Raiders of the Lost Ark* (1981), *Indiana Jones and the Temple of Doom* (1984), and *Indiana Jones and the Last Crusade* (1989)—are modernizations of traditions established by H. Rider Haggard (1856-1925), Rudyard Kipling (1865-1936), and "adventure" pulp magazines from the early decades of the 1900s. Such re-introduction, recontextualizing, and reworking explain much of the critical, cult, and popular success and acclaim of Anne Rice.

Now, this does not by any means diminish the achievements of these distinguished artisans. The "art" in the creative outputs of such storytellers is in the writers' abilities to recontextualize, reinterpret, and recreate their sociohistoric and literary inheritances and the affirmation of these inheritances via their personal life experiences. Clive Barker is exactly correct when he states that there are no new tales, only new ways of telling the old. With this in mind, Anne Rice's "The Master of Rampling Gate" is indeed a masterwork. In this story, the old convention becomes the new invention. Easy enough to do, it would seem. But that is the deception. On closer examination of "The Master of Rampling Gate," the alert reader becomes aware of the deception. There is indeed a great deal of art in this tale. Each word and image is chosen with considerable care. Equally impressive is that the short story has specific constraints and limitations not part of extended novels—Anne Rice's narrative vehicles, it would seem, of choice. So, the art is found in the exploitation of the constraint, the exploitation of the profoundly archetypal. There were works of art in the seemingly limited media of the silent film and in the black and white daily newspaper comic strip, but like Rice's "The Master of Rampling Gate," these were exceptions to the rule, they were the best uses of their respective limited media. Evoking the oldest and most profound of traditions of gothicism, vampirism, and seduction, Anne Rice's "The Master of Rampling Gate" is a classic of modern fiction.

Notes

1. Anne Rice, "The Master of Rampling Gate," *Redbook* Feb. 1984: 50-58.

2. Katherine Ramsland. *The Vampire Companion: The Official Guide to Anne Rice's* The Vampire Chronicles (New York: Ballantine, 1993); Katherine Ramsland. *The Witches' Companion: The Official Guide to Anne Rice's* Lives of the Mayfair Witches (New York: Ballantine, 1994).

3. Katherine Ramsland, *Prism of the Night: A Biography of Anne Rice* (New York: Dutton, 1991), 236.

4. Ibid.

5. Ibid.

6. Ibid.

7. Ibid.

8. Ibid.

9. Richard Dalby, ed. *Vampire Stories* (Secaucus, NJ: Castle Books, 1993); Byron Preiss, ed. *The Ultimate Dracula* (New York: Dell, 1991).

10. *Anne Rice's "The Master of Rampling Gate"* (Wheeling, WV: Innovation Books, 1991). (Adapted from the original manuscript by Anne Rice. An abbreviated version was published in short story form by *Redbook*.) Adapted by James Schlosser, painted by Colleen Doran, lettered by Vickie Williams, edited by David Campiti, cover painting by John Bolton.

11. *The Vampire Companion*, 262.

12. Gary Hoppenstand, *Clive Barker's Short Stories: Imagination as Metaphor in the* Books of Blood *and Other Works* (Jefferson, NC: McFarland 1994), 15.

Development of the Byronic Vampire: Byron, Stoker, Rice

Kathryn McGinley

Tell me the thesis, so that I may apply your knowledge as you go on.
—Dr. Seward's Diary, *Dracula*

Dimly I view its trembling spark—
To-morrow's night shall be more dark—
And I—before its rays appear,
That lifeless thing the living fear.
—from "The Giaour"

An immortal with a mortal's passion, a vampire with a human soul . . .
—*Interview with the Vampire*

The vampire myth has been a part of human culture throughout recorded history. It has existed in some form all over the world, predating ancient Egypt and persisting through modern times. There has rarely been a people on earth who did not incorporate into their legends this idea of a creature that absorbs the life of another into itself through the blood. The earliest recorded evidence comes from Persia and Babylon, but the myth is found in all corners of the world, from the Aztecs in Mexico to the Inuit in Alaska (Marigny 14). Whether or not these cultures were in contact with each other, or with anyone at all, the myth is present. The belief seems to have originated independently as a response to unexplained phenomena common to most cultures (Melton 100). The famous Professor Van Helsing says so quite plainly in Bram Stoker's *Dracula*: "For, let me tell you, he is known everywhere that men have been" (245). This claim therefore raises an interesting question: what is it about the vampire myth that makes it so universal to human experience? And why is this especially true today, in this secular, technical age?

The vampire myth is full of symbolism. Vampires have been seen as a metaphor for everything from AIDS to addictive behavior. Such parallels can certainly be drawn, but there is something more basic at work in the vampire myth; it touches upon the most fundamental questions of humanity. What precisely is death, and what happens to us after we die? What is the nature of good and evil? How are love, guilt, and sexuality part of human life?

Three major authors have attempted to address these universal questions through the use of a vampire character, and in turn, made lasting contributions to its development. This essay will trace the use of the vampire character by three writers: George Gordon, Lord Byron, the first to make use of the vampire legend in literature; Bram Stoker, whose nineteenth-century novel is the most recognized example; and Anne Rice, who has updated the myth for modern times.

Vampires were present in oral history and folklore until about the eighteenth century. Interestingly, it was during this Age of Reason and Enlightenment that the myth reached massive proportions. The first written documents were accounts and treatises that served to spread the legend throughout a vast population and to give it the beginnings of uniform characteristics: a mobile corpse that sucks blood from its victims and can make others of its kind. It is immortal unless destroyed in a specific way, usually a wooden stake through the heart. Toward the end of the eighteenth century, the vampire became a popular subject of literary salons. Eventually science and reason prevailed, but could not extinguish the vampire myth completely.

As the Enlightenment passed into the Romantic Period, which was essentially "a rebellion against the atmosphere of material positivism and an expression of nostalgia for a fascinating and magical past, [writers] lost no time in resuscitating the vampire through literature" (Marigny 61). Goethe and Coleridge both wrote poetry involving vampires at the beginning of this period. The vampire's role soon took on a new significance. Once reason had disproved it as a thing to be feared literally, it became a symbolic creature. This feeling set the mood for all subsequent vampire literature, which includes poetry by Byron, Keats, and Baudelaire, as well as short stories by Poe, Dumas, Maupassant, and Gautier. However, the first novel to be dedicated to the subject of vampires was Bram Stoker's *Dracula* (1897), which is still arguably the quintessential piece of vampire literature, and certainly the most widely known. *Dracula* is very much a product of the Romantic movement, and of Lord Byron in particular.

The Romantic Period produced a related side-genre, labeled gothic literature, which often explores the tormented condition of a creature suspended between the extremes of faith and skepticism, beatitude and horror, being and nothingness, love and hate—and anguished by an indefinable guilt for some crime it cannot remember having committed

(Thompson 33). This definition describes perfectly the Romantic roots of *Dracula*. Such a description recalls the Byronic hero, a charming, seductive, aristocratic character with a diabolical narcissism and desire to control. Dracula, like many other vampire characters, is directly linked with the Byronic hero.

Lord Byron wrote during the Romantic period, in which the gothic novel was extremely popular. The cursed heroes of the gothic novel, endowed with diabolical powers, appealed to many readers of the time, and continue to do so today. This genre had distinct elements, among them the gothic villain, from which the prototypical literary vampire would descend. Byron incorporated this villain into his works, adding to it new characteristics that created what is now called the Byronic Hero. As we shall see, to become a vampire is quite in accordance with one of the developments of the Byronic hero (Praz 43).

Byron's poem "The Giaour" (1813) contains just such a character who has many vampire-like features. He has been described as a hero who is passionate, pessimistic, self-exiled, dark, handsome, melancholic, and mysterious (Skarda 53). This softer, more ambiguous representation of vampire-like heroes, formerly more powerful and harshly diabolical, "blurred the Gothic distinctions of hero and villain and made the self-tortured superman a new Gothic hero, the Byronic hero" (53).

"The Giaour" contains themes similar to those found in Dracula and other vampire literature. The poem centers on the hero's love for a Muslim's wife. The Muslim throws her into the sea for her unfaithfulness, and the Giaour exacts his revenge. Before the Muslim dies, however, he places a curse of vampirism on the Giaour, who is to suffer guilt forever for having committed murder and lost his love. These intertwining themes of love and guilt can be traced throughout the vampire legend.

Byron also wrote "Fragment of a Novel," a sketch later developed into a short story by Polidori. Both dealt with the subject of the Greek version of vampires, or Lamia. As Leonard Wolf writes, "Polidori gave us the prototype vampire as, at least in English literature, we will get him ever after. That is to say, as a nobleman, aloof, brilliant, chilling, fascinating to women, and coolly evil" (Farson 137). But Polidori was drawing on Byron's idea, and even though Byron discredited Polidori's story as an offshoot of his own "Fragment," and disliked the vampire subject in general, it is widely accepted that credit for the development of this character goes to Byron. Twitchell emphasizes the view that to a considerable extent the myth's currency is a tribute to this one man, for by the early nineteenth century the Byronic hero already had many of the mythic qualities of the vampire (75).

Polidori is not to be forgotten, however, for he made one very significant contribution to the myth. He added the characteristic of the "aristocratic vampire—a creature at once arrogant and seductive—of which Stoker's Dracula is an illustrious embodiment" (Marigny 77). By making the vampire an aristocratic gentleman, Stoker emphasizes both the attractive power and the virulence of the character. It is much harder to resist evil when it is presented in an alluring way. In addition, both Byron and Polidori succeeded in bringing the myth to the general population who, for the most part, believed the aristocracy to be corrupt. The association of evil with the aristocracy therefore was the next logical development for the vampire character.

The novel *Dracula* most certainly drew on these influential predecessors, expanding the villain and adding to his development. Its publication marked a true turning point in the history of vampirism in literature, constituting simultaneously a renewal of the gothic genre of the eighteenth century, a return to the orthodox legend of the vampire, and, most important, the founding a myth for modern times (Marigny 83).

Dracula himself is a perfect mingling of the traits of the Byronic hero. Based on the historical Vlad Tepes, the fifteenth-century Romanian count, he is the noble outlaw, a devilish aristocrat with an assertive desire to control, a passion for power and for life itself. He feeds this desire with the blood, essentially the life, of others, thereby either killing or enslaving them. Yet the irony is that he is also extending life simultaneously for those who also become vampires in turn. Dracula wears all black, and has a long mustache. His grip is ice cold. The Count is evil but seductive, and he lives in a dark castle in Eastern Europe. These various features, which define Dracula as the product of gothic villains, came together perfectly to create a wholly new combination, a more modern and complex Byronic hero. Byron's vampire works, as Knight writes, express recurring experiences with mysterious depths of passion and guilt, ecstasy and anguish, of which the Giaour is a powerful example (16-17).

Love and guilt are two such universal human emotions found as themes in the *Dracula* story as well. Love, in particular, is evident, involving the female character relationships, and in the novel, life and love are inextricably linked. The character of Lucy has many suitors vying for her hand in marriage. The three lovers are Dr. Seward, director of the lunatic asylum; Quincey Morris, a Texan; and Arthur Holmwood (later Lord Godalming), an English aristocrat. All three propose to her on the same day. She wishes she could marry all three, but chooses Arthur. The other men pledge eternal love and friendship for her anyway, and even Van Helsing, the wise scientist and father figure of the story, feels an affection for her. All the men in the novel who meet her are drawn to her, including Dracula; indeed, owing to her sleepwalking habit, she becomes his first victim.

Mina Murray is Lucy's dear friend and the fiancée of Jonathan Harker, the first character in the novel who travels to Castle Dracula. Mina's first sightings of Dracula come shortly after Lucy is first bitten, and she describes him as "something dark," "long and black," with "a white face and red, gleaming eyes" (Stoker 101). Whenever he is sighted there is a bright moon overhead, and all perceive him as an evil presence. This circumstance conforms completely to that associated with the Byronic hero for, as in "The Giaour," Byron also associated the moon symbolically with tragedy (West 21). In addition, the Giaour also has a mesmeric quality to his eyes.

Mina notices that the life is slipping away from her friend as, without Mina's knowledge, Dracula drains it each night. Interestingly, not long after the Count's arrival in England, both Lucy's mother and Arthur's father become fatally ill. Dracula is drawing the life forces out of all those around him. He is also, meanwhile, controlling the character of Renfield, a lunatic in the asylum. Renfield acts as both a harbinger of Dracula and his pawn, for Dracula makes use of him in order to get to Mina. Dracula's desire to control and possess is another example of his Byronic traits. Renfield, Dracula's slave and apprentice, displays this same desire in his eating of insects and animals in order to "absorb as many lives as he can" through their blood. Even as Dracula drains the life from his victims, however, some transform into vampires, such as Lucy and the three women in the Castle. Dracula is "continually creating in order to destroy . . . another aspect of Byron's 'heroism'" (Phelps 71). The synonymous creation and destruction characteristic of Dracula is typical of

the "fatal" heroes of Romantic literature . . . [who] diffuse all around them the curse which weighs upon their destiny, they blast . . . those who have the misfortune to meet with them; they destroy themselves, and destroy the unlucky women who come within their orbit. . . . the innumerable Fatal Men . . . came into existence on the pattern of the Byronic hero. (Praz 48-49)

Lucy and Mina represent the innocence in the story, as they are naive and angelic. They also represent purity, at least at the outset, for later they are both corrupted by the evil Dracula. As Lucy weakens, Dr. Van Helsing knows she requires transfusions of blood in order to live. These are donated in turn by her three lovers and finally Van Helsing himself. In this way, Griffin explains, she marries all of them and they become bound to her not only by blood but by friendship and love as well. At this point she is a passive vampire, draining the blood from them indirectly, unlike the women vampires in the Castle (140).

These transfusions make use of the idea of the lover's life's blood. Renfield himself says, "The blood is the life" (Stoker 149), and so it is stated in the Bible. Christianity, like many world religions before it, celebrates blood as a life force. Bram Stoker was not a Catholic himself, but lived in Ireland, a predominantly Catholic country. Therefore he would certainly have made connections between the myth and the Catholic religion. Christ shed His blood that men may drink it and have eternal life: "Whoever eats my Flesh and drinks my Blood, shall have eternal life; and I will raise him up on the last day" (John 6:53). Twitchell identifies this association:

Early literature reflects man's belief that blood was more than a metaphor or a synecdotal description of life; it was life itself . . . in both the Old and New Testaments "the blood is life" [Deuteronomy 12:16] motif is repeated again and again, both as objective statement and psychological truth. (13)

However, it is important to note that the Old Testament also cautions, in multiple passages, against the drinking of blood in an obsessive way, which would be seen as evil. But Renfield displays this obsession, most prominently in the line, "All lives! all red blood, with years of life in it" (Stoker 285), lives which are procured for him by Dracula. As Dr. Seward writes in his diary, "he has assurance of some kind that he will acquire some higher life. He dreads the consequence—the burden of a soul" (Stoker 278).

Bram Stoker agreed that "the blood is life," incorporating not only this trait into his *Dracula* novel, but many other Christian references as well. Most of the Count's limits are imposed by Christian, particularly Catholic, symbols. Dracula is powerfully repelled by crucifixes, rosaries, the Eucharistic host, and holy water. This reaction enforces the vampire image as a demon or devil, unable to prevail against the forces of good. Messent stresses this idea:

The terminology used in this novel consistently opposes the diabolic to the Christian. Dracula, alien to all conventional familial, social, and sexual patterns, has a terrible strength which threatens a supernatural disruption of what we call normality. (14)

If the "blood is life" idea is central to the vampire legend, the connection to love is not far behind. In *Dracula*, all four men are ready to give their blood, essentially their lives, as a measure of their love for Lucy. All of them are strong, powerful, young men, but each time their blood is transfused into her, Lucy's strength wanes. This is because Lucy, in turn, as Dracula's victim, is feeding her lifeblood to her own demon lover.

While Lucy is dying, she becomes more expressive of her sexuality, which is also closely linked with love, but here in a negative way. Lucy whispers to Arthur in a "soft voluptuous voice" they have never heard from her before: "Arthur, Oh my love, I am so glad you have come! Kiss me" (Stoker 167). But Van Helsing keeps Arthur from doing so, knowing what she is, and Lucy becomes her real self long enough to thank Van Helsing for protecting her fiancé. When she dies, she regains the beauty she had in life, so that Arthur doubts she is really dead. In fact, when Van Helsing and Seward open her tomb a week later, she is "more radiantly beautiful than ever" (Stoker 206). It shocks all of them that someone they loved so dearly could become something so evil; but this recognition is in keeping with the influence of the Byronic hero as evident in the Giaour who, by loving, also caused death, just as Dracula so destroys. As McGann points out, Satan, like God, can also work in mysterious ways. One would not expect to find love in a mortal enemy, or death in the heart of love. The Giaour finds both, and once left empty of love, burns for revenge (158).

Arthur also finds both. Van Helsing convinces the other men that Lucy is a vampire and must be killed by a stake through the heart and decaptitation. They lock her out of her tomb by sealing it with the Holy Communion wafer, but at first Arthur will not consent to any mutilation of the body. When they see her at last, she moves towards him saying, "Come, my husband, come" (218). His love, however, soon turns to hate and disgust. As Seward later writes, "Her sweetness was turned to adamantine . . . and the purity to voluptuous wantoness" (217); "There was something diabolically sweet in her tones" (218). It is Arthur who must finally drive the stake through her heart, thus placing her soul at rest. The Christian imagery is continued in a powerfully reversed analogy:

As Dracula is Antichrist, sharing eternal life through a communion/baptism of blood, this scene is a mock Resurrection, where Lucy's apostles find an empty tomb and meet with their risen beloved, as the moon emerges from the clouds. (Griffin 141)

The three young men now feel hatred for Lucy as a vampire because, in this form, her abundant sensuality repulses them. As a vampire, Lucy's physical aspect is emphasized. All her purity of soul now gone, she displays only "the whole carnal and unspiritual appearance, seeming like a devilish mockery of Lucy's sweet purity" (Stoker 220). The killing of her vampire form is really a necessary rite of purification, so that her pure spirit can be freed from the sinful, carnal nature of her body. The return of purity is made clear in the expression of innocent beauty that returns to her face once her soul is at peace. This change also illustrates the point that "the best in the human spirit always triumphs over an evil which is typically, if only symbolically, depicted as sexual" (Roth 128).

The interpretive criticism on sexuality in *Dracula* is prolific, but Roth is right when she says that "only relations with vampires are sexualized in this novel; indeed, a deliberate attempt is made to make sexuality seem unthinkable in 'normal relations' between the sexes" (113). This negative view of sexuality is doubtless due in part to the Christian context of the novel. Sexuality is seen as evil when it is based on sensuality and pleasure alone. Many philosophers throughout history have held this position that excessive pleasure, or any emotion when out of control, is evil. In the case of "Lucy's depiction we see concrete evidence that 'the vampires suggest . . . awakening sexuality.' However, the sexuality, once awakened, is terrifying, requiring for its defeat 'all the resources of society and religion'" (113), which are also needed for the destruction of the vampire. But unrestrained passions are characteristic of the Byronic hero. Dracula is out of control; he absorbs power and exercises it but does not adhere to any laws of control himself. Indeed, his plan is to make all of the characters vampires, and eventually allow his evil to spread throughout the population like a plague. However, such unrestrained emotions and carelessness are not without their price, for as "Richardson states: . . . 'guilt is everywhere, and deep'" (Farson 211).

Meanwhile Mina, being the closest friend of Dracula's last victim, Lucy, becomes his next victim. Just as Lucy was an embodiment of the theme of love and sexuality, Mina exemplifies the theme of guilt. Mina when attacked by Dracula begins to change as her friend did. Renfield, seeing that Mina is no longer the same, knows that "he had been taking the life out of her" (Stoker 286). Van Helsing realizes that Dracula is expanding his circle of power in order to harm innocent people; he is expanding his sphere of influence by using innocent people to accomplish his aims. He used Renfield to gain entry into Seward's house, which is in the asylum, and thereby get to any visitors there, namely Mina.

When they find her being forced by Dracula to drink his blood, she is dressed all in white, symbolizing her purity, while he is all in black. After this incident, Mina feels unclean and untouchable. When Van Helsing touches her with the holy wafer, it sears and burns her forehead. She realizes that she is "unclean," for the stain is a sign of the evil "infection" that was caused by the contamination of Dracula's blood. However, as Weissman points out, Mina is not doomed to the same fate as her friend because Mina fights becoming a vampire much harder than Lucy did, and does not ever become wantonly sexual (75). Griffin adds that

Mina's own purity is defouled now that she has crossed the border into sexuality . . . her reaction in this scene is that of the guilty adultress. . . . The scar, often referred to as a stain, of course duplicates Dracula's, but it is actually closer kin to Hester Prynne's red "A." (146)

The Giaour also, like Dracula and Mina, had a stain comparable to that of Cain, since his murder had made him "a Satanic figure . . . cursed with a curse almost as ancient in biblical terms, the mark of Cain: 'But look—'tis written on my brow!/There read of Cain the curse and crime/ In characters unworn by time' because he was the murderer, indirectly, of his loved one" (qtd. in Doherty 68-69). Indeed, it was not the guilt over killing the Muslim that plagued the Giaour but the guilt that it was his love for Leila that resulted in her murder. He is consumed with guilt over love, tormented because he thinks by loving her he killed her.

While Dracula shows no outward remorse for his actions, it is implied that he can feel something like love. As Hood states, "Even [Dracula] is sometimes overwhelmed by passion" (217). Indeed all the Byronic heros are described as passionate, and the vampire blood-exchange is a metaphor for sexuality, but something deeper is present, for example, in the passage where Dracula speaks to the three vampire women in the Castle: "Moved [by their criticism that he cannot love], Dracula denies the charge, declaring, 'Yes, I too can love; you yourselves can tell it from your past.' . . . Thus Dracula and his fiendish followers cannot quite do without some fossilized affection for one another" (Hood 217). Van Helsing tells the group that Dracula is "more prisoner than . . . the madman in his cell." Other critics agree with the idea of some sort of redemption for the Count. Carter suggests that these passages support some hope for Dracula's eventual salvation, and uses Van Helsing's remark to support her claim: "Oh! if such an one was to come from God, and not the Devil, what a force for good might he not be in this old world of ours" (Carter, *Specter* 113).

Still, Dracula is not really distinguished by feelings of love or guilt; rather the story only implies that he can feel these emotions, while producing them in others. Not until the legend reaches its contemporary incarnation is it possible for the vampires themselves to feel love and guilt for what they are, as we will see.

But salvation for Dracula is perhaps possible, as it was for Lucy at the moment of death. Mina Harker is supportive of some feeling of pity for Dracula:

That poor soul who has wrought all of this misery is the saddest case of all. Just think what will be his joy when he, too, is destroyed in his worser part that his better part may have spiritual immortality. You must be pitiful to him, too. (Stoker 314)

Here Mina feels compassion as well as guilt. She knows that she still bears the unclean stain, and she fears that someday she too may need the same pity she is imploring for Dracula. For there is still the possibility that if the Count escapes, she too will become a vampire. Mina's is the first notable instance of compassion being evoked for the evil villain in a somewhat Christian way. Her compassion for this tortured, desperate Byronic hero is also another way for us as readers to identify with the evil in ourselves, as Roth points out, because she is explicitly comparting both herself and Lucy to Dracula in this passage, evoking our sympathies for villain as well as hero, which are two halves of the one self (126).

When Dracula is at last defeated, these ideas of possible salvation for Dracula are not without fulfillment. Mina, at the moment of Dracula's death, sees in his face "a look of peace," as had been the case with Lucy, and for which Mina will be forever grateful. He has found release from his vampire form at last, and so will she from her own stain once he is dead. The end of the book ties together the themes of love and guilt in Mina, as Griffin writes: "the final sentences of the novel are devoted to the now 'stainless' Mina, the ideal whom 'some men so loved . . . that they did dare so much for her sake'" (148).

The interesting conclusion of this novel is an epilogue that discredits all preceeding events. The epilogue states that there is "hardly one authentic document" left; all are typewritten. Thus the characters can "hardly ask anyone to accept proofs of so wild a story" (Stoker 382). Stoker was one of the first writers to place the vampire story in contemporary settings. The narrative is told realistically, through journals, newspaper clippings, and a ship's log, in order to make it more plausible.

Thus the setting moves out of the fantastical Gothic Transylvania into modern industrial England. In using this technique,

Stoker himself bombards us with reminders that his story's setting is "19th century up-to-date with a vengeance"—shorthand, typing, phonograph recordings, scientific criminology. These technological items . . . set the fantastic events in a highly realistic context. We are constantly reminded that the victims of these strange events . . . are our contemporaries and fellow citizens. We are invited to identify with the protagonists. (Carter, *Specter* 103)

To make the vampire an active part of modern society, instead of the dark, reclusive creature of cemeteries like his predecessors, was an important contribution. It would be much more frightening for readers to think that such evil could exist so close; indeed, that it could be anywhere. It is also important that Stoker does not force belief in the story, but rather lets the reader decide. It must be taken on faith, if at all: "Faith in the unseen world, based on direct experience of the power of love, takes the place of proof" (103). Stoker was using a more modern stylistic tool, by presenting various eyewitness accounts and letting readers make their own judgments based on what would seem to be authentic facts from reliable sources, and not just village legends. This approach adds an extra dimension to *Dracula*, and as Farson states, the Victorian reader would not have seen *Dracula* as a Gothic novel, but one that was daringly modern.

Bram Stoker's *Dracula* became the prototype for the vampire image that has been followed closely ever since. Many other writers have utilized the framework of his novel, specifically the physical appearance and religious limits of the vampire, even to the point of cliché. However, at least one author has moved beyond cliché to new ground, further expanding the vampire legend for our own contemporary society.

Anne Rice, author of *The Vampire Chronicles,* was the first to write from the point of view of the vampires themselves. In doing so, she further modernized the legend, portraying as her protagonists the vampires Louis and Lestat, successively. These vampires are similar to the Dracula character in that they can be destroyed by fire and sunlight, and usually sleep in coffins, though they don't need to necessarily. But garlic, mirrors, and religious articles have no affect on these modern vampires. They are immune because they are no more or less sure of the existence of God than modern mortals are. To be harmed by religious articles would certify an evil, demonic nature, but the Ricean vampires do not have the luxury of this knowledge. Instead they are forced to struggle with questions of good and evil just as the rest of humanity must.

Yet both Louis and Lestat can be seen as modern Byronic heroes, according to some literary critics, such as Peter Thorslev, who distinguish different types of Byronic heroes:

Thorslev rightly insists that we should distinguish them from one another. This is precisely what was not done during the period of their greatest popularity. A composite "Byronic Hero" [was] described . . . as "a man proud, moody, cynical, with defiance on his brow, and misery in his heart, a scorner of his kind, implacable in revenge, yet capable of deep and strong affection." (Jump, *Byron* 87)

Elements of both of Rice's characters, as well as of Dracula and the Giaour, can be found in this composite definition. Often these traits are separated into two distinctly different Byronic heroes.

Lestat is the more classic example, the more like Dracula. He is an eighteenth-century French lord, the son of a marquis, made into a vampire because of his passion for life and his steadfast defiance. He is another noble outlaw, the aristocratic rebel, the one who craves power and independence. Varma's words can be applied to Lestat, for "in him we see also the emergence of the 'Romantic' character—an alien soul solacing itself in occult experiments with forbidden sciences or unscrupulous deeds" (45). Indeed, Lestat breaks all the rules, such as making a child vampire, revealing himself and the other vampires to mortals, and trying to become mortal again. According to Hennelly, "Dracula's revenge ('my revenge is just begun') brands him as Archetypal Rebel . . . as Demiurge or Rival of God . . . compared most often to 'the Evil One' himself" (154-55). Likewise, Lestat is a rebel, having been made a vampire against his will; he is determined to make the best of what he is, and finds vampirism the greatest adventure of his existence. He is referred to as "a perfect devil" and "the damndest creature" even by his fellow vampires. In Lestat, there is a splendidly aristocratic figure who has been corrupted from good to evil, largely by events beyond his own control, a natural leader of men, though basically an independent figure, at odds with others, someone with an unshakable pride, ungovernable passions and a ravaged heart (Doherty 50).

Louis was made a vampire by Lestat but has the opposite qualities. Louis is more akin to the Giaour since he feels an overwhelming sense of guilt at having to kill in order to exist. He, too, exacts revenge for the murder of his loved one. He, too, is more sensitive than Lestat, and the most human of Rice's vampires. Ramsland writes, "However, since he appreciates life and beauty and wants to believe that he can find some measure of goodness, he endures the guilt and hopes one day to transcend it" (168). Varma offers a useful definition for this second type of Byronic hero:

[Another] type presents an "imposing figure." He is an outlaw, a Rousseauistic sentimentalist, a humanitarian who combats life's injustices, follies, and hypocrisies. Haunted by a sense of lonliness, helplessness, and despair . . . [a] victim of Destiny . . . drawn to evil against his better will . . . a character who sentimentalizes over bygone days. (45)

Ricean vampires retain strong human emotions, including love and guilt, that take them a step beyond Dracula. Like Dracula, however, they are both heavily influenced by Catholicism. While traditional religious relics cannot harm them, they agonize over the nature of good and evil in search of solace. The Byronic hero is characteristically marked by guilt. Louis is the most influenced by his moral Catholic upbringing, retaining a respect for it even into his vampire life. This influence becomes the main source of his guilt. Lestat, too, feels guilt, but he no longer believes in God. This important difference makes his guilt different from Louis's, for Lestat does not search for redemption, nor does he let it consume him, as Louis does. The evil of one murder, Lestat claims, is infinite; thus, his guilt is eternal and can never be redeemed. Also, there can be no forgiveness, because there is no one to do the forgiving (Ramsland 168). Therefore, Lestat believes it is wasteful to dwell on one's guilt. He finds his comfort in companionship and, like other Byronic heroes, he "becomes too much committed to present experience to be absorbed by the memory of himself in the last one" (Fleck 170). The words of the Giaour could fit either of them: "If ever evil angel bore/The form of mortal, such he wore:/By all my hope of sins forgiven,/Such looks are not of earth nor heaven!" (11.912-15).

Rice's vampire heroes are also quite capable of feeling love. Though Dracula insisted he could feel love, his version of love was eccentric. Louis states that being a vampire is like being in love, which means to him to take things gently and delicately rather than to rush headlong into the experience (Ramsland 245). These vampires can also love each other, as they need companionship to endure immortality, although Louis believes it is the crowning evil that vampires, who deserve nothing short of destruction, can love each other (Ramsland 246). In addition, these vampires feel love for their victims. As Lestat says, "Drinking up their life, their death, I love them," words that are reminiscent of Renfield (Rice, *Lestat* 231).

The Ricean vampires are similar to the Byronic hero in physical appearance as well. Like the Giaour and Dracula, they are pale with mesmeric eyes: "The eyes stand out from their smooth white faces like 'demonic fire' or 'flames in a skull.' The eyes are variously described as extraordinary, incandescent, and hypnotic to mortals" (Ramsland 451). And like the other Byronic vampires, these are passionate creatures. While they are not sexual in the traditional sense, as with Dracula their blood exchanges are sensual, and the act of sinking their teeth into a victim's neck is pleasurable for both parties (although vampires like Louis, who feel guilty over this pleasure, take their victims more quickly) (Ramsland 445).

This craving for sensation is a particularly Byronic trait, and evident in the Giaour: "I loathed the languor of repose (11.987)" (Jump, *Byron* 69). Byron often felt that he was not living if he was not feeling some overwhelmingly strong emotion, the sufficient magnitude of which was often to be found only in trouble, as Praz explains:

Byron's moral sense functioned only in the exceptional conditions of a crisis, and it was only in the painful functioning of that moral sense that he found the gratification of his particular form of pleasure—"*le bonheur dans le crime.*" To destroy oneself and to destroy others: "My embrace was fatal . . . I loved her, and destroyed her." (47)

It is evident how close this need for intensity and subsequent destruction is to Dracula's, and to that of vampires in general. Lestat, in particular, takes pleasure in crime; he is determined "to be good at being bad." In this way he hopes to serve some function, perhaps even serve a good purpose by displaying himself as definitive evil. He therefore goes to extreme limits of evil, almost hoping to be struck down by God, so at least he would know of His existence. This particularly diabolic quality is also found in Byron's life and works, for Praz tells us that, like Satan, Byron wished to experience the feeling of being struck full force by the vengeance of Heaven, and so he sought to measure the depth of his own guilt (47). This same desire to provoke God is perhaps why Lestat does evil "just to see what would happen."

Just as Byron and his two facets can be found in his own works, so too can Byronic elements be found in the character of Louis. Calvert writes that Byron also "bore about with him an aura of hidden sins and secret griefs, an abysmal melancholy and misanthropy, not altogether at one with his nature. His heroes in successive romances are . . . eternally the victims of brooding misanthropy" (112-13). Louis is most certainly the brooding one, not at all one with his vampire nature. This conflict with his nature and his guilt over having to kill causes Lestat to reprimand and ridicule him. He cannot be completely detached from his conscience, as Dracula is, nor can he make excuses for his existence as Lestat does. Louis is an example of a further development of the Byronic hero, for in him

the Gothic element has declined, and the Gloomy Egoist and the Man of Feeling, both of them eighteenth-century types, have merged to form the Hero of Sensibility, a Romantic type . . . passive, intensely self-analytic, and given to projecting his peculiar ennui and suffering on the whole world of his vision. (Jump, *Byron* 76)

Lestat and Louis are polar opposites, each displaying different sides of the Byronic hero. Jump, who is also distinguishing between different types here, would call Louis the Hero of Sensibility, who typically enjoys tales and songs, he responds to natural beauty, he has humanitarian sympathies, and his love is as tender as it is passionate, containing gentleness and even softness of manner (*Byron* 71). The Hero of Sensibility is very different from the noble outlaw, the man of action, the type of which Lestat and Dracula are examples. Together Louis and Lestat make up the composite Byronic hero previously described by Thorslev. My view is supported in the following words about Byron:

He could feel himself the equal of the greatest sinners—the peer . . . almost of Satan himself . . . the aristocrat and the rebel were all equally satisfied [Lestat]; and so was the romantic lover, whose heart was broken by the loss of the only earthly being still capable of rousing in it the gentler emotions of pity and love [Louis]. (Russell 153)

A final parallel to be drawn between Byron and the vampire legend is the imagery of eternity and immortality. The vampire legend, of course, depends on immortality as part of its allure. The same is true of Byron, for as Knight writes, the image of eternity is present throughout Byron's work: "He is torn between history and tragic insight, mankind and lonely self-conflict, time and eternity . . . each at once symbols of both the natural and the eternal" (29-30). All three generations of the vampire myth examined here depend upon this concept. Dracula and the Ricean vampires are immortal, and the Giaour as well is cursed for eternity.

The concept of immortality and eternity is certainly one of the strongest fascinations of the vampire myth for us today. Humanity has always desired to live forever because of a natural fear of death. This is the same reason vampires frighten us, for they may bring death faster than we expect. For Byronic heroes, however, particularly the Ricean version, immortality can be simultaneously desirable and intolerable. Eternity can seem an overwhelmingly long time; and even they themselves are afraid of death:

Man in this Byronic world longs for "rest, but not to feel 'tis rest" ("Giaour" 995). Thus death is itself an unfulfillment, for all that we know of life is in the restlessness of incompletion. Eternal life beyond death is for them . . . a source of anxiety and sorrow, whereas for us it seems the image of all human needs. (McGann 164)

This very human fear of death, which the vampires retain, is why they need to be a part of human society; not only are mortals a source of sustenance but they are also a source of comfort, which the Byronic heroes need, and of emotions, which they so crave. This need to be near mortals is why Rice's vampires discover that they must live out at least one mortal human lifetime, or they will lack the endurance for immortality:

Man longs to be freed of nature, but once released to imaginitive realms . . . he needs to involve himself back in time and natural cycle. . . . Only in such surroundings can the imagination guarantee itself life. (McGann 164)

Both Louis and Lestat confirm this longing in their love for humans and the products of humanity, such as art and music. This desire to be a part of humanity is also why Lestat believes that the contemporary world needs his new type of evil, which he calls "a new evil for modern times," far beyond that of Dracula. The modern world rejects superstition. He tells a coven of Dracula-like vampires: "Don't you see? . . . It is a new age. It requires a new evil. And I am that new evil . . . I am the vampire for these times" (Rice, *Lestat* 228). The desire to be a part of humanity is also the reason Lestat undertakes an experiment to become mortal again. In making her vampires more human than Dracula, capable of love and suffering under the weight of a guilty conscience, which Dracula did not possess, Rice has modernized the vampire legend even further, while simultaneously returning it to its Byronic roots. As she says herself, the magnetism of her vampires is "the idea that these characters are tragic heroes and heroines, that they have a conscience. They have hearts, they have souls, they suffer lonliness, and they know what they're doing. They don't want to be [killing], and yet it is their nature" (qtd. in Ramsland 446-47).

Just as these vampires have a need and love for mortals, so too do we seem to have a need and love for vampires. Marigny alludes to their lasting presence when he writes that people today find vampires frightening not because they exist but because they embody humanity's most hidden fears and desires (63). Why is this the case? Why has the myth persisted when other stories are long forgotten, or have lost their hold on humanity's imagination?

The vampire has endured throughout recorded history, and it has done so because its details have adapted, as humanity has, to changing times. But the real reason for its endurance is its universal appeal. Farson suggests that many people find a resemblance between themselves and Dracula, and between themselves and vampires in general, thus explaining the myth's popularity (158). The character appeals to human desires for immortality, while being a metaphor for universal human sexuality. Many believe these are the definitive fascinations, along with the added strength and power of the rebellious hero. But the reason why the myth is so relevant to the human condition concerns more than just a desire for unlimited power; the fascination cannot be summed up so simply. The vampire has persisted even today in this technological, secular world, because he represents the alienation the modern world produces in all of us. He is part of humanity, but forever separate.

Messent concurs with this view when he writes that our human universe is changing from one ruled by angels and devils at battle, to one ruled by order and disorder, chaos and anarchy which create a hostile and random universe (14). This common alienation, perhaps, is why we can have some sympathy for the vampire, why we have unfailingly embraced the legend as part of collective human culture. We can identify with him, with his need for love, his feelings of guilt, and even with his evil. Farson writes that the public will never tire of seeing Dracula, because he represents the evil in all of us (147).

The vampire, both in itself and as an example of the Byronic hero, holds a timeless fascination for us. He, like his literary progenitors, can be found directly or indirectly in countless examples of respected literature:

What, at any rate, is certain is that the Byronic [hero] has a continuing and universal relevance. It was no accident, for example, that James Joyce should have introduced . . . the Giaour and other Byronic Heroes into *Finnegan's Wake*, itself a powerful parable of chaos and disorientation. Joyce clearly saw them . . . as prototypes of modern man, wandering exiled and lost in an anarchic universe. (Phelps 74)

Although several critics have noted the Romantic foundations of vampire literature, only Peter Thorslev has explicitly linked the Byronic hero and the vampire myth. Until now, however, none examined the persistence of the connection through the examination of a chronological development of the vampire character from its Romantic roots to its contemporary form with the Byronic hero in mind. In doing so, this essay has attempted to demonstrate the parallel and interdependent development of these two classic literary traditions.

Without Byron's contribution, the vampire might possibly have passed into obscure mythology. Byron had a symbiotic relationship with the vampire, using its qualities of dark mystery to his advantage in his heroes, while at the same time infusing it with his own passion and rebelliousness. He sustained the story, giving it new appeal among the general population during a time of increasing secular materialism when it might have died out. In return the vampire legend has permanently incorporated his spirit:

The heros of . . . the Eastern tales [such as] the Giaour . . . are gloomy, misanthropic, and lonely; . . . they are intrepid, lawless and fiercely passionate. Endowed with illicit desires, guilt, remorse, and revenge, and equipped with fictitious adventures, these outlaw-heroes play their romantic tragedies against a background of Byron's own Eastern experiences. (Trueblood 60)

For all the vital originality of Byron's contribution, however, Bram Stoker is the one most responsible for the prevalence of our image of the vampire today. His complete novel spread a composite version of the legend, making it standard throughout the world. To this day, after nearly a century, Dracula is still the definitive vampire and the authoritative example of the legend in literature:

Dracula has astounding staying power . . . perhaps it is a sign that our folk heroes have become steadily less innocent. . . . With the aimlessness of our values, it seems as though we need Dracula today . . . there is a healthy release from the mundane. Virginia Woolf wrote: "The preternatural has both great advantages and risks: the former, because, no doubt, it eliminates the blows and cuffs that real life deals." (Farson 170)

Dracula serves many functions in modern society. Not only does it offer a release from the ordinary in an exciting way, but through our identification it expresses our own fears and desires as human beings. Through Dracula we can understand the darker side of ourselves; since he, like vampires in general, was once human too, we can relate to him and see a little of ourselves in him.

Dracula not only drew on the Byronic tradition and Romantic heroes of the past but laid the foundations for the continuance of the legend into contemporary times. Although one might think that in a technological age there would be no room for such superstition, some writers such as Anne Rice attempt to make us focus again on the value of the vampire myth, and to see past the commercialism that has surrounded it recently. Ricean vampires not only update the myth for post-Victorian society, but simultaneously return it to its Byronic origins. Still, this development of the character could not have happened had *Dracula* not first defined the hero-villain:

In *Dracula* the concept of a power struggle between universal forces of darkness and light is accented by the figure of the alien, a figure whose features have distinguished literature from "Melmoth the Wanderer" to Anne Rice's *Interview with the Vampire.* (Messent 13)

All three of these writers, Byron, Stoker, and Rice, have made lasting contributions to the vampire legend. Byron gave the vampire its spirit, Stoker its character, and Rice its conscience. Through them all has emerged the image we are so familiar with today.

Through all three stages of its development, Romantic, early modern, and contemporary, the Byronic vampire image has certain constants, the most basic and necessary of which are love and guilt. These themes are common to all the examples used here, to many other pieces of literature, and to human existence itself. They explain the relevance of the myth and its presence in all world cultures and time periods. As emotions they are Romantic themes, but with universal affinities. For this reason the vampire legend has endured, and will continue to do so. For this reason, in human literature and culture, the vampire is immortal.

Selected References

Byron, George Gordon, Lord. "The Giaour." *Childe Harold's Pilgrimage and other Romantic Poems.* Ed. John D. Jump. London: J.M. Dent, 1975. 141-72.

Calvert, William J. *Byron: Romantic Paradox.* New York: Russell, 1962.

Carter, Margaret L., ed. *Dracula: The Vampire and the Critics.* Ann Arbor, MI: UMI Research, 1988.

——. *Specter or Delusion?: The Supernatural in Gothic Fiction.* Ann Arbor, MI: UMI Research, 1987.

Doherty, Frances M. *Byron: Literary Critiques*. New York: Arco, 1969.

Farson, Daniel. *The Man Who Wrote Dracula*. New York: St. Martin's, 1975.

Fleck, P.D. "Romance in Byron's 'The Island.'" Jump 163-83.

Griffin, Gail B. "'Your Girls That You All Love Are Mine': Dracula and the Victorian Male Sexual Imagination." Carter, *Dracula* 138-48.

Hennelly, Mark M., Jr. "*Dracula*: The Gnostic Quest and Victorian Wasteland." Messant 139-55.

Hood, Gwenyth. "Sauron and Dracula." Carter, *Dracula* 215-30.

Jump, John D. *Byron*. London: Routledge, 1972.

——, ed. *Byron: A Symposium*. New York: Barnes, 1975.

Knight, G. Wilson. "The Two Eternities." West 15-30.

Marigny, Jean. *Vampires: Restless Creatures of the Night*. New York: Abrams, 1993.

McGann, Jerome J. *Fiery Dust: Byron's Poetic Development*. Chicago: U of Chicago P, 1968.

Melton, J. Gordon. *The Vampire Book: The Encyclopedia of the Undead*. Detroit: Visible Ink, 1994.

Messent, Peter B., ed. *Literature of the Occult*. Englewood Cliffs, NJ: Prentice, 1981.

Phelps, Gilbert. "The Byronic Byron." Jump 52-75.

Praz, Mario. "Metamorphoses of Satan." West 42-49.

Ramsland, Katherine. *The Vampire Companion*. New York: Ballantine, 1993.

Rice, Anne. *Interview with the Vampire*. 1976. New York: Ballantine, 1987.

——. *The Vampire Lestat*. 1985. New York: Ballantine, 1986.

Roth, Phyllis A. *Bram Stoker*. Boston: Twayne, 1982.

Russell, Bertrand. "Byron." West 151-56.

Skarda, Patricia L., ed. *The Evil Image: Two Centuries of Gothic Short Fiction and Poetry*. New York: Meridian, 1981.

Stoker, Bram. *Dracula*. New York: Signet, 1965.

Thompson, G.R. "A Dark Romanticism: In Quest of a Gothic Monomyth." Messent 31-39.

Trueblood, Paul G. *Lord Byron*. Boston: Twayne, 1977.

Twitchell, James B. *The Living Dead: A Study of the Vampire in Romantic Literature*. Durham, NC: Duke UP, 1981.

Varma, Devendra P. "Quest of the Numinous: The Gothic Flame." Messent 40-50.

Weissman, Judith. "Women and Vampires: Dracula as a Victorian Novel." Carter, *Dracula* 69-77.

West, Paul, ed. *Byron: A Collection of Critical Essays*. Englewood Cliffs, NJ: Prentice-Hall, 1965.

Anne Rice:
Raising Holy Hell, Harlequin Style

Edward J. Ingebretsen

. . . the first maker of the Gods was fear.

—William James,
The Varieties of Religious Experience

Our fiction is not merely a flight from the physical data of the actual world. . . . It is, bewilderingly and embarrassingly, a gothic fiction, non-realistic and negative, sadist and melodramatic—a literature of darkness and the grotesque.

—Leslie Fiedler
Love and Death in the American Novel

what can be imagined can be done

—Anne Rice

The American gothic—like its Old World counterpart—remains a tradition almost obsessively concerned with the hazards of social memory. Fantasy genres, generally devalued and discredited, nonetheless have important work to do; they construct within approved parameters public memory, principally, one could argue, looking ahead and looking behind—formulaic terror on the one hand and formalized nostalgia on the other. Both extremes have been crucial modes of self-reflection in the New World since colonial times.

It is customary to talk about "subtext" and "submerged values" in the gothic tradition (by which, generally, are meant garden-variety Marxist, political ones).[1] However, it is less usual to consider this protean genre from a theologically nuanced perspective—that is, as a genre that questions metaphysical ideologies, in addition to whatever social commentary it may make. Perhaps it is easier to presume that writers of Christian allegory read life through the prescriptive focus of an a priori cosmology. John Bunyan's *The Pilgrim's Progress*, for instance, enacts metaphysics as politics while displacing social conflict into moralized emotions. At first glance it may be less easy to observe that same mystification at work in Robert Heinlein's *Stranger in a Strange Land,* or in Ray Bradbury's *Something Wicked This Way Comes,* or in Anne Rice's *Interview with the Vampire.* Yet all three are equally weighted with moralistic zeal—much of it post-puritanical, even post-Christian.[2]

Nonetheless, theology always had been the ghost rattling in the gothic literary basement. In *Horror Fiction in the Protestant Tradition* Victor Sage points out that the "rhetoric of the horror novel is demonstrably theological in character."[3] Joel Porte explains that in the tradition of Ann Radcliffe, the "proper business of the orthodox novel of Terror was to expand the soul religiously" ("In the Hands of an Angry God" 43).[4] Porte likewise argues for the importance of "Protestant—indeed Calvinist—religious motifs" in the genre of the novel of terror:

Viewing Gothic mystery thus, as a substitute for discredited religious mystery, we may consent to recognize that . . . *le genre noir* represented for its producers and consumers alike a genuine expression of profound religious malaise. (43n)

Porte concludes as "surprising," how little "systematic consideration has been given to Gothic fiction as the expression of a fundamentally Protestant theological or religious disquietude" (43).

Elsewhere (in *Maps of Heaven, Maps of Hell: Religious Terror as Memory from the Puritans to Stephen King*) I extend Porte's observation that gothic texts derive their emotive power from a metaphysical discourse that is fiercely disallowed in public. I argue that the "terroristic literature" (Oral Coad's term) of an Anglophile literary tradition serves as a repository for religious imperatives suppressed by political expediency. A quick glance reflects the still-evident theologies shadowing political fantasies of chosenness, race, and nationalism. For example, Cotton Mather (of Salem infamy), in sermons and apocalyptic theologies, customarily employed a rhetoric of spiritual terror for the purpose of reforming civic order. Jonathan Edwards, likewise, caused civic hysteria through his use of paranoiac religious fantasies. From a more literary perspective, in his short fiction and novels Nathaniel Hawthorne's irony undercuts domestic as well as religious pieties, while Melville's Captain Ahab finds the "pasteboard masks" of illusory reality as formidable an adversary as the white whale. In this century H.P. Lovecraft's breathless apostasies invert this tradition of religious rhetoric, while contemporary markets for horror and sentiment keep raising these restless ghosts. In a determinedly secular age, shadows still exist of a history of divine privilege.

The religious cosmology inspired by the Calvinists and typified in Edwards's classic sermon, "Sinners in the Hands of an Angry God," can be seen, then, to continue as paradigm of American intellectual history. It was abstracted, mystified, and secularized in Emerson and the nineteenth-century tradition of drawing-room poetry. Reappropriated in the fantasies of horrorists like Poe and H.P. Lovecraft, the confusing mix of entrapment, victimization, and expiation typical of this cosmology blended into an enduring and recognizable formula of "religious eroticism" (Germaine Greer qtd. in Russ 676). Such a process is at work in the early days of the horror revival (Friedkin's *The Exorcist*), and more recently, in the breathless tabloid moralisms of Stephen King, Dean Koontz, and in the various gothics of Anne Rice.

Theological disputation, then, remains a traditionally gothic activity, and nowhere is it more in evidence than in Anne Rice's *Interview with the Vampire*. Dictating his life to a young man wielding a tape-recorder (*interview* is not quite the proper term for the one-way nature of the narration), the novel's main character, the vampire Louis, finds himself interleaving theodicies and proofs for the existence of God along with his autobiographical reflections. After much anguished speculation, Louis concludes that his own immortal existence is an ontological impossibility and, therefore, the greatest *proof* of God's absence. Louis recalls the time he wandered into the Cathedral of St. Louis in New Orleans, only to realize that he was the sole supernatural presence in the sacred building. Louis muses, ". . . neither heaven nor hell seemed more than a tormenting fancy. To know, to believe, in one or the other . . . that was perhaps the only salvation for which I could dream" (*Interview* 164). Louis's reflection confirms Maurice Levy's insight that "in some sense the fantastic is a compensation that man provides for himself, at the level of the imagination, for what he has lost at the level of faith" (qtd. in Porte 43). Louis himself says as much when he meets Armand, the powerful Parisian vampire: "after seeing what I have become . . . I can now accept the most fantastical truth of all: that there is no meaning to any of this!" (*Interview* 241).

In its theological self-reflexivity, then, Rice's *Interview* conforms to the theologized gothic identified by Sage, Porte, DeLamotte, and Levy. Yet more remains to be said. Among other problems there remains the difficulty of taxonomizing gothic texts in the first place. David H. Richter's analysis of the gothic mode leaves the way clear for some useful distinctions, particularly between the gothic genre and its hybrid offspring, the text of terror, with which David Punter sees the gothic as "primarily" concerned (*Literature of Terror*).

By 1830, the original impulse of the Gothic was spent, though the tale of terror was to survive both as an influence upon mainstream realistic fiction through the Victorian era and beyond, and in its purest form as a minor subgenre of the novel in both high and popular art right up to the present. (Richter 149)

Richter is correct in distinguishing between the "original impulse of the Gothic" and the "tale of terror" that survived it. The "original impulse," as numerous critics observe, was a reaction to the conservativism of neoclassic literature; the "tale of terror" emerged from a tradition of sermons and broadsides, flourished for a time with the traditional genre, and then finally superseded it in its tabloid and sentimentalized versions. Nonetheless, while I don't share Richter's confidence that "we all know intuitively what the Gothic is" I do agree with him that "it is not one but at least three things" (150). The "Gothic flame," in Devendra Varma's expression, has kindled a number of diverse sparks—including, as Bette Roberts catalogs them, "Gothic science fiction, Gothic detective fiction, Gothic erotica, and other hybrids" (Roberts 18).

In her study of Anne Rice, Bette Roberts argues that Rice follows the "male Gothic" example of Matthew Lewis, noting that his ur-gothic *The Monk* is characterized by "physical horror," rather than by the interiorized drama proper to the Radcliffean tradition. The difference, Roberts writes, is the "distinction between the . . . psychological terror in the female Gothic novels and that of physical horror in those written by men" (16). Yet Rice is accomplished in both modes, as well as being conversant with several others. Although she is best known for her trilogy, *The Vampire Chronicles,* she has also written at least two historical novels and an assortment of other "erotics." In all of these, elements of the gothic—as well as the romance, historical novel, and sentimental tale of confession—mix and conjoin. Consequently, it is often difficult, critically, to place a specific text.[5]

In her gothic texts, for instance, Rice consciously rejects the anti-Catholicism conventionally associated with the genre. As she remarked in a *Playboy* interview with Digby Diehl, it was exposure to the vivid and marvelous lives of the Catholic hagiographic tradition that first interested her in genres of the supernatural. Nor are her unabashedly New World vampires ecclesiaphobic in the accustomed mode of vampires. Louis, good New Orleans Catholic, loves the baroque trappings of church equipage and liturgy: "I was a Catholic; I believed in saints. I lit tapers before their marble statues in churches; I knew their pictures, their symbols, their names" (*Interview* 7-8). Further, speaking to the young man in contemporary San Francisco, Louis mocks his superstition about vampires and crucifixes: "Nonsense . . . I can look on anything I like.

And I rather like looking on crucifixes in particular" (22). Many of his meditations on the failure of religious belief, become, for Louis, meditations on aesthetic first principles rather than problems of metaphysical agency. In this respect Louis seems to speak for his creator; Rice herself observed that the Protestant vision renders the mysteries of life "more sterile" (Roberts 23).

Yet there is another aspect to Rice's eclectic Gothicism that must be considered, and which in some ways is more typical to the complexity of Rice's thought. *Interview with the Vampire* is not only gothic, it is a specifically Americanized version of the genre. First, it signals a departure from claustrophobic familial haunts, as Sage argues them, as well as from the troubled domestic sites customarily associated with the gothic.[6] Rice's fiction considers haunted spaces more broadly construed, perhaps reflecting Fiedler's seminal observation that in New World gothic, wild geographic spaces replace the darkened and deteriorating family castle.[7] Rice is at her best in illuminating the horror of empty metaphysical spaces. Second, the novel is in many respects an ironic exploration of the novel of sensibility, and as such it explores how a commodified flight from the body results in the production, as Joanna Russ describes it in another context, of a "strange fusion of prurience and exaltation" (676).[8] Finally, the form of the novel itself rehearses the captivity narrative—a theological trope rendered contemporary as Louis recounts the metaphysical implications of his seduction and vampiric conversion—first at the hands of the callous, cruel, and indifferent Lestat, and later, by the willful and charming Armand. Louis's anguished and highly moralized recollections of his serial "enslavements" recall a tradition of such confessionary texts, including *Narrative of the Captivity, Sufferings and Remarks of Mrs. Mary Rowlandson; My Life and Bondage* by Frederick Douglass, and others. Characteristic of these texts is a formula of captivity and spiritualized confession that puts deviance on display as moral uplift and theological lesson.[9]

With this history in mind, then, we can turn to Rice's revisions of the gothic and see how she employs its conventions to address a quite different "sensation or 'body' genre."[10] Rice blends the theological moralisms of the captivity with the gothic images of social entrapment in order to argue the genre from what DeLamotte suggests is its original perspective—that of a woman.[11] In addition she combines another staple of the vernacular theological tradition—the sermonizing spectacle of deviances, titillatingly confessed—with the romance genre's formula of sentimentalized sex. At stake here for Rice and her vampires (I use the metaphor advisedly), are the horrific implications of a creature as metaphysically ambiguous as the vampire—the gendered woman, especially as this hapless creature takes form trapped in the repressive representations of the Harlequin romance.

The complex parallels and intersections between the "imitation" that is gender and its enscription in the vampire metaphor rescue Rice's novel from formulaic banality (Butler 21). Louis's tale of his guilt-provoked seduction by Lestat reflects the ontological ambiguity he feels as a vampire and the gendering confusion he experiences in his subsequent relations with Lestat. On the one hand, Louis is the eldest son of a wealthy New Orleans family. At twenty-five, his father dead, Louis was "head of the family" when he meets Lestat (*Interview* 5). He is thus heir to the tradition of male privilege, representing not only the investment of the state but familial primogeniture as well. As agent of state and family in New Orleans, Louis is the visible sign of patriarchy, equally busy about disposing the lands of his estate and arranging for the futures of his sister and mother. (In the waning years of this privilege, that is; Louis's name ironically recalls the ineffectual Louis XVI, who historically, would have been beheaded two years after Louis's transformation as a vampire.)

Yet despite Louis's primogeniture and male birthright, he finds the situation reversed when it comes to telling the story of his turbulent relationship with Lestat—an affair which he couches in the language of romantic pursuit. Significantly, Louis suggests that it was greed for his family's plantation, Pointe Du Lac, that first attracts Lestat's attention to him. Reading between the lines of Louis's narrative, the reader understands that Lestat finds, wooes, and finally, seduces the passive Louis, thus assuming a kind of dowry-like control over the lands and properties of his estate. Thus, Louis's metaphysical anxiety, which takes up so much of his dialogue with himself, finds its more mundane parallel in the confusing, passive, often imitative role he finds himself in vis-à-vis Lestat, his "maker" and, in many respects, his master. Ontological ambiguity is, appropriately enough, mirrored forth in gender, and one suspects Rice of drawing from another tale for this motif—*Frankenstein,* by Mary Shelley. Like Shelley's creature, Louis is created as both copy of and supplement to an ostensibly superior being; further, both are defined and valued from the point of a commandeering, prior, male, and thus seemingly original gaze. Louis, Lestat's companion, in short, is gendered female.

Lestat's primary function as vampire, he says, is to be God-like, a master. Explaining this to Louis he says, "God kills, and so shall we . . . for no creatures under God are as we are, none so like Him as ourselves, dark angels" (*Interview* 89). Lestat, active, male, disposes as he will. Louis, however, cannot kill because he finds it aesthetically revolting. If

Lestat is gendered by action and silence, in typical Harlequin fashion, Louis is gendered feminine in his passivity and his reliance upon words and feelings. In his passivity Louis acquires the feminine—as Roberts notes, the "moral equivalent of virtue" (Roberts 18). Lestat critiques Louis's ethics—as well as his aesthetic sensibilities—as nostalgia for an originary fantasy of being mortal. And yet origins, precisely—or lack of them—are what trouble Louis. Though gendered male as a mortal, as a vampire Louis finds himself stripped of male prerogative; he functions as similacrum, a copy and supplement of an unknown original. Even Lestat is a simulacrum, a copy without original, as Louis finds out to his dismay; whatever origins he has Louis cannot discover.

Doubly troubled by Lestat's apparent lack of origin and by the confusions of his own being, Louis says he "burned with the questions of my own divided nature" (*Interview* 80). Monique Wittig wittily reflects this more mundane aspect of the vampire's discontent in another way: "So what is this divided Being introduced into language through gender? It is an impossible Being, it is a Being that does not exist, an ontological joke" (66). Gender and vampirism are imperfect fits of a role that is always by definition a kind of "theatre," as Clover observes: a role that is always slipping, a role that passes only in dark shadows, and never takes too strongly to the light.[12] Louis remains anxious, even obsessed, about the adequacy of his "passing"; he finds his role as vampire equally a difficult fit, one that demands skills he lacks; the failure of his performance is always a concern to him.[13] Indeed, with good reason; Louis's inability to "pass"—as Armand says—is evident to all: "That you are flawed is obvious to [the other vampires]: you feel too much, you think too much" (*Interview* 254).

Lestat tells Louis that it is his "sensibility" that is the problem, not his vampirism. After hearing Louis proclaim his intention to leave him, Lestat responds dismissively: "I thought as much . . . and I thought as well that you would make a flowery announcement. Tell me what a monster I am; what a vulgar fiend" (*Interview* 80). Lestat's repudiation of Louis's "sensibility" is appropriate, or at least understandable; since throughout the narrative Louis is aestheticized (or, rather, he aesthetizes himself), delineating for himself an inner sphere of emotional fulfillment and need that Lestat says other vampires abhor: "We have no need of your sensitivity." Louis has only the power to feel, and to tell his feelings, which he does, at length. As one critic observes—chiefly about Louis I suspect—a Rice vampire "could talk an adder to death" (Adams 105).

Louis relies upon words to create and sustain his world. He needs the protection of literary mediation; he relies upon feelings to orient himself in the "savage garden" when, as Lestat charges, he should be engaged in making himself a space in it. As he details his turbulent relationship with Lestat to the boy, Louis laments, "You must understand I did not snub him because he did not appreciate his experience. I simply could not understand how such feelings could be wasted" (*Interview* 31). Louis is the quintessential man of feeling, two hundred years beyond his time. And Lestat? As Louis sighs, "Lestat understood nothing." But then, Lestat didn't have to "understand"—his function, as he reminded Louis, was to be a "killer." Louis's passivity and sensitivity accomplish what gender does: confirm and augment the totalizing image of the superior creature, the active male.

In essence, then, Louis's problem is one of gender, metaphysically as well as physically. Roberts argues, wrongly, I think, that Rice's vampires are "genderless" in nature (Roberts 20). Nor does the narrative offer the "gender-free perspective" suggested by one reviewer (qtd. in Roberts 33). To the contrary, Rice's vampires parodically reenact gender conventions and their customary politics. Nowhere is Rice's revision of these gender politics more evident than in the scenes surrounding the vampirization of Claudia, the orphan child. To forestall Louis's threat of leaving him, Lestat vampirizes a young child named Claudia, whose mother has died of plague and left her an orphan. Lestat presents her to Louis, knowing that his need to nurture will bind him to the child, and thus, make him forget about leaving Lestat. This dark parody of reproductory politics as a substitute for male love is only a prelude to what follows, as Lestat, Louis, and Claudia begin a bizarre enactment of the conventional family drama. Bound together by a mix of emotions—death and hatred, need and hunger—Louis describes the three in the romantic imagery of love or, alternately, in the archly sentimental language of domestic bliss. Rice's horror here, one might observe, is family values, seen through a glass, horrifically. Through Louis's eyes Rice chronicles the deathless horror of being trapped for all eternity in an unwanted, or unfulfilling, intimacy, trapped by economics and social need into the formal and horrific replication of an empty structure.

Finally, the question of gender and the possibilities of perversion it makes possible encourages a look at what is thought to be the novel's "homoeroticism." Since Ernest Jones's revisionist Freudianism, which conflated semen with blood in the psychic economy, the vampire theme has a history of identification with homoeroticism. Yet Jones's theory, explains Ellis Hanson, "has the unfortunate consequence of rendering every cocksucker a kind of blood sucker" (328).[14] Accordingly, Rice's novels have developed, at least in the straight press, a reductive gay appeal: "Gays took the book to heart for its homoeroticism . . . guys in

capes sucking each other's blood" (Gates 76). Such a reading only reen-
acts a cultural homophobia; it reflects a taboo against deviant sexuality
except when sexual expression is useful for consumption, erotic titillation, or policement along a normalizing "straight" axis. Sexual repression—a staple of the gothic and of a gothicized commodity culture, it
might be noted—spectacularizes and moralizes the taboo. It thereby
authorizes its expression and exploitation, rather than negating it.

In Rice's *Interview*, for instance, what appear at first to be descriptions (purple, if not quite torrid) of ecstatic union between two males,
Lestat and Louis, become, rather, the traditional assaultative rhetoric of
sex, coded male. Indeed, to reverse the equation Christopher Craft lays
out, in Rice's *Interview* "an implicitly [heteroerotic] desire achieves representation as a monstrous [homosexuality]."[15] With some slight
changes, Rice's novel—like many love-soaked tales of another, closely
allied genre—"reveals the anxieties of women in a subordinate social
position" (Roberts 17).

Anne Rice published *Interview with the Vampire* in 1976—a year
that witnessed, as Ann Snitow notes, a "boom in romantic fiction market
for women," one with a subsequent "growth of 400 percent" in the following years (259). Snitow refers specifically here to the genre of Harle-
quin-type romances, an eponymous genre whose sales now number in
the "several hundred million a year" (259). In "Mass Market Romance"
Snitow analyzes the Harlequin formula, arguing that it offers women
sex—the "one adventure" permitted them in a late-capitalist social order.
Of course, as Snitow lucidly explains, what begins as esteemed privilege
becomes problematic, for when women try to fantasize about sex, the
society offers them "taboos on most of its imaginable expressions except
those that deal directly with arousing and satisfying men" (266). Harle-
quins, Snitow says, "fill a vacuum"; their "romances make bridges"
(266) between the "contradictions" of a society's permitted myths and its
feared nightmares.

But myths and nightmares can easily displace each other; often the
lines blur, and the one completes or becomes the other. In this respect the
"glamor and change" of fantasy and romance genres easily become
recoded in the fears of metamorphosis and instability of another genre
entirely. Much, therefore, is clarified in Rice's ostensible gothicism
when considered from the perspective of "romantic fiction marketed for
women" (Snitow 259). Both are genres of desire and fear, emotions for-
mulaically elicited yet punitively proscribed.[16] Like Louis, the women of
the Harlequin formula are allowed no recourse other than words and the
socially necessary fiction of gender and its spurious prize—the anticipa-

tory illusion of romance. Louis finds that having to pass as mortal is, necessarily, having to reestablish gender and its constraints; although he views them, now, from another perspective, as a waking confinement not unlike the coffin in which he rests.

Like so much of the gothic genre, Rice's novel is a first-person "confessional," and much of what Louis confesses is coded, as we have seen, feminine. Louis's subject is Lestat—his whimsy, capriciousness, his cruelty. Despite the title, Louis is not so much interviewed but just talks—his tone of mixed indignation and rage echoing the fury of Faulkner's Rosa Coldfield, who, as Quentin observes, is still obsessing about Sutpen's crude sexualizing appraisal of her. As Quentin reflects in *Absalom, Absalom!*: "It's because she wants it told" (10). Narrative is the only weapon she has.[17] Similarly, much of Louis's narrative is precisely his attempt to read (first) Lestat and then Armand—to know something more of their origins and their purpose and thus, in some fashion to escape the power of their degradation. Louis's narrative mixes fury and anger and guilt over his seduction, although the narrative derives its power from his retrospective understanding that initially he very much wanted what Lestat had to offer.

Snitow writes that "since all action in the [Harlequins] is described from the female point of view" the reader "identifies with the heroine's efforts to decode the erratic gestures of 'dark, tall and gravely handsome' men" (261). The semiotics of the male is the subject, and as Louis finds out, this is a hermeneutics of suspicion if there ever was one. Lestat is the center of Louis's emotional, often erotically detailed narrative. His first description of Lestat pays careful attention to specifics. Without a sound, says Louis, a "tall fair-skinned man with a mass of blond hair and a graceful, almost feline quality to his movements" entered his room (12), appearing in the manner, as Louis remarks offhandedly, of a "lover" (17). In the impassioned transformation scene Louis recalls that Lestat "put his right arm around me and pulled me close to his chest. Never had I been this close to him before, and in the dim light I could see the magnificent radiance of his eye" (18). Feminized, Louis feels the gaze. The young man who is taping Louis breaks into the narration here and comments, "It sounds as if it was like being in love." Louis's eyes "gleamed" and he responds, "That's correct. It is like love" (31). Of course. Those molded in the Harlequin school of romance know too well the vampiric thrall of love.

Says Snitow, "The books [of the Harlequin formula] are permeated by phallic worship. Male is good, male is exciting. . . . Cruelty, callousness, coldness, menace . . . are all equated with maleness and treated as a necessary part of the package" (261). Lestat is well socialized in male behaviors and conforms easily to Snitow's Harlequinized male, one who, in contradistinction to the woman, is "complete in isolation." Vampires, Lestat tells Louis, are "lone predators and seek for companionship no more than cats in the jungle" (*Interview* 84). What companionships exist will be slave relationships, as Lestat pointedly says, "one will be the slave of the other, the way you are of me" (84). Louis, about to object to this characterization, "realized [he'd] been his slave all along" (84). Indeed, his narrative continually references his slave-like dependency upon Lestat's energy and vampiric knowledge.

Snitow argues that novels following the Harlequin formula "have no plot in the usual sense. All tension and problems arise from the fact that the Harlequin world is inhabited by two species incapable of communicating with each other, male and female" (260). While the the two species in question (male and female) are, from one perspective, fictions represented and enforced by gender, their mutual fictiveness and incomprehensibility are close enough a fit to the melodrama of relations offered in *Interview*. Its hundreds of pages resembles Joanna Russ's description of the modern gothics: "Over-subtle emotions, a 'denseness' of interpersonal texture that is at its most complex, simply baffling, and at its simplest, bathetic" (Russ 681). One could indeed argue that Louis's need for metaphysical clarity—to which he constantly alludes—is in some ways a distraction from the more pressing confusions he experiences as Lestat's companion; historically, as Marx notes, the religious quest has served this purpose, as well as others.

Standing aboard ship en route to Europe, Louis, like Ahab, meditates upon the "great secret" that he had hoped to find revealed in the Old World:

But who was to make this revelation when the sky and sea became indistinguishable and neither any longer was chaos? God? Or Satan? It struck me suddenly what consolation it would be to know Satan, to look upon his face, no matter how terrible that countenance was, to know that I belonged to him totally, and thus put to rest forever the torment of this ignorance. (*Interview* 164)

Good metaphysician, Louis finds his logic based upon a first principle of ignorance. Even in his relations with the Divine, Louis finds he must be passive, accepting—for lack of anything better—what minor consolations he could. Even at a level of metaphysics, then, Louis finds himself responding in gender-determined ways. It is Louis's great crisis that he cannot understand his own existence outside of a framework made possible by the belief in God; as the ontological copy, he has no existence outside that a priori originating (and authorizing) gaze. Yet his relationship with God is as phallic and as controlling, as cruel and emotionally anorexic as Lestat's. In the ironically named St. Louis Cathedral, morally outraged at himself, at his captivity and victimization by Lestat, distressed by the silence of God, Louis thrusts himself at the priest and cries, "Do you see what I am! Why, if God exists, does He suffer me to exist!" (*Interview* 148).

One might attribute Rice's blurring of the lines between gothic and Harlequin formulas to mere chance, or as a coincidental intersection of cultural tropes. But one can also view Rice's *Vampire Chronicles* as—at least in part—an elaborate and deft satire of the inherently vampiric nature of a commodity culture, especially one in which gender is chief fantasy as well as chief commodity. Victorian culture was "gender anxious" (Craft 219), agonizing over the fluidity of gender roles; and in the words of one of its greatest scholars, the vampire's blood exchange "stands for every conceivable union of men with women, men with men, women with women"—every "permutation, normal, subnormal, hypernormal, or supernatural."[18] Contemporary American culture has not left that anxiety in the dark, gothic repositories of Victorian history; indeed, that fear is still socially formative. The vampire is a reigning cultural metaphor encoding numerous, often contradictory, social emotions. Reflecting upon the themes of her *Chronicles*, Rice calls the vampire a "fathomless well of metaphor," adding that "once I was looking through the vampire's eyes . . . I was able to describe the world as I really saw it."[19] Rice's horror revisits an uncanny scene, one too familiar and routinely idealized (or essentialized) out of consciousness. The world Rice sees is ontologically odd, constructed of seemingly fixed gender roles— or, at least, roles with an apparent necessary political fixity. Whether as text, as vampire, or as the rote duties of a "gendrified" shopper, it's all done with mirrors, a kind of slavish imitation; and as Lestat observes with satisfaction, "that's how vampires increase . . . through slavery" (*Interview* 84).

Snitow writes that one of the culture's "most intense myths"—the "ideal of an individual who is brave and complete in isolation"—is "for men, only." Women, on the other hand, "are grounded, enmeshed in civilization, in social connection, in family, and in love. . . . Their one socially acceptable moment of transcendence is romance" (266). In "Compulsory Heterosexuality" Adrienne Rich makes a similar point: "heterosexual romance has been represented as the great female adventure, duty, and fulfillment" (242). The formula romance books, observes Snitow, fill a vacuum created by social conditions. When women try to picture excitement, the society offers them one vision, romance. When women try to imagine companionship, the society offers them one vision, male, sexual companionship. When women try to fantasize about success, mastery, the society offers them one vision, the power to attract a man. (266)

This observation suggests why Rice's *The Vampire Chronicles,* though ostensibly gothic, are horror rewritten in a Harlequin mode— and why, as Adrienne Rich observes in another context, they are horrific: "The ideology of heterosexual romance, beamed at [the woman] from childhood out of fairy tales, television, films, advertising, popular songs, wedding pageantry, is a tool ready to the procurer's hand" (237). Rice's Harlequin horrors are romance rather than horror; or better, they are the horror of romance in which, as Russ observes, "'Occupation: Housewife' is simultaneously avoided, glamorized, and vindicated" (675).

Christopher Craft suggests that the power of the vampire is its power of "subversion of the stable and lucid distinctions of gender" (218). Robin Wood observes that the power of the vampire mythology lies in its "privileged focus for any inquiry into the possibilities of liberation within Western civilization" (175). Vampires conventionally serve as icon of desire unfilled, and Rice's great achievement is to find another icon for that desire much closer to home. Her image is much more recognizable—yet for all that, one as horrific. The endless chain of unfilled desire, elicited yet voided in Harlequin fiction is comparable to the endless fear of fulfilled desire that so often is the subtext of gothic horror. Vampires, in particular, are endlessly adaptable, as resurrectable as the gothic genre itself. Yet both "sensation" genres under discussion are noted for their conservatism. Writes Stephen King in *Danse Macabre:* "The writer of horror fiction is neither more nor less than an agent of the status quo" (51); the horror story, he writes, contains a "moral code so strong it would make a Puritan smile" (368). In Anne Rice's case, the moral seems equally clear.

It is customary to denigrate the gothic genre, to accuse it of being a kind of "book lite," zombie fodder for the unthinking (although heavily shopping) masses. It has even been called by critic Peter Parisi closet pornography, for "people ashamed to read pornography" (qtd. in Snitow 267). But then, this sort of dismissal is consistent with, and similar to, arguments made against other forms of cultural dissimulations called, oddly enough, "diversions." Of course, the chief of these arguments is the extent to which violence is the pornography of choice in a culture that repudiates sex—except when it can be seamlessly inserted into cultural semiotics of consumption. Claudia, by accident of her youth, is less tied to mortal sensibilities than is her guardian, Louis. In her innocence of these constraints she speaks to the point of both horror and pornography: "I seduce [humans], draw them close to me, with an insatiable hunger, a constant never-ending search for something . . . something, I don't know what it is" (*Interview* 125). Desire is the thing; it is the nature of desire, always, to replicate itself, to become the copy of the copy—to remain in itself unknown, even unknowable, vampiric. Thus, as Parisi argues (in Snitow 267), if sex is the reason for Harlequin romance, similar things might be said for the moralization of other "sensibilitist" genres in which eros is fetishized, rather than enacted, either in violent representation or in romantic mystification.

Finally, as Carol Clover notes, "Abject terror . . . is gendered feminine, and the more concerned a given film with that condition—and it is the essence of modern horror—the more likely the femaleness of the victim" (117). The American tradition of gothic eroticizes this victimization; it draws attention to its constitutive place in a social metaphysics, in practical effect, derivatively Christian. That is, any problematic gendering—female, vampire, or homosexuality—is arraigned as transgressive and public, and thus available both for spectacle as well as policement.

Of course, critics of pornography argue that such systemic victimization is the essence of pornography, too. Yet pornography is another genre of fantasy, busy about doing culture's unspeakable business. Carol Clover writes, "Pornography . . . has to do with sex (the act) and horror with gender" (93). None of this is news to Rice, of course, who comes to gothic fiction with side interests in S&M soft porn, under the name of A.N. Roquelaure, published by E.P. Dutton, and two other erotic novels under the name Anne Rampling. Rice does it all. To return to an earlier question, then, Rice's first two vampire novels can indeed be considered gothic, though possibly for all the improper reasons. Her horrorification of the Harlequin formula of "travel, glamor, sex" disguises a deeper level in which the vampire's ontological crisis of existence reflects the greater horror of the Harlequin sentimentalized dead end—which itself derives from debased social metaphysics. Even Armand observes, perhaps with some irony, that Louis speaks for his age: "'You reflect your age differently. You reflect its broken heart'" (*Interview* 312). Rice's vampire novels are, in essence, parables of gender horror, in which the metaphor of vampire shows the extent to which gender is the great vampire, the "imitation," as Judith Butler argues, *"for which there is no original"* (21) (Butler's emphasis).

Perhaps this is why Louis torches the Theatre Des Vampires in Paris, realizing that only fire can effectively kill a vampire. In vampires and in genders, there are only copies without originals, and desire without basis or fulfillment. He understands then, the true horror of vampirism—eternal life without eternal rest, always hungry, never full. In this context I recall a popular country western song in which an abused and long-suffering wife, on Independence Day, burns down the house in which (presumably) she has been held by force of patriotic custom and law. In Rice's clever revaluation of domestic gothic, life in the afterlife of gendered mortality is not unlike a more mundane domesticity—as DeLamotte puts it, it is a "guise of transcendence" that "may be only a version of that old Gothic peril, domestic entrapment" (ix). *Interview with the Vampire* is, then, however disguised, yet one more book about a woman "who just can't seem to get out of the house" (DeLamotte 10). Whether a slave to love or a slave to terror, Hell is better than no hell, even for a vampire.

Notes

1. See Frank McConnell, "Rough Beast Slouching." McConnell writes, "The horror film is. . . . a remarkable instance of submerged value, precisely because that value has come to consciousness and full articulation not through the development of critical intelligence but through the development of art itself" (110).

2. Bradbury, however, is a particular example of the close connection between terror and sentimental nostalgia. In *Trillion Year Spree,* Brian Aldiss writes, "Bradbury is of the house of Poe. The sickness of which [Bradbury] writes takes the form of glowing rosy-cheeked health" (248).

3. Sage writes, "Horror fiction gives the reader a unique insight into the way these factors [in the psychology of individual writers] operate, because the interaction betweeen cultural homogeneity and political divergence is displayed in a peculiarly clear form in the language of these texts" (xvi). Differing from Freud, Sage argues that "the cause and the effect of the horror experience in English culture is a form of 'theological uncertainty,' an anxiety which is recognizable at many different levels of consciousness" (xvii).

4. See David Punter, *The Hidden Script.*

5. In the matter of religion, for example, while the earlier of Anne Rice's *Chronicles* most directly invoke the metaphysical inscrutabilities involved here, her metaphysic (for lack of a better word) is considerably less moralistic—and considerably more "Catholic"—than Stephen King's *'Salem's Lot* (a tribute to

Stoker's *Dracula*). These differences, alone, would provide an illuminating study.

6. See Sage, *Horror Fiction;* see also Eugenia DeLamotte's feminist reading of the genre, *Perils of the Night.*

7. See Fiedler, *Love and Death in the American Novel.*

8. See Russ: "No longer bodiless and yet within the code of romance—the result is a very strange fusion of prurience and exaltation, i.e., the confusion of values described by Firestone (sex = personal worth) [*The Dialectic of Sex*, 1970] combines with the 'religious' eroticism Greer [*The Female Eunuch*, 1970] notes in romance stories" (676).

9. See Marilla Battilana, *The Colonial Roots of American Fiction.*

10. Carol J. Clover, "Her Body, Himself: Gender in the Slasher Film" (93); Clover lists other "body" genres as "horror and pornography, in that order."

11. DeLamotte argues this perspective, saying that "women were (and are) the primary readers, protagonists, and creators of the genre" (8).

12. In "Her Body, Himself," Clover writes, "The idea that appearance and behavior do not necessarily indicate sex—indeed, can misindicate sex—is predicated on the understanding that sex is one thing and gender another; in practice, that sex is life, a less-than-interesting given, but that gender is theatre" (123).

13. Which is one reason, among others, Louis prefers the night. Indeed, when we hear Louis reflecting about "passing," it is always in the context of some potentially glamorous mortal setting, although at night—an evening at the theatre, restaurant, ball. Claudia, then, has additional troubles passing—either as vampire or as women, which is reflected in Louis's thinking about her: "Doll, doll." If he is a copy of a copy, she, more perversely, is even more derivative.

14. See Ernest Jones, *On the Nightmare* 119; Ellis Hanson, "Undead"; see also Sue-Ellen Chase, "Tracking the Vampire."

15. Craft argues that "the sexual threat that this novel first evokes, manipulates, sustains, but never finally represents is that Dracula will seduce, penetrate, drain another male" (218). *Dracula*, then, is another parable of gender-confusion.

16. See William Patrick Day, *In the Circles of Fear and Desire: A Study of Gothic Fantasy.*

17. Louis, who records his on a tape recorder for the reader, must, as the book's title explains, tell it all. Throughout the novel he finds himself unburdening to passing strangers, repeatedly confessing his captivity and freedom to anyone who will listen—first to Claudia, then to Lestat himself, then, later to a priest—and finally, as the novel makes clear, the narrator, and the reader. (Indeed, Louis attempts to "care for" the narrator. This reverses the customary gendering formula in fairy tale, in which the "bad girls" do all the talking while "good girls" are notable for their silence.)

18. Leonard Wolf, qtd. in "Fangs for Nothing," Tom Mathews with Lucille Beachy, *Newsweek* 30 Nov. 1992: 75.

19. Qtd. in "Fangs for Nothing," Mathews and Beachy, *Newsweek* 30 Nov. 1992: 74.

Works Cited

Adams, Phoebe-Lou. Rev. of *Interview with the Vampire*. *Atlantic Monthly* June 1976: 105.

Aldiss, Brian. *Trillion Year Spree: The History of Science Fiction*. New York: Avon, 1986.

Battilana, Marilla. *The Colonial Roots of American Fiction: Notes Toward a New Theory*. Florence, IT: Olschki, 1988.

Butler, Judith. "Imitation and Gender Insubordination." Fuss 13-31.

Chase, Sue-Ellen. "Tracking the Vampire." *Differences* 3.2 (1991): 1-21.

Clover, Carol J. "Her Body, Himself: Gender in the Slasher Film." *Fantasy and the Cinema*. Ed. James Donald. London: British Film Institute, 1989. 91-133.

Coad, Oral Sumner. "The Gothic Element in American Literature Before 1835." *Journal of English and German Philology* 25 (1925): 72-93.

Craft, Christopher. " 'Kiss Me with Those Red Lips': Gender and Inversion in Bram Stoker's *Dracula*." *Speaking of Gender*. Ed. Elaine Showalter. New York: Routledge, 1989. 216-42.

Day, William Patrick. *In the Circles of Fear and Desire: A Study of Gothic Fantasy*. Chicago: U of Chicago P, 1985.

DeLamotte, Eugenia. *Perils of the Night: A Feminist Study of the Nineteenth-Century Gothic*. New York: Oxford UP, 1990.

Diehl, Digby. "Playboy Interview: Anne Rice." *Playboy* Mar. 1993: 53-64.

Faulkner, William. *Absalom, Absalom!* New York: Modern Library, 1964.

Fiedler, Leslie. *Love and Death in the American Novel*. Rev. ed. New York: Dell, 1966.

Fuss, Diana. *Inside/Out: Lesbian Theories, Gay Theories*. New York: Routledge, 1991.

Gates, David. "Queen of the Spellbinders." *Newsweek* 5 Nov. 1990: 76.

Hanson, Ellis. "Undead." Fuss 324-41.

Ingebretsen, Edward, S.J., ed. *Maps of Heaven, Maps of Hell: Religious Terror as Memory from the Puritans to Stephen King*. New York: M.E. Sharpe, 1996.

James, William. *The Varieties of Religious Experience*. Ed. Martin Marty. New York: Penguin, 1982.

Jones, Ernest. *On the Nightmare*. New York: Liveright, 1951.

King, Stephen. *Danse Macabre.* New York: Berkley, 1982.

McConnell, Frank. "Rough Beast Slouching: A Note on Horror Movies." *Kenyon Review* 1 (1970): 109-20.

Porte, Joel. "In the Hands of an Angry God: Religious Terror in Gothic Fiction." *The Gothic Imagination: Essays in Dark Romanticism.* Ed. G.R. Thompson. Pullman: U of Washington P, 1974. 1-10.

Punter, David. *The Hidden Script: Writing and the Unconscious.* Boston: Routledge, 1985.

——. *The Literature of Terror: A History of Gothic Fictions from 1765 to the Present Day.* New York: Longmans, 1980.

Rice, Anne. *Interview with the Vampire.* New York: Ballantine, 1976.

Rich, Adrienne. "Compulsory Heterosexuality and Lesbian Existence." *The Lesbian and Gay Studies Reader.* Ed. Henry Abelove, Michele Aina Barali, and David M. Halperin. New York: Routledge, 1993. 227-54.

Richter, David H. "Gothic Fantasia: The Monsters and the Myths, a Review-Article." *Eighteenth Century* 28.2 (1987): 149-70.

Roberts, Bette B. *Anne Rice.* New York: Twayne, 1994.

Russ, Joanna. "Someone's Trying to Kill Me and I Think It's My Husband: The Modern Gothic." *Journal of Popular Culture* 6.4 (1973): 666-91.

Sage, Victor. *Horror Fiction in the Protestant Tradition.* New York: St. Martin's, 1988.

Snitow, Ann Barr. "Mass Market Romance: Pornography for Women Is Different." *Passion and Power: Sexuality in History.* Ed. Kathy Peiss and Christina Simmons. Philadelphia: Temple UP, 1989.

Varma, Devendra P. *The Gothic Flame.* New York: Russell, 1966.

Wittig, Monique. "The Mark of Gender." *The Poetics of Gender.* Ed. Nancy K. Miller. New York: Columbia UP, 1986. 62-73.

Wood, Robin. "Burying the Undead: The Use and Obsolescense of Count Dracula." *Mosaic* 16.1-2 (1983): 175-87.

Eroticism as Moral Fulcrum in Rice's *Vampire Chronicles*

Terri R. Liberman

Not least of the reasons for the great popularity of Rice's *Vampire Chronicles* is their erotic allure. That eroticism, however, serves not merely to titillate but as a fulcrum for moral awareness. Through the choice of erotic object, Rice challenges moral taboos, suggesting that morality must be defined anew.

Eroticism for Rice's vampires is expressed most dramatically in two acts, "the kill" and the making of another vampire. Though nongenital in nature, these acts are, unmistakably, quite overwhelmingly, sexual ones. These blood acts comprise the locus of morality in *The Vampire Chronicles* and function in two distinct ways. First, the books offer moral commentary on the nature of evil, seen in very human terms by many of the vampires, as the taking of human life. (Notice how antithetical this position is to the amoral one of the vampire as a natural predator.) Traditional human values are upheld at times by Louis, Lestat, and other vampires, who even drink the blood of rats to avoid killing humans. However, at other times, Lestat in particular revels in his evil acts and insists on seeing himself as evil. Although traditional definitions of good and evil are adhered to on this matter of taking life, the vampire's attitude toward evil is rather continually in flux in *The Chronicles*. Evil is both repulsive and fascinating, to be avoided and to be immersed in. This unresolved ambivalence is a recurrent theme running through all four books of *The Chronicles*.

If traditional human morality is upheld in the vampire's belief that killing is inherently evil, then morality is viewed less traditionally when it moves to the choice of erotic object, the second vehicle for moral commentary. Although the vampires do make some moral distinctions about their victims, for example, at times choosing criminals or other "evil" people, rather than good people, other sorts of traditional moral taboos are happily ignored by the vampires. Quite a number of erotic combinations seem not only possible for the vampire, but quite acceptable, including bestiality, homosexuality, and incest. Indeed the vampires seem quite freed from the limitations of traditional human heterosexu-

109

ality, and much of the erotic impact of the four books lies in the breaking of these sexual taboos. The great popularity of *The Vampire Chronicles,* in fact, is most likely due to this breaching of traditional morality rather than the upholding of it. Evil is either indulged in or redefined on such a dazzlingly large and glamorous scale, with a cast of characters that is so exquisitely beautiful, wealthy, and indeed, immortal, that the books entrance. The total freedom of immorality along with its great material rewards speaks to the dark side in us all. But while evil is made thoroughly seductive in *The Chronicles,* and may account for their immediate appeal, Rice's dialectic in the novels leads us back to far more complex assessments, although often not the common assessment, of moral issues. Rice's morality is never simplistic, as her treatment of childhood eroticism reveals. Although the creation of the child vampire, Claudia, and her subsequent erotic attachment to her two vampire fathers, Louis and Lestat, provide a good deal of the erotic titillation of the first half of *Interview with the Vampire,* ultimately the making of a child vampire is revealed as a vampire "sin," as the child vampire remains trapped forever in a child's body, unable to care for itself in the world. This "sin" may be seen as parallel to our general abhorrence of child pornography because of the way it victimizes and violates the innocent. Rice affirms some aspects of traditional moral behavior while rejecting others.

Rice's vampire novels are connected loosely by characters, plot, and themes. The story of the first book, *Interview with the Vampire,* told in the form of an interview the vampire Louis gives to a mortal reporter, concerns Louis's initiation into the world of the undead that begins in New Orleans in 1791. The second book, *The Vampire Lestat,* focuses on Lestat, creator and mentor of Louis, and also gives a mythical history of vampires that reaches all the way back to ancient Egypt. The third book, *The Queen of the Damned,* includes Louis, Lestat, and many other vampires met in earlier books. The fourth, *The Tale of the Body Thief* centers on Lestat and his mortal friend David Talbot, who has appeared in earlier books as well.

The central issue of all four books is the struggle between good and evil. The basic assumption the vampires make is that humans and human values, such as compassion, kindness, and love, are good, while vampires and what they represent as killers are evil. Rice's vampires are still tied to their human roots. They do not become a totally separate race as is the case in other vampire stories, for example, in the film *The Hunger.* Louis, the protagonist of *Interview with the Vampire,* is the least willing of any of the vampires to give up his humanity in his vampire transformation. He struggles to maintain his human goodness in his vampire form, tormented by the necessity to perform evil acts to insure his own survival. Through most of the novel, Louis questions the possibility of a relationship between vampires and the Devil. If he were possessed by the Devil—damned—the concept of evil would be simpler to understand. But Armand, the four-hundred-year-old vampire Louis meets and loves, tells Louis he knows nothing of the Devil, and indeed doubts the existence of the Devil or God. So Louis remains tormented by "the awful, ancient, hounding question of evil" (*Interview* 238). The vampire, a natural predator like an animal, must kill, but Louis cannot accept this amoral attitude toward the kill; he cannot be a good existential vampire. To him, taking human life is the most serious evil, and he tries throughout the book to bring some good out of that evil. Although Lestat attempts to convince Louis that evil is a point of view, and a Parisian vampire, Estelle, reminds him that men are capable of far greater evil than vampires, Louis persists in seeing evil from a human's point of view, not a vampire's. The fact that vampires kill only to live and that men often kill and maim for pleasure has little impact on Louis's moral outlook.

Even at the end of the novel Louis is still tormented by his dilemma. "I wanted love and goodness in this which is living death," he tells us. "It was impossible from the beginning because you cannot have love and goodness when you do what you know to be evil" (*Interview* 339-40). Louis sees himself as damned in his own soul.

The attraction of the book's themes arises from Louis's vampire obsession with the nature of evil mirroring in a more extreme form the same human concerns.

Mortals thrill at the possibility of immortality, at the possibility that a grand and beautiful being could be utterly evil, that he could feel and know all things yet choose willingly to feed his dark appetite. Maybe they wish they could be that lusciously evil creature. How simple it all seems. And it is the simplicity of it that they want,

proclaims the vampire Lestat in Anne Rice's novel *The Vampire Lestat* (466). Most films and novels dealing with vampires employ the point of view of humans; from a human point for view, vampires are obviously evil. Definitions of evil in these cases are clear, and the world is seen as a relatively simple place. In *Interview with the Vampire*, the vampire is drawn into the moral dilemma of the twentieth century. The question of good and evil is not simple, much as these questions are not simple for mortals in the modern world. Thus, the novel is not only about the philosophical struggles of vampires, but about very human efforts to define difficult moral concepts at a time when evil seems not to have absolute meaning.

As the vampire Lestat tells his story in the novel of that name, he reveals much of the same conflict between good and evil that Louis endured. In his mortal life, Lestat was already obsessed with this issue. Lestat tells his friend Nicki, "I can live without God. I can even come to live with the idea there is no life after. But I do not think I could go on if I did not believe in the possibility of goodness" (*Lestat* 72). When Lestat becomes a vampire he at first, like Louis, kills only those mortals he perceives as sinful. "What a sublime idiocy that I had dragged that paltry morality with me, striking down the damned ones only—seeking to be saved in spite of it all" (*Lestat* 135). But he obviously questions that morality.

Like Louis, Lestat seeks answers from other vampires. Gabrielle, Lestat's mother and the first vampire he makes, becomes a pure predator, much like a cat. For her there was meaning in the world, laws and inevitability, but they had nothing to do with morality, only to do with aesthetics. Satan for Gabrielle is humanity's invention, a name for the force that seeks to overthrow the civilized order of things. For Gabrielle there are no absolutes of good and evil. She is the most totally amoral of all the vampires in *The Chronicles*.

The coven of vampires Lestat meets in the cemeteries of eighteenth-century Paris are living like vampires did centuries before. They believe they are damned souls, Satan's creatures, who exist only by the will of God to make mortals suffer for God's glory. They see their immorality as given to them only at the price of suffering and torment. Concepts of good and evil, heaven and hell, are very clear and very simple for them. But the eighteenth-century Lestat cannot accept these medieval notions.

Speculation about good and evil and the nature of vampires, perhaps the most valuable in the book, comes from Marius. The most ancient of vampires, Marius came into existence during the reign of Caesar Augustus of Rome, and he explains to Lestat the origins of vampires: how they were Isis and Osiris to the Egyptians, Dionysus to the Greeks, and the dark gods to the Kelts. The perversion of the Children of Darkness, Marius explains, came through Christianity when vampires began to be seen not as gods but as serving the Christian Devil, and then they began to give value to evil, to believe in its power in the scheme of things. Christianity was thus first to see the vampire as evil. The historical overview that Marius provides reminds us of the relativity of all concepts of good and evil.

Lestat in the eighteenth century sees himself as "the vampire for these times" (*Lestat* 228). He is able to say the very same thing when he is metamorphosed as quite a different sort of vampire, a twentieth-century rock star. In the 1980s sections of the novel, questions of good and evil have been somewhat resolved. Lestat finds the sinless, secular morality of the modern world much to his liking. He becomes a wildly successful rock star dealing with issues such as good and evil, angel and devil in rock songs but living in a world where pure evil has no place.

The Queen of the Damned is more episodic in structure than either of the other books as it deals with a number of different vampires, some of whom have been prominent in the earlier novels. However, it still deals with varieties of the same moral issues. "So hurtful to be again the outsider, forever on the fringes, struggling with good and evil in the age-old private hell of body and soul," Lestat proclaims early in the novel (*Queen* 5).

In spite of Lestat's continuing angst, the allure of the vampire is as strong as ever in this third book of *The Chronicles*. Perhaps this is best seen in the character of Daniel, the mortal lover of Armand, who yearns to become like Armand, a vampire.

He loved its [Armand's] smooth white skin, its great dark brown eyes. He loved it not because it looked like a gentle, thoughtful young man, but because it was ghastly and awful and loathsome, and beautiful at the same time. He loved it the way people loved evil, because it thrills them to the core of their souls. Imagine, killing like that, just taking life anytime you want it, just doing it, sinking your teeth into another and taking all that that person can possibly give. (*Queen* 85)

Despite Daniel's yearning to become a vampire, Armand, like most of the other older vampires who appear in *The Queen of the Damned,* is opposed to making new vampires. And despite Daniel's yearning to be evil, in this novel there seems to be "evil" and then again "evil." In some unexplained way, there are great numbers of young vampires inhabiting the United States. These young vampires seem to be truly immoral; that is, they kill without compunction or conscience. To make sure we realize their villainous nature, Rice has them conspire to kill our hero, Lestat. Rice clearly draws moral distinctions among her vampires in this novel. There are definite vampire rules that must be followed: vampires must not make children into vampires; vampires must not kill their makers; vampires must not reveal other vampires to humans. And later in *The Tale of the Body Thief*: don't make new vampires; don't wonder off without a trace; do cover up the kill. Perhaps more than in any other of *The Chronicles*, in *The Queen of the Damned* Rice has obviously "good vampires"—most of the older ones—and just as obviously "bad vampires"—most of the young. There is also moral retribution. Akasha, the queen of the damned, destroys most of the evil young vampires and is then herself destroyed.

Wakened by Lestat's music, Akasha formulates a grandiose plan to break the cycle of human violence in the world by destroying most of the males of the human species. Akasha's intention, to use her power to kill for what she perceives as a moral purpose, is opposed by the other old vampires, Maharet, Mael, Marius, Khayman, Armand, Louis, and others, who come together to oppose Akasha.

This conclave of wise old vampires perhaps states the general moral position of the whole of *The Chronicles* when Lestat tells Akasha

History is a litany of injustice, no one denies it. But when has a simple solution ever been anything but evil? Only in complexity do we find answers. Through complexity men struggle towards fairness. It is slow and clumsy, but it's the only way. Simplicity demands too great a sacrifice. It always has. (*Queen* 407)

This concept of complexity governs Rice's moral vision. Questions of good and evil, as well as of erotic attachments, must be viewed from this vantage point. Lestat and others see Akasha's answers as too simplistic. Wholesale extermination is too great a price to pay for peace. Although Akasha's power to kill is superhuman, the issue itself is clearly human. The debate has shifted from the morality of the single human kill in the earliest novel to the morality of genocide in his one.

The Tale of the Body Thief opens with Lestat poised as a dark avenging angel. Living in Miami, Lestat preys on killers:

Track him, wait for him, catch him just at the moment that he would bring death to his next victim, and take him slowly, painfully, feasting upon his wickedness as you do it, glimpsing through the filthy lens of his soul all his earlier victims. . . . Nevertheless I like saving those innocents from their fate." (*Tale* 12)

What is certain is only that their victims don't deserve it, and that they, the killers deserve to meet with me. (*Tale* 14)

Convinced of his own evil and eternal guilt, Lestat still makes moral distinctions about his victims. However, this position is not consistent either from novel to novel or within any given novel, for mixed in with these "moral" murders are always some capricious, wanton killings, such as the death of the old woman Lestat had set out to save in *The Tale of the Body Thief*. The small scale of this fourth novel in *The Chronicles* is in contrast to the large panorama of vampires and time periods in *The Queen of the Damned.*

The Tale of the Body Thief allows for many philosophical discussions between Lestat and David Talbot, head of the Talamasca, and Lestat and Gretchen, the nurse/nun who saves his mortal life, about issues such as the existence of God and the Devil, definitions of good and evil, and appropriate ways to live one's life.

I do think God exists. I don't like to say so. But I do. And probably some form of Devil exists as well. . . . And you know. I think your view of them—an imperfect God and a learning Devil—is just about as good as anyone else's interpretation. I think you've hit on it (*Tale* 76-77),

Lestat tells David—although, he's just as apt at other points in the novel (as well as in other places in *The Chronicles*) to say he doesn't believe in either God or the Devil. This inconsistency in Lestat's statements of his beliefs is never explained or dealt with in *The Chronicles*, but he is not a particularly consistent character in many regards. One way in which he is consistent, though, is in his strong sense of the uniqueness of the self. When Gretchen explains to him that she lives her life to lessen the misery in the world, he counters: "I must shine; and I must reach for the very ecstasy that you've denied—the very intensity from which you've fled! That to me is transcendence" (*Tale* 252).

The philosophical sections of *The Tale of the Body Thief* are draped over a framework of action that centers on the activities of Raglan James, the body thief, who has managed to convince Lestat to exchange bodies with him and then refused to return to the proper body. Stuck in a mortal body for far longer then he likes, Lestat has ample opportunity to compare the mortal and vampire lifestyles, and he is determined to get his vampire body back again. His moral dilemma over whether he should seize on this opportunity to live out a mortal lifetime is short lived: "all of my dreams of mortal life had been a lie. . . . I had taken my dark power so for granted that I did not realize the vantage point it had given me" (*Tale* 303).

My greatest sin has always been that I have a wonderful time being myself. My guilt is always there; my moral abhorrence for myself is always there; but I have a good time . . . you see that's the core of the dilemma for me—how can I enjoy being a vampire so much, how can I enjoy it if it's evil? (*Tale* 235)

Once Lestat is ensconced back in his vampire body, his final moral dilemma of the novel concerns whether or not he should make David Talbot a vampire. David has consistently refused the dark trick but when

Lestat finds the seventy-four-year-old David in the beautiful young body of a twenty-six-year-old man, Lestat can't resist making David his immortal companion. Ambivalent as usual, Lestat is sunk into misery, feeling his evil to the fullest. But David finally admits he is thrilled with the dark gift and the two men along with Louis plan happily to go off to carnival in Rio.

Although the Lestat of *The Tale of the Body Thief* debates about the nature of evil as much as ever in this novel, he seems less tortured by his vampire dilemma than in earlier novels. For the most part, he lives the life of a "good" vampire, killing those who deserve to die. His adventure with Raglan James may break vampire rules, but James deserves what he gets. And finally, though he forces the dark trick on David Talbot, David ultimately seems pleased with the outcome.

A total assessment of Lestat here and elsewhere arises from a paradoxical combination of conflicting statements of what Lestat says about himself and what David says about him. Lestat talks about his guilt over his evil, greedy vampire ways, and we respond to his human aspect of conscience, but we are even more strongly drawn to agree with David's perceptions of Lestat the vampire as not evil or greedy, but someone whose soul is "immense . . . fierce, and indomitable and outside time" (*Tale* 314).

The morality of the kill, which is a central theme of all four novels, is paralleled in all four by the strongly erotic nature of the kill. The kill itself, as well as the exchange of blood between vampires, is expressed always in highly erotic terms.

His lips moved over the neck and over the chest and over the tiny nipple of the chest and then, putting his other arm into the open shirt so that the boy lay hopelessly wound in both arms, he drew the boy up tight and sank his teeth into his throat. . . . and Lestat knelt, the boy pressed against him, sucking hard, his own back arched and rigid, his body rocking back and forth, carrying the boy, his long moans rising and falling in time with the slow rocking until suddenly his whole body tensed. (*Interview* 136)

The parallel between the kill and sexual intercourse becomes obvious here. The choice of erotic object provides Rice's second vehicle for moral commentary. The erotic in these cases encompasses all possibilities, homosexual as well as heterosexual, children as well as adults. Louis's relationship to the beautiful child vampire, Claudia, show the latter case and is further complicated by incestuous overtones. "I had killed her," he tells us, taken her life from her, had drunk all of her life's blood in that fatal embrace . . . but she lived to put her arms around my neck and press her tiny cupid's bow to my lips and put her gleaming eye to my eye until our lashes touched and, laughing, we reeled about the room as if to the wildest waltz. Father and Daughter. Lover and Lover. (*Interview* 102)

The sexual relationship between Claudia and Louis shocks and titillates at the same time as moral taboos are broken. Less shocking, though more pervasive, are the homoerotic relationships in the novel. Louis has an ambivalent, love/hate relationship with Lestat, a strong passionate attachment to Armand, and a brief erotic moment with Armand's mortal boy.

Unlike the nature of the kill, which poses such moral difficulties for Louis and Lestat, the amorality of erotic choice seems not to present a problem; all sorts of pairings seem permissible. This tantalizing openness of choice only increases the erotic atmosphere of the novels by making mortal's ideas of what is forbidden—possible.

The unrelentingly erotic nature of *Interview with the Vampire* continues in *The Vampire Lestat*. If the first book shocks with the sensual relationship between adult and child, and the pervasive homosexuality, the second book offers the literally incestuous relationship between Lestat and his human mother made vampire, Gabrielle. As Lestat recounts, "And jetting up into the current came the thrust, not obliterating but heating every concept of her, until she was flesh and blood and mother and lover and all things beneath the cruel pressure of my fingers and my lips, everything I had ever desired" (*Lestat* 157). Being free of the normal taboos of incest adds to the dark, attractive eroticism of the vampire.

As the Theatre des Vampires reveals, the eroticism can seduce an entire mortal audience. The actors in this eighteenth-century Parisian theatre are all vampires. During a performance, a vampire dressed as Death lures a beautiful mortal woman on stage, gradually removes all her clothes, and incorporates her tortuous death into what seems to the mortal audience to be an act, but is all too real.

But she was looking into his eyes now, and her pain bathed her in a beauteous light, a light which made her irresistibly alluring. It was this that held the jaded audience, this terrible pain. . . . She stiffened, cried out as he sank his teeth, and her face was still as the dark theatre reverberated with shared passion. (*Interview* 224)

The voyeuristic audience participation in this chilling scene of death serves to heighten its pulsating eroticism.

Not only is the Theatre des Vampires audience mesmerized, but so are we as we experience both the erotic atmosphere and the seductive evocation of evil in the novels. *The Queen of the Damned* continues the erotic spell of the vampire. The relationship between Daniel and Armand explores the erotic pairing of human and vampire. Though this is not the first time we have seen this combination, it is more fully expressed in this novel. It is also a homosexual relationship, which is by now quite common in *The Chronicles*. This novel like all the rest clearly speaks for the acceptance of diversity in erotic choice.

All the vampires in the large cast of characters in *The Queen of the Damned* are seductively beautiful, none more so than Akasha herself, who tantalizes Lestat with her combination of beauty and power.

She was something fit for the most lavish palace of the imagination; something both sensuous and divine. I wanted her blood again, the blood without fragrance and without killing. I wanted to go to her and lift my hand and touch the skin which seemed absolutely impenetrable, but which would break suddenly like the most fragile crust. (*Queen* 331)

Akasha's powerful erotic allure poses a moral dilemma for Lestat as he is torn between his desire for her and his abhorrence of her plans for the world. "Her blood and my blood. And the deafening thunder of her heart, yes! And it was ecstasy and yet I couldn't yield; I couldn't do it; and she knew it" (*Queen* 363). Here the erotic takes second place to the moral. Here are immoral beings, vampires, acting like extremely responsible, extremely human beings. They don't object to Akasha's plan because it is eliminating their vampire prey (which is what the reader might expect, if this were a different kind of vampire story), but because it is humanly wrong.

The vampire sensibility has become essentially identical with a human sensibility at this point in *The Chronicles*. Akasha's death at the hands of Mekare functions as poetic justice; Akasha pays for her past sins again Mekare and Maharet as well as for her present abuse of power. Justice is done. As much as Lestat likes to proclaim how evil he is, he clearly does not lead simply a lawless life. His formidable erotic attachment to Akasha is forfeited as he sides with the other vampires for the sake of the moral good.

In *The Tale of the Body Thief* Lestat has an opportunity to experience once again the sensual experiences of the human body. He is lured into making the body switch by the promise of seeing sunshine again, of eating, drinking, and making love. But, he hardly knows how to eat or drink at first and quickly gets quite ill. "The truth was, I'd envisioned pleasure, a variety of pleasures—eating, drinking, a woman in my bed, then a man. But none of what I'd experienced was even vaguely pleasurable so far" (*Tale* 183). Lestat's first sexual act in his new human body is a disaster as he rapes the woman with whom he has gone home.

Lestat compares human sex with vampire sex:

No, it's not going to be that easy, or that consuming. It's going to be between the legs and more like a shiver. . . . One moment it was eternal; the next it was finished, as if it had never begun. I lay exhausted on top of her, drenched with sweat, of course, and faintly annoyed by the stickiness of the whole evening and her panic-stricken screams. (*Tale* 188-89)

"The whole thing seemed overwhelmingly dismal. It filled me with despair. The pleasure itself had been nothing" (*Tale* 190). This first human sexual experience is a disaster for Lestat partly because he is inexperienced in his human body and partly because being human seems puny after being a vampire. Lestat does have a more successful sexual relationship with Gretchen, described with Rice's usual skilled erotic handling. But Lestat still anxious to return to his vampire state leaves Gretchen. Rice's stretching of erotic boundaries in this novel continues as she plays with varieties of previous couplings. Lestat's attachment to David Talbot presents the kind of human/vampire bond seen in slightly different form between Armand and Daniel in *The Queen of the Damned*. Although Armand and the mortal Daniel are lovers, and Lestat and the mortal David are not, the latter pair are certainly "wanna-bes." The intensity of the intellectual bond between Lestat and David has spilled over into erotic feeling and even into love. "Oh, every time you ever came to me, you touched me; you wrung from me a deep protectiveness. You made me feel love" (*Tale* 434), David tells Lestat. Despite his feelings for Lestat, David differs from Daniel in that he does not want to become a vampire, and David does, with a parallel difference between Lestat's desire to give David the dark gift and Armand's refusal. It is only when critical circumstances hit both pairs that the two new vampires are made.

The one new moral issue that is raised in Lestat's making of David is that Lestat violates the real bond of friendship and trust he had had for years with the mortal David when he makes him a vampire against his will. In his mind this act is a kind of rape. In Lestat's relationship with Akasha in *The Queen of the Damned*, Lestat puts morality before his erotic needs. In Lestat's relation with David he puts his erotic needs before morality. Lestat's inconsistency is characteristic of him; he is after all both vampire and human, both immoral and moral. The moral issues raised by Lestat's "rape" of a close and trusted friend is vitiated in large part by David's own attraction and admiration for that exquisite twenty-six-year-old body before it was even his and by his admission after the vampire transformation has occurred of his delight in his new state. Lestat has freed him from making a difficult moral choice. So after all Lestat had done well.

The delight in young bodies is evident throughout Rice. Although the vampires who were made when they were middle age, like Marius, are conceived to be beautiful and sexually desirable, most of the vampires in *The Chronicles* are incarnated in young mortal bodies—Lestat and Louis were both in their twenties, Armand, merely sixteen. The appeal of youth in the novels reflects this youth-obsessed age we inhabit. David Talbot is a man of seventy-four. Interestingly, Lestat is able to resist making David a vampire as long as David's body is also seventy-four. It is not until the body thief swaps bodies with David, and David has that gorgeous twenty-six-year-old-body that Lestat finds him irresistible. "I nuzzled in against his neck, licking it, smelling it, and then sinking my teeth for the third time. Hmmm . . . this is ecstasy. Could that other body, worn with age, have ever yielded such a feast?" (Tale 422). Lestat would seem to succumb to the prejudices of our times that equate youth and desirability.

Unlike most earlier vampires, Rice's vampires are complex and individual. They are not simple, evil creatures who feed upon humans, but are generally some combination of amoral, immoral, and moral. They tantalize us by their freedom to break the rules, human and even vampire rules. They celebrate amorality in their choice of sexual object. And most important, they don't usually have to pay a price for it. Unlike earlier vampires, they are not automatically punished at the end of their stories. Rice's vampires are not the first to have an erotic dimension. Bram Stoker certainly understood the connection between terror and the erotic as his Dracula seduced and charmed his victims. Although most of the early vampire eroticism was pointedly heterosexual, Stoker did hint at an erotic attraction between Dracula and Jonathan Harker. It is Rice, however, who fully homoeroticizes vampires; she consistently breaks down boundaries of erotic choice, although she focuses largely on men, specifically young, white men. She shows few relationships between women and no interracial couplings. Despite this limitation, the overall impact of Rice's erotic pairings is to suggest choice and diversity and a breaking away from traditional moral judgment. Once again Rice's vampires are dressed in garments of human morality.

In all of the novels, Rice's grand and beautiful vampires appear perversely attractive. Lusciously evil beings who can make moral choices seem somehow preferable to the puny psychopaths who inhabit the twentieth century. The tantalizing combination of evil and eroticism exerts a powerful grip over the modern imagination. But no matter how much we may be dazzled by the titillating glamor of the surface, we ought not fail to look beneath that dazzle of the vampires at the genuinely serious human moral issues at the core of *The Chronicles*.

Works Cited

Rice, Anne. *Interview with the Vampire*. New York: Ballantine, 1976.
——. *The Queen of the Damned*. New York: Knopf, 1988.
——. *The Tale of the Body Thief*. New York: Ballantine, 1992.
——. *The Vampire Lestat*. New York: Ballantine, 1985.

Anne Rice's *Interview with the Vampire*: Novel Versus Film

Diana C. Reep, Joseph F. Ceccio, William A. Francis

Interview with the Vampire was Anne Rice's first novel, marking the beginning of her successful career as a modern gothic writer. The novel presents a darkly erotic, guilt-ridden yet amoral, contemporary version of the ancient vampire myth. In transfering the novel to the screen, film-makers had to deal with a story, drenched in luxurious decadence, covering some two hundred years, and shifting back and forth between two continents. Moreover, by the time filming began, the novel had been thrilling readers for seventeen years, and the built-in audience for the film had intense feelings about the characters and how they should be portrayed. Finally, Rice herself had strong opinions about how she wanted her story to appear on the screen. A monumental task faced any filmmakers who were bold enough to take on the project.

This study of the transformation of Rice's novel into a $50 million Hollywood film focuses on three central elements. Part I explores the film's interpretation of the characters and the ways in which subtle shifts in emphasis or minor changes reinvented Rice's vampires for general film audiences. Part II deals with the plot changes, both omissions and additions, and how those changes affect Rice's overall story on the screen. Part III investigates the New Orleans setting and identifies the specific locations and specific techniques used by the filmmakers to recreate the New Orleans of Rice's novel.

Part I
Shadows in the Night: Characters

Diana C. Reep

The vampire is, arguably, the most intriguing and appealing of the traditional horror figures in literature and film. Although early writings, such as Bram Stoker's *Dracula*, and silent films, such as *Nosferatu*, made in Germany in 1922, presented the vampire as an ancient, decaying, walking corpse with distorted features, razor-sharp fangs, and extended fingers, the predominant twentieth-century image has been that established by Bela Lugosi in the 1931 film *Dracula,* in which the vampire became a pale, middle-aged aristocrat with a nonspecific European accent. After Lugosi set the standard for vampire portrayal, the vampire in film was usually the best-dressed man in the room, suave, sophisticated, charming, and with an interest in the women that implied more than merely opening a vein. Women characters nearly always exhibited an erotic attraction to the vampire, and the scene in which the vampire finally drains the woman he has been "courting" is usually filled with sensual tension as the woman seems to experience ecstasy while losing her life's blood.

However erotic the implication of the bloodsucking scene, however, Lugosi's vampire and those that followed, if not outwardly ancient, had a maturity that signified a long existence. In addition, the vampire, when he was not out in society, usually lived in decaying, uncomfortable quarters amid cobwebs, spiders, and bats, and slept in a coffin. In spite of his immortality, the vampire was not invulnerable. He feared sunlight, religious objects, and garlic bulbs and spent most of his time fending off the attempts of the nonvampire men in the film to uncover his secret and destroy him. He always failed. At the end of the story, the vampire, as the representation of evil, was destroyed, if not permanently, at least until the sequel.

When Anne Rice published *Interview with the Vampire* in 1976, she broke this long-established pattern. Her male vampires were as well dressed as the earlier vampires, but in addition, they were young, handsome, passionate figures, who lived in luxury and—except for Louis—delighted in their vampire immortality. Most important, Rice told the story from the vampire's point of view, making her vampires not only sympathetic but also glamorous and exciting. In another departure from traditional vampire figures, Rice created a child vampire—a pretty little killer. Finally, to the delight of her readers, Rice's vampires were not vanquished by normal humans; her vampires flourished, under little threat from ordinary mortals who appeared in her novel primarily as convenient victims of the vampires' daily hunger.

Hollywood was immediately attracted to the novel, and Rice sold the film rights to Paramount in 1976, but development of a viable script was slow in coming until David Geffen of Geffen Pictures and Warner Brothers put together the project. Because of the popularity of Rice's work, casting for *Interview with the Vampire* became an active interest for fans and then developed into a controversy that lasted until the film finished production.

Even before hiring Neil Jordan as director, Geffen cast Brad Pitt as Louis de Pointe du Lac, the aristocrat who becomes a vampire but never loses his guilt over the vampires' inevitable blood lust and killing of human beings (Abramowitz 70). The role of Claudia, the five-year-old child vampire who can never grow up, was more difficult to cast. More than 5,000 children auditioned, most of whom simply could not handle the dynamics of the role. Director Jordan wanted a professional child actress because he was afraid the part had so many dark implications, an amateur could be psychologically harmed (Abramowitz 72). Finally, Kirsten Dunst, an eleven-year-old actress, was cast. The role of the reporter who listens to Louis's story was initially filled by River Phoenix, but Phoenix died of a drug overdose two weeks into the shooting, and Christian Slater took over the part (Abramowitz 72).

As Rice fans know, the controversy in casting erupted when Tom Cruise, known for playing all-American hero parts, accepted the role of Lestat de Lioncourt, the hedonistic, lascivious vampire who turned Louis and Claudia into vampires. Rice's distress at Cruise playing Lestat was noted by the press every time the film was mentioned, especially since Rice made no secret of her feelings whenever a reporter was in the vicinity. Then, two months before the film's premiere on November 11, 1994, Rice viewed a videotape of the completed production and announced that her fears had been groundless. She took a full-page ad in several newspapers and trade publications to say how pleased she was with the film overall and with Cruise's portrayal in particular (Barton 56).

Rice was not alone in her satisfaction. *Entertainment Weekly* reported that the film received overall positive reviews from critics, and after eight weeks in release, it had grossed over $100 million ("Box Office," "Critical Mass").

At least part of the success of the film can be attributed to the interpretation of Rice's characters. Louis and Lestat in the film provide the precise emotional contrast shown in Rice's novel. Louis is soul-searching, anguished, and thoughtful; Lestat is flamboyant, energetic, and lusty. No film version of a novel, however, completely replicates the original, and this film also contains changes that affect the portrayals of the major characters.

Louis, twenty-five years old in the novel and twenty-four in the film, is the central figure in *Interview with the Vampire*. He tells his story to the young reporter, and it is his point of view that dominates the film. Tall, dark, slender, Brad Pitt is physically appropriate as the sensitive and suffering Louis.

In the novel, Louis, in spite of his revulsion over his vampire nature, experiences sensual pleasure from draining blood and is attracted to other male vampires in the homoerotic atmosphere Rice is known for creating in her vampire novels. In the film, however, several changes reduce and nearly eliminate the homoerotic in the character of Louis.

Although in the novel, Louis's initial depression was caused by the death of his brother, a religious fanatic, in the film Louis is in despair because his wife and child have died, thus establishing Louis as a widower and emphasizing the traditional heterosexuality of such a position. Lestat, in the film, attacks Louis for the first time while he is with a prostitute who is performing oral sex—a scene not in the novel. Louis's first human victim in the novel is a male slave. The film, however, changes the character to Yvette, a beautiful female slave, who asks Louis why he doesn't come to the slave quarters any more, implying a past sexual liaison. Moreover, she tells Louis she is worried about him and urges him to send Lestat away. Louis calls her "ma cher," echoing her implication of a sexual relationship in the past. As a vampire, he is attracted to her pulsing veins and succumbs to temptation, making her his first victim. These changes, which emphasize Louis's heterosexuality when he was human, make it easier for audiences to ignore any homoerotic implications in Louis's character that arise from the portrayal of the close companionship experienced by the male vampires in the film.

Although Rice's vampires do not have sex, the novel emphasizes the erotic closeness of the male vampires, and the kill is Rice's metaphor for sexual satisfaction. Lestat makes Louis a vampire because he is beautiful and Lestat wants a companion. In the novel, Louis has to share Lestat's coffin when he is first made a vampire, sleeping on top of Lestat, face down. In the film, Louis has his own coffin at once.

When Louis meets Armand in Paris, Armand offers him a human boy, who allows the vampires to drink from him. In the novel, Louis drinks and experiences ecstasy:

I sank my teeth into his skin, my body rigid, that hard sex driving against me, and I lifted him in passion off the floor. Wave after wave of his beating heart passed into me as, weightless, I rocked with him, devouring him, his ecstasy, his conscious pleasure. (231)

That same moment in the film creates a very different image of Louis. When offered the young boy, Louis lifts the boy's hand and grimaces when he sees previous puncture marks. He turns the boy's hand to an unmarked spot and briefly sucks, his face a testament to his revulsion. Instead of a homoerotic moment, the scene becomes another instance of Louis being unable to enjoy his vampire nature and drinking from the boy only as a courteous guest might take coffee when offered it.

The novel specifically stresses Louis's intense attraction to Armand in Paris. He tells the reporter, "I felt a longing for him so strong that it took all my strength to contain it, merely to sit there gazing at him, fighting it" (256). And he later tells Claudia that he loves Armand (294).

In the film, however, Louis's interest in Armand is presented largely as a hope that he has found someone who will tell him all the vampire history and lore. And when Armand engineers Claudia's death, Louis, although he admits Armand's companionship might be tempting, rejects Armand immediately rather than traveling with him for years as in the novel. Both Lestat and Armand want a male companion, but Louis rejects them and seeks escape from the vampire life. In the film, once Claudia dies, Louis prefers to be alone, telling the reporter, "All my passion went with the golden hair."

Lestat, as played by Tom Cruise, is the opposite of Louis in the novel and on the screen. Shorter than Brad Pitt, Cruise, even with blond hair, does not match the novel's description of "a tall, fair-skinned man with a mass of blond hair and a graceful, almost feline quality to his movements" (12). Cruise's portrayal of Lestat stresses his physical energy, as when he bounces on the coffin holding the dying prostitute, and his raffish charm, as when he urges Louis to enjoy his vampire powers.

The reduction of homoerotic implications in Louis's character increases the disparity between Louis and Lestat in the film. In a scene not in the novel, Louis and Lestat visit the Widow LeClair (Madame St. Clair in the film) and her young foppish lover. While Louis strolls with the widow, kisses her neck and, unwilling to kill her, finally sinks his teeth into her poodles, Lestat strokes the cheek of the rouged youth and then drains his blood. The addition of this scene to the film seems designed to show Lestat's erotic enjoyment of killing young men, a preference both the novel and the film emphasize, while Louis has no desire to follow Lestat's lead.

However, other changes in the film reduce Lestat's homoerotic connections. The film omits Lestat's obsession with and killing of Freniere, a young plantation owner. This episode in the novel again highlights the essential incompatibility between Louis, who tries to stop Lestat, and Lestat, who lusts for the youth and spirits him away into the swamp to kill him.

This incompatibility of spirit between Louis and Lestat is illustrated in the film when Lestat kills two prostitutes. After bringing the prostitutes to his apartment, Lestat kills one woman outright and seduces the second woman, draining her to the point of death. Then Lestat toys with her while Louis begs him to end the woman's suffering and she begs for her life. In the novel, Louis finally drains the woman to stop her terror and pain, but in the film, he does not, again showing the audience Louis's horror at Lestat's actions. This scene with two female prostitutes puts Lestat in a traditional heterosexual context, and the woman's initial ecstasy as Lestat drains her increases the sensual implications of his "kiss." As in the novel, this scene also shows Lestat's basic acceptance of his vampire nature and his indifference to the suffering of his human victims.

The film emphasizes Lestat's father role as the maker of both Louis and Claudia. Louis, in the novel, tells the reporter, "I was educating Claudia" (100). In the film, however, Lestat is the teacher. He trains Claudia how to kill as a vampire does, and he sees to her cultural education, taking over the piano lessons after she kills her teacher, taking her out socially as if she were his daughter, arranging for a dressmaker. Lestat slaps Claudia's hand to discipline her, teaches her vampire rules ("Never [kill] in the house"), and brings her dolls on her "birthday"—the anniversary of the night he made her into a vampire.

Most important in the film, Lestat is not present during the Paris events and, therefore, bears no guilt for Claudia's death. In the novel, he comes to Paris seeking revenge for Claudia's attempt to kill him. "She has to die!" Lestat tells Louis (299). In the film, Lestat tells Claudia she has been a "very naughty little girl" after her first attempt to kill him, thus maintaining the parental role he has assumed, a role which increases the audience's sympathy for him.

Eliminating Lestat's involvement in Claudia's death is an essential change if there are to be film versions of Rice's other vampire novels, which focus on Lestat. Responsibility for killing a child, even a vampire child, would tarnish Lestat's character with audiences, perhaps beyond acceptance. The reduction of homoerotic implications in both the characters of Louis and Lestat serves two purposes. It makes the film more acceptable and enjoyable to general audiences who may wish to ignore those implications, and it protects the leading-man status of Brad Pitt and Tom Cruise, both of whom have the responsibility of appealing to wide audiences in other expensive films.

The filmmakers, however, probably mindful of the widespread popularity of Rice's novels in gay circles, try to have it both ways, and the character of Armand fulfills this goal. Antonio Banderas, a favorite with gays, does not physically suit the role of Armand. Armand in the novel has auburn hair and is described as "very young" (239). (Rice's later novels establish Armand as seventeen years old.) Banderas has nearly waist-length black hair and is in his thirties. The film uses the character of Armand to maintain the homoerotic tone of the novel, and Banderas has a dominant, compelling presence in the scenes with Louis—an effect a teenage actor probably could not achieve.

In the novel, Armand's attraction to Louis and his desire to have Louis with him is intense. He tells Louis, "I want you. I want you more than anything in the world" (284). He urges Louis to leave Claudia. The film also shows Armand's jealousy of Louis's relationship with Claudia. When Louis describes Claudia as his "daughter," Armand immediately responds, accusingly, "your lover." Claudia, as in the novel, understands immediately that she is in danger, telling Louis that Armand wants him as a companion.

The film makes it clear that Armand arranges Claudia's death as a way of eliminating her as his rival for Louis's affections. While Louis, Claudia, and Madeleine are being dragged through the Theatre des Vampires, we see Armand calmly listening to their screams for help. When he knows it is too late to save Claudia from the sun's rays, Armand rescues Louis from the coffin he has been buried in and says they cannot rescue Claudia. By making Armand the one primarily responsible for Claudia's death, the film emphasizes his overwhelming desire for Louis, thus preserving Rice's strong emphasis on erotic bonding between the male vampires.

In the film, the strongest erotic bonding is between Louis and Claudia. Claudia, five years old in the novel, is made a vampire by Lestat who realizes Louis is on the verge of breaking away. Lestat knows Louis will love Claudia and stay with her as long as she needs him. When Claudia has her first taste of blood and echoes Oliver Twist, another orphan, in saying "I want some more," the audience sees her as a child determined to survive.

Claudia becomes a tragic character when she develops the mind of a woman while remaining trapped in a child's body, unable to grow up. Claudia's older age, necessitated by the need to find an actress who could play the role, intensifies her dilemma for the audience. She is physically just on the threshold of puberty but is unable to move into adulthood. However, as years pass, her mind matures, and she becomes a woman emotionally. The pathos of her situation is illustrated in the film by an episode not in the novel.

When Claudia sees a lovely Creole woman bathing herself, she tells Louis and Lestat she wants to grow up to be like the woman. They avoid telling her she can never grow, but Claudia guesses. When Lestat brings her another doll, she flies into a rage and reveals that she has killed the Creole woman and brought her body to her bedroom—her action a symbolic attempt to possess the woman's age and beauty. In a fury, Claudia cuts her childish curls off, but her hair grows back in an instant as the film demonstrates to the audience that Claudia can never change the physical shape she had when Lestat turned her into a vampire.

Rice's description of the love between Claudia and Louis brought criticism about pedophilia. In the novel, Louis frequently kisses Claudia and pets her. Claudia tells Louis, "I would die rather than live without you . . . I cannot bear it if you do not love me" (142). Louis tells the reporter that, when they reached Paris, "We were alive again. We were in love" (205). And when Claudia tells Louis that Armand wants him, Louis replies, "Love holds me to you . . . we are wed" (250).

When Louis and Claudia go to Paris, the film creates a romantic atmosphere for them. Claudia has abandoned her childish dresses and curls and now wears gowns that are smaller versions of those worn by adult women; her hair is upswept with elaborate hair decorations. She and Louis dance at the Paris Opera House, and he tells the reporter that he was so euphoric then he could deny her nothing.

The film, in using an eleven-year-old actress instead of a five-year-old, strengthens the pedophilia implications that appear in the novel and, at the same time, creates the image of a tragic love affair. In spite of their devotion to each other, Claudia can never quite be a full companion to Louis because her body cannot match her emotions, and she needs him to take care of her in a world that sees her as a child. When she realizes she will lose Louis to Armand and demands that Louis make Madeleine into a vampire so she will have a companion to help her, Dunst, as Claudia, projects the despair of the woman trapped in a child's body. To emphasize her understanding of the hopelessness of her situation, the film shows her gently kissing Louis goodby an instant before she is seized by the vampires who will kill her.

In spite of the initial controversy over casting, the actors in *Interview with the Vampire* successfully capture the essence of Rice's characters in the novel. In the film, the physical appearance of the actors proves less important than their reflection of the characters' emotions and desires. Louis's despair, Lestat's zest, Claudia's fury, and Armand's desire are all perfectly revealed on the screen, and the film adds new and haunting images to those in the novel.

Part II
Dark Journey: Plot

Joseph F. Ceccio

Director Neil Jordan's film *Interview with the Vampire* received two Academy Award nominations on February 14, 1995: one for art direction and one for original music score. On the other hand, *Forrest Gump* received thirteen nominations, and *Pulp Fiction* received seven. Yet the latter two are not necessarily better films or even the most carefully crafted. As often happens in Hollywood popularity contests, the superior film may not receive the most acclaim.

According to film critic Steve Murray, "If you're worried whether *Interview with the Vampire* . . . suffered drastic changes in reaching the screen, the answer is, no. Well, mainly no" (C7). As we know, Rice herself wrote the screenplay. Of course, there had to be changes in translating the 346-page novel into a two-hour film. And we understand that Jordan made some changes in Rice's screenplay. Still, the film is remarkably faithful to the book, often using key lines of dialogue such as Claudia's "Oh . . . *really?*" in response to Louis's warning, "He will not let us go" (119). But often, too, the film moves quickly, skipping over certain events and large passages of description in the novel.

In spite of the first impression of film critics, such as Murray, and the relative faithfulness to dialogue from the novel, the film *does* contain significant changes in story and emphases from the novel. While the term *plot* may refer simply to the events in a story, the definition offered by critics X.J. Kennedy and Dana Gioia more precisely characterizes *plot* as "the artistic arrangement of those events" (10).

The film retains the frame structure of Rice's novel as Louis tells his story to the boy in a single night. The lighting in the film emphasizes this frame and also highlights the dark world of Rice's vampires. The opening of the film takes place just after sunset, the light fading to darkness as the camera finds Louis and the boy in the stark hotel room. Louis tells his story surrounded by the darkness of the night, relying on artificial light. As Louis's story ends and the film closes, the sun rises and the sky grows lighter and lighter as the credits run. The film's use of light in the frame sequences emphasizes the vampires' dark world. Louis appears with the darkness and must disappear with the light. Using Rice's frame device in the film indicates that the filmmakers wanted to retain her overall structure. When the film departs from Rice's novel, we must ask why it has done so.

A major change from novel to film comes in the significant cuts in content and characters. These cuts both streamline the story to fit the two-hour running time and also enhance the rich atmosphere of the New Orleans and Paris settings.

The film eliminates the characters in the opening plantation setting—Lestat's father, the Frenieres (including Babette), and Louis's brother, Paul. Cutting these characters helps the film focus on Louis and Lestat and also prevents the audience from becoming involved with characters who will disappear after the first third of the story without having had any lasting effect on the overall tale that Louis relates. The cuts also allow a more rapid movement to the third primary character—Claudia, the child vampire. The plot complications in the novel, particularly in the section dealing with Babette, would slow the pace of the film, and audiences of adventure/horror films generally expect a swift linear movement through major action points. Lestat's treatment of his father is also problematic in that audiences might respond negatively to a hero—even a vampire—who is not respectful of his father.

The director's attention to story pace is evident in the changes made in events when Louis and Lestat find Claudia. In the novel, Lestat gets Claudia out of the New Orleans sick ward, leaves money for her, and poses as her father. In the film, these events are simply dropped, and Lestat asks Louis to come home with him where Claudia waits in bed and is quickly made into their vampire child.

In a major cut, the film omits Part II of the novel, approximately forty pages. In the novel, after Louis and Claudia burn Lestat and flee New Orleans to cross the Atlantic, they wonder how Lestat could have risen from the swamp—perhaps he fed on various "creatures" around him to gain strength (165). The film, however, makes clear that it was the alligator that started Lestat on the road to recovery. Other Part II sequences—Louis's and Claudia's European adventures in search of other vampires, the tragic story of Morgan and Emily, and the mindless European vampire in the ruins—are deleted from the film. The film takes us quickly to Paris with only a glimpse of Claudia's sketches to indicate that she and Louis have traveled to other places first.

Cutting the adventures in central Europe obviously helps keep the film to its ideal running length, but the cuts here also seem essential to maintaining the generally sophisticated, rich atmosphere created by the two primary settings of New Orleans and Paris. The central Europe section in the novel involves peasants, gloomy and decayed settings, and hideous, mindless corpses. As Louis describes his struggle with one of these creatures in the novel, he says, "The two huge eyes bulged from naked sockets and two small, hideous holes made up his nose; only a putrid, leathery flesh enclosed his skull, and the rank, rotting rags that covered his frame were thick with earth and slime and blood. I was battling a mindless, animated corpse" (192). This image may be appropriate for a traditional horror film, but *Interview with the Vampire* is a film centered on the beauty of the vampires and the physical attractiveness of their surroundings as they enjoy luxurious quarters and travel in high society. Cutting the central Europe sequence maintains this focus.

Perhaps the most significant cut the film makes is the elimination of the intense scene from the novel in which Louis kills the priest who hears his confession in the cathedral. In a sense, the priest is the first interviewer, but he is killed (unlike the boy in San Francisco who has no need to fear Louis). For seventy years, Louis confesses, "I have walked the streets of New Orleans like the Grim Reaper and fed on human life for my own existence. I am not mortal, father, but immortal and damned, like angels put in hell by God. I am a vampire" (148). The film had earlier omitted Louis's excessively religious brother, Paul; then the film drops the priest-killing scene, thus avoiding the religious (or antireligious) emphasis often found in Rice's novel. Of course, Louis's stature in the film (and audience sympathy) would have been diminished if he had killed a priest on screen.

Another major difference between the film and the novel is the way the film highlights vampire violence. Although the vampires' existence is necessarily violent as they kill daily, the film creates a strange beauty in the rich color and drama of violence. This emphasis actually allows the film to *feel* more violent than does the novel.

Lestat's thumbpiece, the silver claw he deftly uses to cut or puncture his victims' veins, appears in the film, but not in the book. In the novel, Lestat uses his teeth or a knife. The claw is fascinating as a beautiful weapon. Viewers may feel more sympathy for the humans in the film than they do for the humans in the novel because they actually see and hear their suffering and death. The novel is told almost always from the vampire's point of view; frequently the film moves into the dramatic point of view, allowing the viewer to shift sympathy from vampire to human (and perhaps back again). Hence the scene involving Lestat, Louis, and the two prostitutes appears both in the book and in the film, but in the film the second prostitute's role is played so strongly, so movingly that the audience feels more sympathy for her than might the reader of the passage in the novel. The prostitute begs for life, tears streaking her makeup, her bodice bloodstained—a vivid picture. Lestat comes across as an evil and eager killer in this scene from the film. Still later in the film, we watch the terrible—yet brilliantly colorful—death scene of Claudia and Madeleine, as the sun's rays burn them. (Madeleine is treated much more fully in the novel than she is in the film.) Rice's novel does not describe this death scene, although Louis does later view the ashes of Claudia and Madeleine. In the film, the death scene presents a sculpture created by the ashes of Claudia and Madeleine, showing them in each other's arms. When Louis touches the ashes, the sculpture crumbles.

To maintain this link between beauty and violence, the film adds scenes not in the novel. An early killing is outdoors at a performance of the Comedia del Arte watched by diners. The colorful costumes and festive atmosphere surround the two vampires as they feast on a beautiful prostitute. The sequence at the plantation with Louis, Lestat, Widow St. Clair, and her young fop attending a ball with fashionable members of the aristocracy again emphasizes elaborate costumes and a lavish setting as Lestat tries to initiate Louis into appropriate killing. Here Lestat uses his silver claw on the youth. Lestat kills the widow later after Louis fails to do so, and the vampires then fight under the huge oaks on the grounds. Two people lie dead, yet the violence occurs in a setting so attractive that the audience is fascinated rather than repelled. The novel merely mentions Madame LeClair as a patron of the musical arts; the film creates a fuller character in order to develop a dramatic and violent sequence.

After the intense sequence in which Louis burns the Theatre des Vampires, the film adds a beautiful scene in dusky light. It is nearly daybreak. Gradually we hear—then see—Armand's carriage and black-plumed horses emerging from the foggy darkness to rescue Louis. Armand's young boy is driving the carriage. In the novel, the young boy is already dead, and Louis arranges for his own getaway carriage. The film's emphasis on black reflects the deaths that have just occurred, but the film creates yet another dramatic moment with the rushing black carriage and the fog.

The end of Part I in the novel is the moment when Louis and Claudia start a fire to escape from Lestat, who has risen from the swamp after they think they have killed him. The fire in the novel appears to be confined to their rooms. The fire in the film spreads across the waterfront in a raging conflagration as Louis and Claudia reach the ship. Thus the film heightens their frantic escape to Europe and creates a brilliant scene of destruction.

Jordan's film does especially well with special effects that recreate the paranormal events Rice features in her novel. At long last, Rice fans can see and hear the blood drinking they could only imagine from reading the text. Particularly effective are scenes that show some of the victim's blood on the vampire's mouth after drinking. Then that blood fades away in the next scene. The effect is startling. On occasion, the soundtrack even provides the distinct sound of the thumping heart.

On other occasions, the film creates special effects that are not in the novel. The film adds a brief flying scene when Lestat first takes Louis, for they rise up into the masts of a ship. But there is no such scene or vampire flying in the first of Rice's *Vampire Chronicles.* However, Rice and Jordan know from the later vampire novels that some vampires can fly and that Lestat learns to fly from Akasha in *The Queen of the Damned* and continues to fly about in the fourth vampire novel, *The Tale of the Body Thief.*

The film also adds special effects dealing with Claudia's hair. After she is made a vampire by Lestat, her transformation includes not only her teeth, as we would expect, but also her hair, which magically arranges itself into lovely golden curls. Yet in the novel, Lestat himself "had his comb out and was running it through her hair" (94). Moreover, the film adds material on Claudia's hair not found in the novel. When she realizes that she is not growing up and not changing into a woman, she cuts her long hair, runs into the next room, and then emerges scream-ing—for her hair has quickly grown back. A vampire (in Rice's world) cannot change appearance from the time it was made. There is no such haircutting scene in the novel; but *The Vampire Lestat*, the second book of *The Vampire Chronicles,* does include a scene in which Gabrielle, Lestat's mother-made-vampire, cuts her long blonde hair, only to have it grow back. She, too, screams at the return of the hair (180). When there is a sequel filmed, it will be important to have Rice on board to sort out such matters.

One failure in the special effects department must be noted. It may be the director's fault. Surely Rice would not allow her vampires to shed clear tears. Tears appear twice in the film, more frequently in the novel. First, Claudia sheds tears as she demands that Louis help her by making Madeleine a vampire to love and care for her. Second, Louis sheds tears when telling the boy about Claudia's death. These clear tear drops should be red or red tinted. In the novel, Rice includes phrases such as "tears that were tinted with blood . . . the faint touch of red" (141), "the stain of tears, tinged with mortal blood" (260-61), and "the red film that covered her eyes" (264). Rice aficionados demand perfection or close to it. Their approach to Rice's work explains part of the initial furor over Tom Cruise being cast as Lestat. The lack of red tears here is a distinct oversight.

Elliot Goldenthal's original soundtrack is also a feature not possible within a fictional text. His music has "adventure" elements such as are heard in the music from *Batman;* there are also "mystery" elements reminiscent of the soundtracks of Alfred Hitchcock's *Psycho* and *Vertigo*. There was even a mysterious one-month delay in getting out the soundtrack, for the album was not released until December 13, 1994. Some stores had the soundtrack earlier but would not display it until the appointed date. The final track is the Guns n' Roses rendition of "Sympathy for the Devil," a rock tune that paves the way for Lestat to enter the modern era and probably to be the focus of the sequel.

And a sequel there must be.

To date, Rice has written five novels about vampires and their lives, deaths, joys, and sufferings. After *Interview with the Vampire*, Lestat becomes Rice's central character. The film's subtitle, *The Vampire Chronicles,* echoes the subtitle of her novels and foreshadows the sequel starring, we expect, Tom Cruise. Moreover, the film's ending with Lestat and the reporter driving away in San Francisco to the tune of "Sympathy for the Devil" allows Lestat to join the modern age, perhaps as a rock star as he does in Rice's second novel in the series, *The Vampire Lestat.* In 1976 Rice may not have dreamed of a sequel to her first novel; but now her readers and the film's viewers know there is much more to the story than what Louis relates in his interview. Lestat's old "line" to the boy at film's end, "I'll give you the choice I never had," has still not been explained to the audience.

Jordan's film has a framing unity of place, for it begins and ends in San Francisco. The novel ends a bit differently with the boy running out into the San Francisco day with the goal of somehow finding Lestat in New Orleans. Although "the boy" (the reporter) is not named in the novel or in the film, the credits interestingly list his name as "Molloy" (played by Christian Slater). Only in a later novel does Rice name the boy Daniel Molloy. When Cruise's Lestat looks invigorated after drinking from the boy and when he pulls out his lace cuffs while driving off to the rock music, we have left Louis's painful story and set the stage for learning more about Lestat's past and future adventures.

True, Louis appears from time to time in the other *Vampire Chronicles*, but they are told from Lestat's point of view, for Lestat becomes Rice's new hero, her new focus. In the fourth vampire novel, *The Tale of the Body Thief*, Lestat may have at last found a worthy companion in David Talbot. Yet even then, Louis plays a role in the story.

In *The Vampire Lestat,* Rice allows Lestat to tell his own story, and at the end Lestat adds some comments about how Louis made mistakes in *Interview with the Vampire*. According to Lestat,

When he [Louis] says I played with innocent strangers, befriending them and then killing them, how was he to know that I hunted almost exclusively among the gamblers, the thieves, and the killers, being more faithful to my unspoken vow to kill the evildoer than even I had hoped I would be? (499)

For example, a different perspective on the scene involving Louis, Lestat, and the two prostitutes is given by Lestat who says, "The whores I feasted upon in front of Louis once, to spite him, had drugged and robbed many a seaman who was never seen alive again" (499). Indeed, there are two sides to the story—and to Lestat.

Finally, the newspaper advertisement for *Interview with the Vampire* provides some clues about the film's focus. Cruise's Lestat is pictured, and the words "Drink from me and live forever" appear. But while a human-made-a-vampire in the film may live forever (unless obliterated by fire or the sun or otherwise killed), such a being may not be happy. He or she may, in fact, be severely tormented and discontented. Louis, Claudia, Armand, and even Lestat are not happy. Living "forever" as one was when made a vampire has a high price. Perhaps that being cannot change with the times. And, of course, the humans of one age die while the vampire outlives them. Ironically, vampires need companionship, but they often don't get along too well with each other. The theme of the film (and perhaps, too, of the novel) may be that no state of existence is perfect or without torment; all beings must wander the earth searching for love, happiness, and fulfillment. Yet despite the troubles of vampire existence, it still holds great attractiveness, as evidenced at the end of both the film and the novel by the boy who desires "The power to see and feel and live forever!" (343).

In sum, the film does make significant changes in the novel's content, primarily through omission, and modern film techniques are able to turn Rice's tales of vampire violence into visually stunning sequences.

Part III
The New Orleans Setting

William A. Francis

In 1972, Anne and Stan Rice lost their five-year-old daughter, Michele, to leukemia. The long period of grief was unbearable for the couple. Seeking a way to end her despair, Anne decided to resume writing full time. Rather than start a new story, she turned to an unfinished one about a New Orleans vampire. In the course of the writing she introduced a little girl named Claudia. Susan Ferraro writes that Anne was "unaware . . . of the significance of what she was doing [when] she added a beautiful little girl with golden curls (like Michele), whom the vampires save from mortal death by making her a vampire" (74). As the story developed and the voice of Louis grew stronger, Rice saw with his eyes her beloved New Orleans. For Louis and for Anne Rice, "New Orleans [was] a magical and magnificent place to live" (40). It was an old, history-laden city that had been shaped by the river, devastating plagues, greed for sugar and cotton profits, slavery and revolution. Bewitching and complicated by its exotic contradictions, New Orleans is a city of French and Spanish Creoles, Irish and German immigrants, Indians on the levee, slaves from Africa in their tribal robes, and people of mixed blood "who produced a magnificent and unique caste of crafts-men, artists, poets, and renowned feminine beauty" (39). In this magical place, where "ships appeared to float against the sky" (39), Lestat, Louis and Claudia blend into the crowds of "exotic creatures" (40) in the narrow, dark streets.

When director Neil Jordan decided to film *Interview with the Vampire*, he chose Dante Ferretti to be his production designer. Ferretti had made a name for himself in many period films, including *The Age of Innocence, And the Ship Sails On*, and *The Name of the Rose*. James Schulman observes that Ferretti set out to create New Orleans as it was in the 1790s (29), a city established by France in 1718 and ruled by French kings until 1762, when Louis XV ceded it to his Spanish cousin, Charles III. Ferretti made artistic decisions to ensure that New Orleans would look old and dark, with street lamps giving but a feeble light absorbed by the fog-laden night. Schulman notes that fiberglass columns painted to look like wood were used to cover the Spanish style ironwork of the galleries and their supporting iron columns (30). In the evening, before the filming began, crews spread dirt on Rue Bourbon to comple-ment Rice's description: "The streets were muddy then, the actual blocks islands above the gutters" (73). At dawn, when filming stopped, the dirt was picked up and held for the next evening's filming. Ferretti worked closely with Philippe Rousselot, the director of photography, to make sure "that the film's light source, predominantly Chinese paper lanterns, helped create the painted, fantastic look Ferretti hoped to achieve" (Schulman 29). Through their artistic collaboration they created a haunt-ing microcosm of nocturnal fog, swamps, tropical rain, mud, disease, death and decay—all contributing to an oppressive, stifling atmosphere of claustrophobic enclosures. In essence, Rice's love for New Orleans was not lost on Ferretti, whose "historical authenticity and vivid fantasy" served his higher purpose of creating "self-contained worlds with a pal-pable sense of reality" (Barbour 4).

To complement his New Orleans settings, Ferretti insisted upon the historical authenticity of costumes worn by the many scores of extras. According to Linda Gardar, the set costumer for the film's extras, some seventy boxes of costumes were brought in from England, Italy, and Los Angeles. More than two hundred extras were carefully dressed in appropriate costumes for the period ranging from the 1790s to the 1820s.

Similar concern for authenticity was seen in the dressing of soldiers in a variety of period uniforms. Military historian Timothy Pickles, who supervised the costuming of soldiers, chose Spanish Colonial uniforms of 1798, which had seen service in Stanley Kubrick's *Barry Lyndon*. New Orleans City Guard uniforms of 1800 were also used, along with cocked hats and black leather equipment. For the fire scene in which the vampires flee New Orleans, French-fashion uniforms were chosen. They were based on those worn by Jean Baptiste Plauche's Uniformed Battalion of Creole gentlemen, who fought beside General Jackson in the Battle of New Orleans.

In scenes filmed outside the city of New Orleans, Ferretti was dedicated to capturing late-eighteenth-century plantation and river life. To accomplish this he took great care in the artistic rendering of Oak Alley Plantation, Laurel Valley Plantation, Home Place, Destrehan Plantation, and an authentic river town he constructed behind Jackson Barracks, which is the New Orleans headquarters of the Louisiana National Guard.

Oak Alley in Vacherie, Louisiana, built between 1837 and 1839, was the site chosen for the Pointe du Lac family plantation, where Louis was born to darkness in 1791. Schulman observes that since Oak Alley had recently been renovated, it was necessary to apply an artificial mildew solution to the front of the house to make it appear old and weathered (29). The tropical atmosphere was enhanced when additional strands of Spanish moss were draped along the lower branches of the famous trees that gave the plantation its name ("In a Local Vein" E7). Sugar cane was planted on the levee, and a dock was built along the river for an old sailing ship to be moored. It is from the masts of this ship that Louis's stunt double falls after Lestat offers him a taste of death.

Filming at Oak Alley lasted for one week and was limited to exterior scenes. Jordan's request to have fires set in Oak Alley's front windows was turned down by Zeb Mayhew, Jr., administrative director of Oak Alley, who feared that the building's old timbers would ignite. Jordan offered to show Mayhew the safety precautions being employed in fire scenes in the French Quarter, but Mayhew still refused to allow fires to burn in the windows. Jordan did get permission to blow an aerosol smoke from the windows, to which flames were later added by digital enhancement. Mayhew also permitted Louis's torch to be carried through the front door a number of times until the final take was achieved. Interior fire scenes were filmed at Pinewood Studios. A quarter-scale replica of Oak Alley was used for the culminating fire which destroyed the plantation home. Film of the burning replica, which was actually a firebox, was composited onto a live-action plate of the original plantation home (Shay 49).

The Oak Alley slave quarter was filmed at Laurel Valley near Thibodaux, Louisiana, the largest surviving nineteenth-century plantation complex in the United States. (The plantation home was burned by Union soldiers.) According to Jerry McKee, general manager of Laurel Valley, where sugar cane is still harvested, filming lasted for three nights. There were scenes of stunt doubles on jumping horses, and of bodies of Lestat's victims being pulled from a stream at dawn by weeping slaves. McKee added that several slave quarter interiors were dressed for filming, but no interior scenes were used in the film. Another scene that was eventually cut showed Lestat and Louis walking in the moonlit sugar cane fields.

Since slaves labored from sunrise to sunset, when vampires slept, very little is revealed about slave life. But the transplanted sugar cane by the levee at Oak Alley suggests that sugar made the Pointe du Lac fortune. In the novel, however, the Pointe du Lacs settled on not one but two plantations, and their fortune came from the cultivation of indigo. But according to James Pitot in his *Observations on the Colony of Louisiana from 1796 to 1802*, indigo was a risky commodity, for the Louisiana soil, weather, and insects tended to make victims of indigo planters (68).

Louis's transformation into a vampire is consummated in the family cemetery constructed on Oak Alley grounds. However, the three nights of filming in the cemetery were unproductive because the vampire makeup did not film well in the hot, humid night air, which was filled with annoying insects. Rather than continue the expensive filming, Jordan had the cemetery props dismantled and shipped to London, where the scene of Louis's transformation was finally filmed. In the novel, Lestat first attacks Louis a few steps from the Pointe du Lac town house in New Orleans. Louis finally receives Lestat's dark gift on one of the indigo plantations.

The most extensive sets to be constructed in New Orleans were a river town and a huge floating dock located behind Jackson Barracks. Period ships, visible in the distance, were "accomplished with a digital matte painting and model ships composited onto a live-action crane shot of the moonlit harbor" (Shay 46). One of the principle sets in the river town was the tavern called Du Chat Noir, where despondent Louis wins at cards while longing for death. Louis bares his chest and dares the gambler to shoot him. Denied the death he longed for but could not bring upon himself, Louis leaves the tavern in the company of a prostitute. As they cross a long bridge connecting the levee to the dock they are accosted by a man wielding a knife. But before Louis can decide whether to surrender his money or his life, Lestat breaks the thug's neck, dispatches the prostitute and sinks his teeth into Louis's neck. Then, with the music of Elliot Goldenthal's "Born to Darkness" building in a crescendo, Lestat rises with Louis some fifty feet into the masts of a ship (actually docked at Oak Alley), where Louis has his taste of death before Lestat drops him into the river.

The floating dock constructed at the Jackson Barracks levee was necessary because the period ships could not float in the shallow water close to the shore (Schulman 30). Durward Dunn, a marine contractor, stated that the dock was constructed by connecting two barges, which together measured 240 feet by 30 feet. Then a long bridge was built to connect the levee with the floating dock. To hold everything steady in the swift Mississippi current workers drove pilings into the river bank and the river bottom. Barges were then fastened to the pilings by heavy cables. A period ship was moored on the outside of the floating dock, as were barges, which were dressed to look like river rafts.

The river town serves a second important function: it doubles as New Orleans set ablaze by Louis when he breaks an oil lamp at Lestat's feet and engulfs him in flames. Although the entire city appears to be on fire, only a few river town buildings were actually "burned" through special effects. Digital artist Adam Stark observed that because the filming of the fire went on for a long time, he was able through his computer to select different buildings and "move them around to get a complete burning waterfront" (Shay 53). Maria LoVasco, public affairs officer with the Louisiana National Guard, observed that one of the buildings was purposely burned to the ground; the surviving buildings, including the tavern, were dismantled and the materials became the property of the national guard.

The scenes filmed at the river town and on the floating dock are visually stunning, beautifully illuminated by torch and candle light, and evocative of a wild and primitive time on the river long ago. Although these scenes have no counterparts in the novel, they are in harmony with Louis's celebration of New Orleans, to which we may add: "And drifting through all, through this medley of languages and colors, were the people of the port, the sailors of the ships, who came in great waves to spend their money in the cabarets" (39).

Home Place in Hahnville is the setting for an outdoor tavern, where Louis and Lestat witness a performance of the Comedia del Arte, a scene not found in the novel. According to Richard Keller, who owns the French Colonial–style house, six weeks of preparation were required to set up a dozen large poles supporting a large tent by the side porch of the building. A stage had to be built and dressed to look aged. The filming lasted from sunset to dawn. Keller noted that approximately seventy-five extras were used to cheer the Comedia del Arte performers in their sexual farce. The scene testifies to the vampires' fondness for theatrical performances, whether classical or vulgar. In addition to mitigating Louis's increasing morbidity and underscoring Lestat's need for what he calls "real sport," the scene stands in opposition to the grotesque vampire seduction and marriage Louis witnesses with Claudia in the Theatre des Vampires.

Lestat and Louis, newly born to darkness, attend an elegant ball filmed over three nights at Destrehan Plantation in Destrehan, Louisiana. This plantation, some twenty-five miles from New Orleans, was built between 1787 and 1790 in the French Colonial style. It is the oldest documented plantation in the lower Mississippi Valley. In the nineteenth century, the plantation was transformed into the fashionable Greek Revival style through the addition of wings and a second story. Ferretti did not attempt to disguise the Greek Revival features for he had learned from Pier Paolo Pasolini that a production designer of a period film must sometimes work with certain unalterable limitations or else risk becoming "academic or pedantic" (Schulman 30). According to Irene Tastet, plantation administrator and executive director of the River Road Historical Society, set dressers fitted the ballroom with elaborate Parisian draperies and art work, which did not accurately reflect the austere decor of Destrehan Plantation during this period. (Jean Noel d'Estrehan owned a more fashionable residence in Rue Chartres, where the decor reflected the fashion of the day.)

In a memorable episode filmed on the Destrehan Plantation grounds, the Widow St. Clair, her twin poodles, and her foppish beau are victims of Louis and Lestat. Recalling a number of the scenes, Irene Tastet tells of a karate expert who tutored Cruise in the proper moves necessary to snap the Widow St. Clair's neck, and she, or more precisely the actress Lyla Hay Owen, was required to collapse on the ground over a number of takes.

For Brad Pitt the fake poodle hair covered with fake blood was especially annoying. Tastet describes the special effects employed in the scene in which Louis attacks Lestat, lifting him high in the air and running him into a live oak tree. To accomplish this feat, technicians strung a wire between two ancient trees. Then a stunt man was attached to the wire and whisked along it to the other tree. In such a manner did the vampires "duel" under the live oaks. This scene, like the earlier one in which Lestat levitates with Louis, underscores the power of New World vampires.

After the Pointe du Lac plantation burns, the vampires move into a large Creole Spanish–style house, which is located at 731 Rue Royale in New Orleans. Since the house dates to at least 1799, Ferretti fulfilled his wish for architectural authenticity. Known as Maison Montegut, this brick house was erected shortly after the disastrous fire of 1794, which destroyed over two hundred houses, many of which had been built to replace some of the 856 houses destroyed by fire in 1788. To prevent another such disaster, the Spanish governor, Carondelet, "issued an order that all future buildings of two or more stories erected in the center of the city should be of brick" (Federal Writers' Project Staff 265). Evidence of Spanish architecture in the French Quarter today can be seen in the "heavily walled brick houses, two-storied, tile-roofed, with wide arches, fanlights and Spanish-style courtyards" (Kane 83).

As a reminder of the significant Spanish political and architectural influence in New Orleans, a tile plaque was placed on the facade of 731 Rue Royale to note that under Spanish rule Rue Royale was known as Calle Real. In the novel Louis speaks of the great fire "a long time ago" (153), and of the predominant Spanish architecture that displaced the French style of construction.

In the novel Rice has Louis and Lestat settle into a suite at a "new Spanish hotel" (71) where, in a vivid scene, Lestat drains the blood of one woman and places another, half dead, in a coffin. This scene is presented in the film, too, but it takes place in Maison Montegut. Louis describes the "new Spanish town houses in the Rue Royale," with its "long, lavish upstairs flat . . . a hidden garden court . . . [and] a wall secure against the street, with fitted wooden shutters and a barred carriage door" (99). Katherine Ramsland writes that Rice modeled the town house after the Gallier House at 1132 Royal Street (153), which was built in 1857. For the film, however, the older Maison Montegut is an ideal setting. With its two French windows, barred carriage door, spiral stairs, upstairs apartments, and garden court behind the house, it closely matches Rice's description of the vampires' town house. Extensive filming was done at Maison Montegut, and permission was given for fire to be filmed at the windows. According to Elston James Howard, assistant location manager, the house was dressed appropriately to retard the force of the flames, and the exterior of the building was hosed down as an added precaution. The interior fire scenes were filmed at Pinewood Studios.

Claudia, whose actions are largely responsible for the fire, is a fearless killer in the novel and the film. One of the briefest scenes of her killing, for which there is no counterpart in the novel, was filmed in an antique doll store at 241 Rue Chartres, where the dollmaker tells the little girl that his dolls are probably too expensive for her. Within seconds, however, Claudia is on her way home with a lovely doll, and the fate of the dollmaker requires no explanation. Although this is a brief scene, it nevertheless prepares viewers for the grotesque Creole doll-corpse Claudia buries in her collection in her room.

In her early days as a vampire Claudia sits "alone in the dark square waiting for the kindly gentleman or woman to find her" (101). These words from the novel are dramatized in the film in the square before the Presbytere next to the Saint Louis Cathedral. As Lestat proudly looks on, Claudia the child-doll feigns tears that melt the heart of her matronly victim. Claudia also took pleasure in devouring an entire family. In the novel Louis says that "Claudia had a family . . . which she took one by one" (104-05). The comparable film scene was shot at two New Orleans locations. First, there is an establishing shot of an old French Colonial–style house known today as Madame John's Legacy, 632 Rue Dumaine, which George Washington Cable made famous in *Old Creole Days*. Second, the scene supposedly taking place in Rue Dumaine, Claudia's piano recital, is actually filmed in the Pitot House, an old plantation house at 1440 Moss Street, the residence of James Pitot, author of *Observations on the Colony of Louisiana*. The hosts for the musical evening are systematically devoured (off camera), and we see their coffins, some carried across the second floor gallery and others from the street-level entrance of Madame John's Legacy. This house, which was spared in the Great Fire of 1794, is one of the oldest in the Mississippi Valley.

Nearly a century after Louis's catastrophic trip to Paris, where Claudia dies, we find Louis home again in New Orleans. The year is 1988, three years short of his vampire bicentenary. Although he is now stronger, wiser, and resigned to what he is, he still longs to see the sun rise. He realizes his wish by watching the dawn recorded in numerous films, and we discover him leaving the Coliseum theatre, where the feature film is *Tequila Sunrise*. The Coliseum theater, 1233 Coliseum Street, was built in the early 1920s. Now it is the home of Coliseum & Motion, a special effects company. Kenny Morrison and his business partner renovated the theater and preserved its art deco design ("Fifty People to Watch" 58).

As Louis leaves the Coliseum, he hears the traffic noises and the police sirens on the Camp Street ramp leading to the Mississippi River

Bridge. The closeness of the ramp to the theater and the piercing traffic noise emphasize the film's claustrophobic atmosphere, which is mitigated as the camera rises for an aerial shot and finds the illuminated steeple and spire of St. Theresa of Avila Church. Kevin Althans, effects designer for Coliseum & Motion, observed that the church gives depth and dimension to the once-fashionable neighborhood, which has known better days.

The sirens link this scene with the following one where Louis senses the presence of Lestat in a dilapidated uptown house on Prytania Street. In the novel Louis returns to New Orleans specifically to renew acquaintance with Lestat, whom he finds "stooped and shivering" (329) and terrified by sirens and flashing red emergency lights (332). In the film, however, Louis returns to New Orleans out of "curiosity, boredom, who knows what." He happens upon Lestat in a house on Prytania Street, but the scene is actually filmed in an old two-story house at 1519 Esplanade Avenue near the French Quarter. On the east side of the house is a large yard in which six fake tree trunks were erected for the film. They are about twelve feet tall and have only the stubs of low branches. According to William Tanguis, who is restoring the house, braces were attached to the trunk tops. Boards were fastened to the braces to link the trees and provide a framework for the set dressers. The wrought-iron fence viewed in the scene was fake, as were the columns by the rear door of the house. According to Howard, this yard through which Louis passes was dressed by greensmen with shrubs and other plants to condense its haunted and forlorn nocturnal atmosphere.

Through the upstairs windows on the west side of the house viewers see and hear the vehicles driven by extras on nearby Interstate 10. Next to the house is a service station, which was shut down for the filming to allow a helicopter to come in low and close to the house. According to Bob Zajonic, the aerial coordinator who piloted the helicopter, some electrical lines and a station lamp were removed to allow the helicopter to fly within two feet of the upstairs windows. A tree close to the house was trimmed and ivy was removed from the windows. The shuddering noise and intense light of the helicopter, which terrorize Lestat, provided the cue for the action in the large, barren ballroom of the old house.

With this scene, the New Orleans episodes conclude. Louis (and Lestat) move on to San Francisco. The film ends on a tentative, taunting note as Guns n' Roses squeal and laugh to a rock beat in lyrics about "wealth and taste," the Crucifixion, and a satanic "goat boy"—the recipe for the sequel in *The Vampire Chronicles*.

In conclusion, the decision to film *Interview with the Vampire* in New Orleans was one welcomed by Rice fans, who would have been incensed to see their beloved novel brought to cinematic life in any other setting. To satisfy the fans as well as Anne Rice, Jordan and Ferretti insisted upon historically accurate settings, which were enhanced through special dressings and props. The French Quarter was filmed extensively, as were a number of Louisiana plantations. Crude bars and brothels were created to dramatize the tumultuous and terrifying life on the river. Ferretti's superbly dark and sensual New Orleans embraces the decadent, erotic vampires, whose internecine battles build in a crescendo to the majestic conflagration that sends them off to adventures on the old continent.

Director Neil Jordan commented that Rice's vampires had to be played by the "best young Hollywood actors" because vampires have "glamour, indestructibility, and eternal youth" ("Fall Movie Preview" 58). Along with that youthful beauty and intriguing immortality, the film also captures what Rice describes as the underlying theme of her novel. "It's about being orphaned," Rice says (Abramowitz 68). The vampires exist in conflicted isolation even when they are with each other. Lestat wants to embrace the vampire existence, but his search for a companion to enjoy it with him is futile because the companions he creates—Louis and Claudia—do not want to stay with him. Claudia is isolated in her own, too-small body. Louis wanders alone through the centuries, consumed with his feelings of spiritual damnation. The film captures what the novel shows as the surprising pain of immortality, and when Louis ends his story, he says to the reporter that there is nothing more to tell.

The film moves beyond Louis's story, however, and the final scene shows Lestat, rejuvenated from drinking the reporter's blood and taking over the wheel of his car on the Golden Gate bridge. Lestat is driving into the sequel—with fresh energy and the promise of new adventures.

Works Consulted

Abramowitz, Rachel. "Love Bites: *Interview with the Vampire*." *Premiere* Nov. 1994: 63-72, 116.

Althans, Kevin. Telephone interview. 8 Mar. 1995. New Orleans, LA.

Barbour, David. Letter. *Theatre Crafts International* 29.2 (1995): 4.

Barton, Rick. "The Big Bite." *New Orleans Magazine* Nov. 1994: 54-58.

"Box Office." *Entertainment Weekly* 13 Jan. 1995: 41.

"Critical Mass." *Entertainment Weekly* 18 Nov. 1994: 81.

Dunn, Durward. Telephone interview. 3 Mar. 1995. New Orleans, LA.

Federal Writers' Project Staff. *New Orleans City Guide.* Boston: Houghton Mifflin, 1938.

"Fall Movie Preview." *Entertainment Weekly* 26 Aug./2 Sept. 1994: 56-58.

Ferraro, Susan. "Novels You Can Sink Your Teeth Into." *New York Times Magazine* 14 Oct. 1990: 27+.

"Fifty People to Watch." *New Orleans Magazine* July 1994: 54-67.

Gardar, Linda. Telephone interview. 24 Feb. 1995. New Orleans, LA.

Howard, Elston James. Telephone interview. 27 Feb. 1995. New Orleans, LA.

"In a Local Vein." *The Times-Picayune* [New Orleans] 10 Nov. 1995: E7+

Interview with the Vampire. Dir. Neil Jordan. With Tom Cruise, Brad Pitt, Christian Slater, Antonio Banderas, and Kirsten Dunst. Warner, 1994.

Kane, Harnett T. *Queen New Orleans: City by the River.* New York: Morrow, 1949.

Keller, Richard. Telephone interview. 2 Mar. 1995. Hahnville, LA.

Kennedy, X.J., and Dana Gioia. *Literature: An Introduction to Fiction, Poetry, and Drama.* 6th ed. New York: HarperCollins, 1995.

LoVasco, Maria. Telephone interview. 13 Mar. 1995. New Orleans, LA.

Mayhew, Zeb, Jr. Telephone interview. 14 Mar. 1995. Vacherie, LA.

McKee, Jerry. Telephone interview. 3 May 1995. Thibodaux, LA.

Melton, J. Gordon. *The Vampire Book: The Encyclopedia of the Undead.* Detroit: Visible Ink, 1994.

Murray, Steve. "Changes Don't Draw Blood in 'Vampire.'" *Akron Beacon Journal* 28 Nov. 1994: C7.

Nosferatu. Dir. F.W. Murnau. With Max Schreck. Germany, 1922.

Pickles, Timothy. Telephone interview. 27 Feb. 1995. New Orleans, LA.

Pitot, James. *Observations on the Colony of Louisiana from 1796 to 1802.* Trans. Henry C. Pitot. Baton Rouge: Louisiana State UP, 1979.

Ramsland, Katherine. *Prism of the Night.* New York: Dutton, 1991.

Rice, Anne. *Interview with the Vampire.* 1976. New York: Ballantine, 1993.

——. *The Vampire Lestat.* 1985. New York: Ballantine, 1989.

Schulman, James. "The Vampire." *Theatre Crafts International* 29.2 (1995): 29-30.

Shay, Estelle. "Mortal Images." *Cinefex* Mar. 1995: 38-57.

Skal, David J. *The Monster Show: A Cultural History of Horror.* New York: Norton, 1993.

Tastet, Irene. Telephone interview. 27 Feb. 1995. Destrehan, LA.

Tanguis, William. Telephone interview. 10 Mar. 1995. Chalmette, LA.

Zajonic, Bob. Telephone interview. 10 Mar. 1995. San Anselmo, CA.

Let Us Prey:
Religious Codes and Rituals
in *The Vampire Lestat*

Aileen Chris Shafer

In his examination of the gothic novel, Robert D. Hume notes a change that occurred in the mid-eighteenth century when gothic novels moved beyond the melodramatic shock value that evoked terror to the more complex, troubling, or appalling situations that involved the reader in new psychological ways. These changing gothic novels still included the supernatural, but they began to escalate from terror to horror. Significantly, the change also reflected a concern with moral ambiguity, for example, in *The Castle of Otranto*. The confusion of good and evil produced non-Christian or anticlerical feeling in the changing gothic novels: Hume attributes the change to the cultural shift in conceptions of good and evil. In poetry this shift might be found in Blake's *The Marriage of Heaven and Hell*; in fiction, *Frankenstein* provides "real psychological insight" as Frankenstein's monster mirrors Frankenstein's problems with love and his inability to respond to human feeling. Moral ambiguity, the inversion of Christian ritual, as well as other features of the changed horror-gothic as described by Hume classify *The Vampire Lestat* well within the genre.

Rice's gothic *Vampire Chronicles* demonstrate that the gothic novel continues to evolve as culture changes. The greatest divergence from the classic gothic novel in the *Chronicles* is the shift from the hero-villain protagonist, who confronts the monster vampire, to the consciousness of the vampire himself. This innovation in the genre is noted by Stefan Dziemianowicz who indicates

Ever since Anne Rice made the protagonist of her 1976 novel *Interview with the Vampire* deserving of reader sympathy writers of vampire fiction have felt compelled to humanize their monsters. Some do so by portraying the vampire as a tragic victim of circumstance, others by showing that vampire behavior is no less predatory than many types of human conduct.

In *The Vampire Lestat*, Rice moves beyond a humanized monstrous consciousness in her innovative development of Lestat who takes on heroic proportions. Lestat fits both the classical definition and the Nietzschean definitions of a hero. He fulfills the classical definition both as a mortal and as a vampire, for he is an aristocrat whose heroic deeds place him above others, yet he is flawed because of his reckless impetuousness. His heroism continues into his vampire existence, for among other heroic actions he attempts to drink from and kill only murderers and outlaws and he battles and attempts to convert the vampires who are "Children of Darkness." Lestat also fits the Nietzschean definition of a hero or *Übermensch* described by Katherine Ramsland, as one that replaces Christianity with new values, "a being of moral courage who could face the total collapse of meaning required to replace [Christianity] and could shoulder the burdensome responsibility of creating new standards of right and wrong" (258). Nietzsche saw this replacing of old meaning by new as cyclical throughout history. Because *The Vampire Lestat* includes the creation story of vampires that harkens back to an early Egyptian period, when Egyptians were cannibals, as described in the novel, Lestat learns of cyclical changes as this novel traces religious beliefs and practices, factual and fictional, and concepts of good and evil from that period until 1984. It is through Lestat's experiences, and those of other vampires throughout their history that Rice's novel reveals Lestat's heroic search for meaning, purpose, and belief in a world that is a "savage garden."

Lestat, who was a mortal prior to the French Revolution, echoes changing Enlightenment views of man and becomes Rice's personification, or vampirization, of a call for new beliefs to fit changing times. Prior to his transformation he had become exposed to the ideas of Diderot, Voltaire, Rousseau, and other intellectuals who were changing humanity's concept of people and of God, ideas he carries into his vampire existence. Although Lestat questions the existence of a deity throughout the novel, he affirms belief in a positive force or power. Not all of the vampires are as enlightened as Lestat, for, as he eventually learns, the nature of vampires, like that of mortals, is individualistic and stems from their cultural milieu as humans before their creation as vampires. Thus, the early vampires were, and many remain, inclined toward placing no value on human life and in perpetuating superstitions about themselves as vampires. Lestat, for the most part, attempts to victimize only murderers and evildoers, and on the occasions that he resorts to killing innocent victims, he is troubled by his action. Also, he creates his own vampiric standards because he had been given no codes nor rules after Magnus performed the "dark trick" on him and made him a vampire. When he eventually confronts a coven of vampires, termed "the children of darkness," they call him "heretic" because he doesn't follow the old ways of vampires.

Dr. Polidori's *Vampyre*, Sheridan Le Fanu's *Carmilla*, and Bram Stoker's *Dracula* created vampire lore related to mirrors, crucifixes, and garlic, while their "dark trick" is traditionally performed on the opposite sex. *The Vampire Lestat* retains enough of the vampire mythology to establish a link to the earlier vampires; however, much of the lore is demythologized, as Lestat looks into mirrors, sleeps under a church altar, has no fear of crosses. Lestat's deconstruction of these rituals serves as metonomy for Lestat's iconoclasm throughout the novel. Significantly, unlike traditional vampires whose "love bite" is heterosexual, Lestat activities are bisexual and include transforming his mother and two men he loves into vampires. Lestat, who unlike traditional vampires still loves mortals after his transformation, grapples with the concepts of good and evil.

Although the novel encompasses centuries, it begins in 1984 and then flashes back to Lestat's mortal existence in the eighteenth century. In 1984, the vampire Lestat arises from a self-imposed underground exile, which he began in 1929. In keeping with the language of beliefs and religion, the name of the rock band whose sounds awaken him is Satan's Night Out. Lestat had already concluded that the devil is the creation of both men and vampires who cling to the old ways: the Devil, which is part of the "savage garden," he believes, exists in men's minds. Lestat sees a manifestation of the savage garden in 1984 as he watches the movie *Apocalypse Now:* he muses ". . . it sang of the age old battle of the Western world against evil." He hears the mad commander in the savage garden of Cambodia say, "You must make a friend of horror and moral terror." Lestat reflects, "to which the Western man answers as he has always answered: 'No.'" Lestat's conflict lies in knowing he is a monstrous anomaly as he questions the "savage garden," within the minds of men and vampires. "No. Horror and moral terror can never be exonerated. They have no real value. Pure evil has no real place. And that means doesn't it that I have no real place" (10). Because of Lestat's heroic morality, he recognizes the inherent evil of being a parasite who survives by draining blood from men and whose very nature places him in opposition to men.

Ironically, Lestat establishes himself in the Satan's Night Out rock band for which he writes music and in which he performs. His expertise and his promotion of the group catapults them into national prominence. Additionally, Lestat gains prominence when he decides to write a book rebutting *Interview with the Vampire*, written by Louis, a vampire he had created and who had attempted to destroy him. His book, too, will break the code of vampires since they are forbidden to tell mortals of their existence; however, Lestat creates his own standards. When his book and the group's videos evoke hostility among some vampires the world over, they express their fury with threatening messages. Then the novel shifts back to Lestat's story.

As a heroic mortal in the eighteenth century, Lestat, who had been born into the French aristocracy prior to the French Revolution, had tried to escape his provincial home twice but been brought back. Once he had been sent to a monastery to study, a place he treasured because there he was beginning to learn to read and write. When Lestat decided to become a priest, he was brought back by his family because the family couldn't financially support his movement up into bishop or other position of distinction, a status that would befit his family's position. The second time he had tried to flee, he ran off with a troupe of Italian actors, but once again he was brought back, because the theater had the "taint of the devil," for "Even the great Moliere had not been given a Christian burial" (35).

Despite the evil that is ascribed to the theater, when Lestat later recounts his experiences with the acting troupe to his friend Nicolas he overturns the existing view as he states, "Actors and actresses make magic. . . . They make things happen on the stage; they invent; they create. . . . Actors and musicians—they're saints to me" (51). When Nicolas questions Lestat's view, Lestat responds, "I'm speaking of those who won't accept a useless lie, just because they were born to it. I mean those who would be something better. . . . There is blessedness in that. . . . There's sanctity. And God or no God, there is goodness in it" (52).

In further extolling the virtue of the theater (a value Rice extends to the other arts), Lestat notes, " 'Now how could it not have been good,' I asked, 'to give and receive such happiness? We brought to life that town when we put on our play. Magic, I tell you. It could heal the sick, it could' " (52). Both Katherine Ramsland and Bette B. Roberts liken Lestat to Dionysus; as Ramsland indicates, "the god represents both the eternal spirit of passion and energy worshiped by the Greeks in frenzied ritual," as well as being the god of theater (51). By extolling the nobility and virtue of the arts and creativity, Rice further dramatizes Lestat's heroic qualities.

Following his experiences with the monastery and theater, both aborted by his less-than-heroic family, Lestat carries out his most recognized heroic deed as a mortal. He achieves celebrity in the town by single-handedly killing a pack of wolves. Because of his feat, he receives recognition from the townspeople who give him a magnificent fur-lined velvet cape. In town, he meets Nicolas who has studied in Paris and who also plays the violin, a meeting that changes his life. Nicolas's father, a wealthy merchant, wants him to continue his education rather than indulge in a frivolity like violin playing, for which he threatens to break Nicolas's hands. Nicholas's father's attitude reflects his mercantile mentality; whereas Lestat is moved by the emotions Nicolas evokes in him with his playing and is entranced with Nicolas's stories of Paris, stories that reinforce the anticlerical stance of the novel. Nicolas informs him that in Paris "educated people didn't believe in God, that they were infinitely more interested in science, that the aristocracy was much in ill favor, and so was the Church. These were the times of reason, not superstition" (46).

Although these seem to be the times of reason, superstition lingers. Nicolas reminds Lestat of a time when they were boys and Lestat had cried when a priest had taken them to see a place where witches had been burned. Lestat remembers the episode he hasn't thought of in years,

It was the place itself I thought about whenever I drew near it—the thicket of blackened stakes, the images of men women and children burnt alive.

Nicolas was studying me. "When your mother came to get you, she said it was all ignorance and cruelty. She was so angry with the priest for telling us the old tales."

I nodded.

The final horror to hear they had all died for nothing, those long-forgotten people of our own village, that they had been innocent. "Victims of superstition," she had said. "There were no real witches." No wonder I had screamed and screamed. (48)

Lestat's mother's enlightened view expressed in his description is contrasted to Nicolas's mother's primitive attitude, for Nicholas's mother had "told a different story, that the witches had been in league with the devil, that they'd blighted the crops, and in the guise of wolves killed the sheep and children—." To which Lestat responds, "And won't the world be better if no one is ever again burnt in the name of God? . . . If there is no more faith in God to make men do that to each other. What is the danger in a secular world where horrors like that don't happen?" (48). This episode, like others throughout the novel, questions the relationship between religion and superstition.

In his discussion of religion with Nicolas, Lestat, the humanist, notes that no one in his family believes much in God, saying, "Even in the monastery I had not believed in God. I had believed in the monks around me" (47). Lestat learns that Nicolas's family is fervently religious; Nicolas queries, "But can men live without these beliefs?" (47). In their discussions of good and evil, Lestat tells Nicolas he can't live without the concept of goodness; whereas Nicolas says, "I'm evil and revel in it" (72). Once again Lestat exhibits his heroic moral superiority in contrast to Nicolas's expression of embracing evil. Ironically, it is Nicolas who when he eventually becomes a vampire cannot cope with his nature; as Lestat later indicates, Nicolas cannot overcome the stronghold of Christianity and its belief in original sin and guilt.

Lestat in his angst over discussions with Nicolas and in his increased awareness of his mortality goes through a dark period, agonizing over the meaninglessness of life and the possibility that after death we still will not have an answer. Conveying his mood to Nicolas he states that "we're going to die and not even know. We'll never know, and all this meaninglessness will just go on and on and on. . . . We'll just be gone, dead, dead, dead, without ever knowing!" (55). His despondence about the meaning of life leads him to seek an answer from the priest, but the responses from the priest offer him no solace. He says of his despair about not knowing, "It never did pass, really" (58). Later as an immortal, Lestat continues to seek answers to his questions throughout the centuries and craves hope in his times of despair.

During his depression, Lestat avoids his mother because he doesn't want to discuss death and chaos. But his mother comes to his room the first Sunday of Lent as he is watching a big bonfire about which he says,

It had a ghastly aspect to it—the roaring flames, the dancing, and singing, the peasants going afterwards through the orchards with their torches to the tune of their strange chanting.

We had a priest for a little while who called it pagan. But they got rid of him fast enough. The farmers of our mountains kept to their old rituals. It was to make the trees bear and the crops grow, all this. And on this occasion, more than any other, I felt I saw the kind of men and women who could burn witches. (59-60)

Rice superimposes the old superstitions on to the Lenten festivities as she foreshadows and echoes other rituals and ceremonies described later in the novel. These cyclical repetitions develop a motif of the human need for ritual and ceremony to serve needs or to affirm meaning in people's and in vampires' lives. Prime examples of the desire for ritual and ceremony are depicted when Marius, the most heroic vampire in the novel, is converted to a vampire as part of a Druidic ritual and during the rock concert at the conclusion of the novel when the audience cheers and wails.

Lestat's mother, Gabrielle, the educated one in the family, allies herself with Lestat who, unlike the rest of the indolent family, attempts to improve the estate and educate himself. She sells her jewels to buy him hunting dogs and to provide him with money for his ventures. It is she who provides money for him to escape with Nicolas to Paris. Although Lestat's and Nicolas's financial means in Paris are limited, they eventually join the ranks of a small theater where Lestat performs and Nicolas plays his violin. As he becomes more successful as an actor, Lestat senses that someone in the audience is calling him "Wolfkiller"; the epithet seems to be emanating from a strange figure in the audience.

One night Magnus, an "old" vampire who had been observing him, awakens Lestat from sleep and whisks him away to his castle to perform the dark trick on him. Despite Lestat's agnosticism, when panic and fear overcome him, he pleads with Magnus, "In God's name get away!" As he internalizes, "I had to believe in God now. I had to. That was the only hope. I went to make the sign of the Cross" (87). Magnus watches as he continues to call to God.

Eventually after Magnus has taken blood from Lestat and is about to give him his blood to convert him to a vampire, Magnus breathes, "The wine of all wines. . . . This is my Body, this is my Blood." Lestat notes, "And then his arms surrounded me they drew me to him and I felt a great warmth emanating from him, and he seemed to be filled not with blood but with love for me" (89). This is one of a number of episodes in which Rice inverts Christian ritual, including the rituals when Lestat transforms his mother to vampire and during Lestat's rock performance, when, according to Ramsland, as the concert is depicted in *Queen of the Damned*, he becomes a Christ figure as blood pours down his face while he calls for the destruction of evil (298).

Magnus destroys himself by going into a fire, leaving Lestat little information about vampires but providing him a castle and centuries of wealth. Lestat's thirst propels him toward Paris, clothed in elegance taken from Magnus's treasure trove. While en route he enters a church and reaches into the ciborium to remove the consecrated Communion Hosts. Despite his superhuman senses, he notes, "No, there was no power here, nothing that I could feel or see or know with any of my monstrous senses, nothing that responded to me. There were wafers and gold and wax and light." Lestat closes everything up "So nobody would know a sacrilege had been committed" (113). Lestat once again questions religious traditions and seeks answers to religious verities.

Lestat's newly acquired treasure enables him to send gifts to his family, to purchase the theater where he had performed, and to buy Nicolas a Stradivarius violin and other gifts. His generosity reveals a generosity uncharacteristic of most other vampires. When he learns that his mother is critically ill, he arranges to send her to Venice; however, on her request Nicolas brings her to Paris. Rice continues her use of religious terminology, calling the section in which Lestat's mother is about to die "Viaticum for the Marquise." His mother's Viaticum, or final communion, is with Lestat's blood as he gives her eternal life, at her request, rather than let her die. This inversion of a Catholic ritual becomes even more subversive as his conversion of his mother is described in erotic language: "And jetting up into the current came the thirst . . . until she was flesh and blood and mother and lover and all things beneath the cruel pressure of my fingers and my lips, everything I had ever desired" (157). Rice's use of the vampire paradigm enables her to break taboos and to tap in to primal emotions.

On their trip to the castle and back to Paris, Gabrielle and Lestat are attacked by a band of malevolents, vampires who pursue and attack them shouting epithets such as, "A Curse on you, blasphemer" and "May the wrath of God punish the profane" (186). Although Gabrielle and Lestat know nothing of these creatures, they read the images and communication from the malevolents as Gabrielle tells Lestat that the creatures damn Gabrielle and Lestat for entering churches. Gabrielle and Lestat find refuge in a church, where Gabrielle fearfully questions, "What if they're right . . . And we don't belong in the House of God." To which Lestat responds, "Gibberish and nonsense. God isn't in the House of God" as once again Lestat questions religious trappings and symbolism (190). When the creatures pursue Lestat and Gabrielle into Paris, the two seek safety in Notre Dame cathedral. Despite the taboo forbidding vampires to enter churches, the leader of the coven, Armand, does enter Notre Dame where he battles with Lestat and Gabrielle. When Lestat is thrown out of the cathedral, he and Gabrielle accompany the "Children of Darkness" peacefully.

Gabrielle and Lestat confront the coven who live among graves like ghouls in *Les Innocents*, a burial ground under which the Children of Darkness, who are unkempt and dressed in rags, reside. The coven, which has captured Nicolas and holds him prisoner, accuse Lestat of being a profaner because among other offenses, he moves among mortals, profanes holy places and performs the "dark trick" without the proper ritual (187). Lestat learns that his creator Magnus also had scorned the old rules, that he, too, was a dissident. When he is warned that he will bring down the wrath of God on all of them, Lestat responds, "If you fear so much the power of God, . . . then the teachings of the Church aren't unknown to you. You must know that the forms of goodness change with the ages, that there are saints for all times under heaven," a Nietzschean concept of cycles of change that permeates the novel. The Children of Darkness believe they are children of the Devil, live in filth, and avoid mortals. Lestat tells them, "you waste your gifts! . . . And worse, you waste your immortality! Nothing in all the world is so nonsensical and contradictory, save mortals, that is, who live in the grip of the superstitions of the past" (222).

After the coven disbands, Armand who had led the coven wants to travel with Gabrielle and Lestat. We learn that Armand, who was born on the Russion Steppes and carried away by marauding Tartars into slavery at an early age, was turned into a vampire by Marius a wise "old one." But from Santino in the Roman catacombs Armand had learned the code for vampires; many of these "thou shalt nots" seem arbitrary to Lestat, rules he had broken (301). Lestat and Gabrielle refuse to take Armand with them for, among other reasons, Lestat states, "I've been a rebel always . . . you've been the slave of everything that ever claimed you." Armand had been a toady to Marius who created him and then to the arbitrary rules and the coven he had directed. Armand in his desire to go with Lestat argues, "Guidance is what you need. . . . You've only begun your adventure and you have no beliefs to hold you. You cannot live without some guidance." To which Gabrielle responds with her pantheistic view,

Millions live without belief or guidance. It is you who cannot live without some guidance. . . . there are things I must know. I cannot live without some embracing philosophy but it has nothing to do with old beliefs in gods or devils. . . . I want to know, for example, why beauty exists . . . why nature continues to contrive it, and what is the link between the life of a lightning storm with the feeling these things inspire in us? If God does not exist, if these things are not unified into one metaphorical system, then why do they retain for us such symbolic power? Lestat calls it the Savage Garden, but for me that is not enough. (288-89)

Armand tells Gabrielle that they are the abandoned of God, she asks him, "Do you believe in God?" To which Armand replies, "Yes, always in God. . . . It is Satan—our master—who is the fiction and that is the fiction which has betrayed me" (310). As in many instances in the novel, there is equivocation about the belief in a deity.

Armand informs them of Marius, the almost god-like vampire, who,

found a way to imitate mortal life. To be one with mortals, he slew only the evildoer, and he painted as mortals paint. Angels and blue skies. . . . He created good things. I see wisdom in him and a lack of vanity. . . . He had lived a thousand years and he believed more in the vistas of heaven that he painted than in himself. (310)

Lestat feels compelled to know about Marius and about the references Armand makes to "those who are kept." To achieve his goal of finding Marius, Lestat travels the "Devil's Road from Paris to Egypt" with Gabrielle.

Lestat's trip includes numerous and prolonged stops in various geographical areas on his journey to Egypt, including a confrontation with his mother, who begs him not to go to New Orleans to join his father. He then burrows underground, an act that resulted in part from his pain over killing a young man. Marius, who knows Lestat is seeking him, comes to his underground retreat and reveals himself to Lestat, saying,

Very few beings seek knowledge in this world. Mortal or immortal, few really ask. On the contrary, they try to wring from the unknown the answers that they have already shaped in their minds—justifications, confirmations, forms of consolation without which they can't go on. To really ask is to open the door to the whirlwind. The answer may annihilate the question and the questioner. (380)

Marius, who becomes Rice's voice of change and hope, in his mortal life had been the illegitimate son of a Roman nobleman and a Keltoi (Celtic) slave. He had been captured and taken to where the Keltoi lived, was imprisoned, and then prepared to become an immortal. His conversion is to occur during a Druidic ceremony where the "holy one," a vampire, had been kept in a gigantic tree, as the cycle of superstition, belief, and ritual continues. The Druids had kept evildoers to sacrifice to the immortal who resided in the tree, and after the immortal had feasted on the victims, they were attached to a large framework and destroyed by ritual fire.

The immortal who had performed the magic trick on Marius had a blackened appearance, and he had insisted that Marius escape from the Druids who have kept him imprisoned as their god, telling Marius that he must go down into Egypt to find out why vampires have been burned, and to make the discovery he must find "those who must be kept" (416).

Marius reveals his history, describing belief in the Roman gods during his mortal life and elaborating on changes that have occurred during his centuries as an immortal, the evolutionary changes in man's values and beliefs and the angst of being an immortal.

It is the belief in the value of human life that has caused the torture chambers and the stake and the more ghastly means of execution to be abandoned all over

Europe in that time. And it is the belief in the value of human life that carries man out of the monarchy into the republics of America and France.

Of course, we cannot know what will happen as the old religion thoroughly dies out. Christianity rose on the ashes of paganism, only to carry forth the old worship in new form. Maybe a new religion will rise now. Maybe without it, man will crumble in cynicism and selfishness because he really needs his gods.

And maybe something more wonderful will take its place; the world will truly move forward, past all gods and goddesses, past all devils and angels. And in such a world, Lestat, we will have less of a place that we have ever had. . . . and in this world the vampire is only a Dark God. He is a Child of Darkness. He can't be anything else. And if he wields any power upon the minds of men, it is only because the human imagination is a secret place of primitive memories and unconfessed desires. (465)

Marius informs Lestat that "the mind of each man is a Savage Garden, to use your phrase, in which all manner of creatures rise and fall, and anthems are sung and things imagined that must finally be condemned and disavowed" (465). A contemporary example of a cycle of savagery can be seen in an essay on fascism by Umberto Eco, pointing out how cycles of fascism can recur. Eco recalls the fascism of the 1930s and '40s as he cautions, "Ur-fascism is still around us. . . . [It] can come back under the most innocent of guises" (15).

Marius also relates the creation story of vampires who are mutants, created when Akasha and Enkil (later known as Osiris and Isis in myth) ruled. They were benevolent rulers who taught their people agriculture and banned cannibalism. Akasha and Enkil had entered a house inhabited by a spirit that moves things about, a poltergeist, in an effort to control the spirit. Evildoers, resenting their new ways, attempted to murder them, but the spirit entered their bodies and mutants, vampires, were created. To keep secret their state, they created moonlight worship and cloaked themselves with the myth of Isis and Osiris. Eventually, evil reappeared as one of the elders took them out to the desert into the sun. All of the existing vampires at the time were burned, but Akasha and Enkil turned a deep bronze and took on a statuelike form. Since then, they have been "those who must be kept." When Marius goes to Egypt he becomes their keeper after he learns that the elders who were their caretakers were plotting to destroy them as the cycle of evil once again surfaces.

Marius takes Lestat to the Greek island where Akasha and Enkil are being kept in a sumptuous underground dwelling. When impetuous Lestat disobeys Marius by going to the room in which they repose, he plays Nicolas's Stradivarius. Akasha responds to the music and to him and when they exchange blood, Enkil almost kills him. Rescued by Marius, he travels to New Orleans where his father fled from the French Revolution. Eventually Lestat creates two vampires, Louis and Claudia, both of whom would have died without his intervention. When the two turn on him and attempt to destroy him, it is only the power of Akasha's blood, which she had given to him, that saves him.

After a trip to Paris and his return to New Orleans, in despair he goes under the earth in 1929. When he returns above ground and achieves success with the rock band, now called the Vampire Lestat, he plans a rock concert in San Francisco. But the vampires—who feel he has betrayed the code by writing his autobiography and by acknowledging himself in the band—begin to threaten him, even though the viewers of his videos think that the vampire bit is simply a theatrical effect. Louis, who has been in Paris, shows up and offers to assist him when the other immortals may attack.

As the concert gets underway, the audience stamps and claps in unison as the vocalist, Tough Cookie, "wrung her head round and around in a circle, her hair flopping down to touch the boards in front of her feet, her guitar jerking lasciviously like a giant phallus" (538). And as Lestat sings words that echo his conflict with his own private hell, his conflict of good and evil.

CHILDREN OF DARKNESS,
MEET THE CHILDREN OF LIGHT,
CHILDREN OF LIGHT,
FIGHT THE CHILDREN OF THE NIGHT

The crowd goes wild, "they cheered and bellowed and wailed, unmindful of the words." Lestat compares their behavior to rituals of old: "Could the old Keltoi have cut loose with lustier ululations on the verge of massacre?" Despite this seeming need for ritual and release, Lestat notes, "But again there was no massacre, there was no burnt offering. Passion rolled towards the images of evil, not evil" (539). His sentiments reveal his belief that this type of ritual has replaced the old in a movement toward change since it does not lead to bloodshed or violence.

As Lestat and Louis leave the concert, Gabrielle returns to aid them, but they are assailed by the vampires seeking their destruction. Some powerful force saves them as the attacking immortals burst into flame enabling Lestat, Louis, and Gabrielle to escape. Lestat finally comes to the conclusion that it is Akasha who has saved them, an action opening the way for the sequel that follows, *The Queen of the Damned.*

The Vampire Lestat is not a philosophical nor a religious treatise but a gothic novel that addresses the issue of moral ambiguity through the use of a mutant, an immortal who has been a mortal but must now adapt his old heroic values to a situation that requires him to murder. Throughout the novel, Lestat must reconcile himself to life as the "other" to find a code to live by and to determine the nature and/or origin of vampires. His existentialism, then, is based on needs and characteristics that differ from mortals and on experiences that cover centuries, yet his agonizing decisions about his actions and his beliefs call to question mortal situations. Yet there are times when Lestat, like most mortals, acts impulsively, without giving adequate thought to his actions. Most significantly, he challenges religious rites and codes as he questions old rules and behaviors. Ramsland notes Rice's incorporation of the Nietzschean view that there is a "cycle of rising and falling, of old meaning replaced by new . . . mirroring continuous resurrection throughout history" (258). Paralleling the Nietzschean theme of cycles of change, Robert D. Hume, in defining the gothic novel, focuses on its changing form. While Rice keeps within the genre of the gothic in her use of the supernatural and the horrific, she moves beyond most gothic novels in her creation of a heroic monster and her depiction of issues of religious codes and rituals. Her mutation of the genre goes beyond those issues, as expressed by Ramsland in Rice's reference to vampire novels: "People responded to the psychological depth and philosophical explorations in the search for values on the part of a creature who hovered at the boundaries of humanity" (*xiii*).

Works Cited

Dziemianowicz, Stefan. "Vampire in the Library." Rev. of *The Book of Common Dread. Washington Post Book World* 25 July 1993.

Eco, Umberto. "Ur-Fascism." *New York Review of Books* 22 June 1995: 12-15.

Hume, Robert D. "Gothic Versus Romantic: A Revaluation of the Gothic Novel." *PMLA* 84 (1969): 282-90.

Ramsland, Katherine. *Prism of the Night.* New York: Plume, 1992.

Rice, Anne. *The Vampire Lestat.* New York: Ballantine, 1986.

Roberts, Bette B. *Anne Rice.* New York: Twayne, 1994.

Anne Rice's *The Tale of the Body Thief* and the Astral Projection Literary Tradition

Joseph F. Ceccio

One fruitful way to evaluate Anne Rice's work is to avoid simple praise or blame and instead to focus on seeing where and how the fuller meaning of just one recent novel, *The Tale of the Body Thief* (1992), is revealed through her creative handling of certain sources, inspirations, and allusions. Knowing an author's sources or inspirations—and seeing how well an author shapes and transforms those materials to a new or higher purpose—is surely one important measure for evaluating an author's achievement. Shakespeare's art, for one example, has often been illuminated using such a method.

The Tale of the Body Thief, Rice's thirteenth novel, may be profitably approached from several angles. Of course, it is book four of the popular *Vampire Chronicles* that began with *Interview with the Vampire* and continued with *The Vampire Lestat* and *The Queen of the Damned*. On another level, *The Tale of the Body Thief* offers a unique blend of philosophical discussions (with a special role for Goethe's *Faust*) and popular settings (with a special role for the *Queen Elizabeth 2*). However, it is the astral projection literary tradition that may well be the best context to help readers unlock many of the mysteries of Rice's recent novel.

Through several specific allusions by Lestat, Rice seems to invite readers to search out and discover for themselves two earlier short stories about body switching that convey ominous overtones and that play an important part in her novel. The first tale delivered by the Body Thief as a clue for Lestat is H.P. Lovecraft's "The Thing on the Doorstep," published in 1936 in *Weird Tales*. The second tale delivered by the Body Thief as a clue for Lestat is Robert Bloch's "The Eyes of the Mummy," published in 1938 in *Weird Tales*.

This chapter will discuss ways in which these two short stories foreshadow and illuminate several events and themes in *The Tale of the Body Thief*. In addition, this chapter will look selectively at other short fictional works on the astral body motif that typify the literary tradition Rice attempts to surpass.

163

Rice's Use of Lovecraft and Bloch

At the outset, we should recall three key passages from *The Tale of the Body Thief*. The first excerpt takes place in Miami. Lestat feels as if he "might be squeezed right out of" himself (26). In fact, Raglan James, the Body Thief, has just attacked Lestat and tried to switch bodies. Then James tosses a thick envelope at Lestat's feet. The envelope contains the Lovecraft story.

I picked up the envelope. . . . Inside, I found, of all things, a printed short story clipped apparently from a paperback book.

It made a small thick wad of pulp pages, stapled together in the upper-left-hand corner. No personal note at all. The author of the story was a lovable creature I knew well, H.P. Lovecraft by name, a writer of the supernatural and the macabre. In fact, I knew the story, too, and could never forget its title: "The Thing on the Doorstep." It had made me laugh.

"The Thing on the Doorstep." I was smiling now. Yes, I remembered the story, that it was clever, that it had been fun.

But why would this strange mortal give such a story to me? It was ludicrous. And suddenly I was angry again. (28)

The second excerpt takes place in London. Again, Lestat feels as if he is being "forced" (82) out of himself. Then another envelope is delivered to him. This one contains the Bloch story.

I tore open the envelope. My hands were suddenly shaking. It was another little printed short story, clipped out of a book exactly as the first one had been, and stapled at the upper-left-hand corner in precisely the same way!

. . . "Eyes of the Mummy" was the title, author Robert Bloch. A clever little tale, but what could it possibly mean to me? I thought of the Lovecraft, which had been much longer and seemed wholly different. What on earth could all this signify? (83-84)

The third excerpt takes place in Paris. Here Lestat and his mortal friend, David Talbot, discuss the possible meaning of "these little stories" (92).

"Well, in the Lovecraft piece, Asenath, this diabolical woman, switches bodies with her husband. She runs about the town using his male body, while he is stuck at home in her body, miserable and confused. I thought it was a hoot, actually. Just wonderfully clever, and of course Asenath isn't Asenath, as I recall, but her father, who has switched bodies with her. And then it all becomes very Lovecraftian, with slimy half-human demons and such."

"That may be the irrelevant part. And the Egyptian story?"

"Completely different. The moldering dead, which still possess life, you know . . ."

"Yes, but the plot."

"Well, the soul of the mummy manages to get possession of the body of the archaeologist, and he, the poor devil, is put in the rotted body of the mummy—"

"Yes?"

"Good Lord . . . it's about body switching as well. [The] stories are about the same thing."

"Exactly."

"Christ, David. It's all coming clear. I don't know why I didn't see it. But . . ."

"This man is trying to get you to believe that he knows something about this body switching. He's trying to entice you with the suggestion that such a thing can be done." (92-93)

Naturally, Lestat will pursue the possibility of body switching in the adventure that follows. Had he not been so proud and so foolish, he might have thought more clearly about the Lovecraft and Bloch stories in his possession. And he might have remembered the surprise last-minute switches in both Lovecraft and Bloch—exactly what Rice will have happen at the end of her novel, when Raglan James is jolted out of Lestat's body but takes over David's.

Lovecraft's "The Thing on the Doorstep"

Lovecraft, a writer of supernatural fiction, was popular in the 1930s. As we have seen, Lestat summarizes "The Thing on the Doorstep" to David, adding, "I thought it was a hoot, actually" (92). Earlier in the novel, Lestat had said that this story "had made me laugh . . . it was clever . . . it had been fun" (28). Lestat had also mentioned to David that "the story doesn't mean a thing" (46).

Still, one insight that Lestat *does* gain through this story is that Raglan James, the Body Thief, isn't really in his own body. James has stolen a handsome young body from a garage mechanic. And in this body he tempts Lestat to switch bodies for a short time. The restless Lestat foolishly agrees. But if he had remembered his Lovecraft more clearly, he would have seen how poorly body switching turns out there—not so much funny as tragic, really, for all concerned.

In the Lovecraft story, the narrator remarks on how Asenath is beginning to take over Edward's body:

It was in the third year of the marriage that Edward began to hint openly to me of a certain fear and dissatisfaction. He would let fall remarks about things "going too far," and would talk darkly about the need of "gaining his identity." . . . in time I began to question him guardedly, remembering what my friend's daughter had said about Asenath's hypnotic influence over the other girls at school—the cases where students had thought they were in her body looking across the room at themselves. (111)

Here Rice's borrowing is apparent, for she endows Raglan James with hypnotic powers, calling him a "sorcerer" (142). Moreover, Edward tells Dan, the story's narrator, that his wife Asenath (actually old Ephraim [her father]-in-Asenath) plans to be immortal: "On, on, on, on—body to body to body—he means never to die" (117). This passage should have alerted Lestat to be more fully aware of the Body Thief's danger: Raglan James wants Lestat's vampire body *permanently* so he can become immortal. Then Lestat would be left in the mortal body of the young mechanic. David cautions Lestat against any dealings with Raglan James, a former member of the mysterious Talamasca. But Lestat goes ahead with his body-switching plans.

In addition, while Lovecraft is rather vague about just how astral projection (spirit traveling) occurs, Rice develops the topic and the details more explicitly, more completely, using a theory of the participants' need to cooperate as they will their higher souls to rise and anchor in the other's body. Here Rice goes beyond the vague prose of Lovecraft to discuss the body-soul connection, the presence of two souls in the body, the mechanics of switching, and how to jolt another out of his body. Her prose style—descriptive, evocative, intense—makes everything more believable, more possible, and so less comic, more serious than the Lovecraft source.

But here's a twist: Rice has Lestat refer to this short story as a "small thick wad of pulp pages, stapled together" (28). Rice clearly wants to go beyond her "pulp" source, the story that first appeared in *Weird Tales* magazine.

Here's another twist: In a 1990 *Newsweek* article, David Gates writes about Rice's literary ambitions, as follows:

Given her literary ambitions, Anne Rice might consider it faint praise to be called America's classiest Gothic novelist. Then again, she likes to remind people that Poe and Hawthorne are canonical American writers and that Mary Shelley's "Frankenstein" is a novel of ideas. "Only in our time," says Rice, "is Gothic fiction associated with low-level writers like H.P. Lovecraft. I mean, I love him, but he's a hack." (76)

Of course, we cannot help noticing her ambivalent attitude toward Lovecraft, one of her important literary sources.

Bloch's "The Eyes of the Mummy"

Bloch's earliest work was influenced by Lovecraft. But we probably know Bloch best through his novel *Psycho* (1959), which director Alfred Hitchcock made into a famous film in 1960.

In *The Tale of the Body Thief*, Lestat receives a second short story from the Body Thief. "Trembling with annoyance" (84), he scans it, notices that it is shorter than Lovecraft's story, and wonders what it could "possibly mean to me" (84). Later, Lestat summarizes the story's plot for David, mentioning that the soul of the mummy manages to take possession of the body of the archaeologist, "and he, the poor devil, is put in the rotted body of the mummy" (93). Lestat ignores the terrible implications of Bloch's story, namely, that the Body Thief could well keep Lestat's vampire body for himself after any "trial" switch. Lestat instead pursues the idea of body switching in order once again to be "a mortal man" (95). The much wiser David tries to caution Lestat: "Would you kindly wake up and pay attention to me, please! This is not a matter of comical stories and Lovecraftian pieces of gothic romance" (96). However, Lestat's pride gets in the way of clear reasoning.

In several ways, Bloch's story may be more important to Rice than is Lovecraft's. First, "The Eyes of the Mummy" is told in the first person by the main character, as is Rice's novel. In the story, the "I" is able to tell—and even type out—his tale before he finally crumbles in the mummy's body at the end. Lestat should have seen how disastrous such switching could be.

Second, the "I" of the short story is tricked into the disastrous Cairo expedition by Professor Weildan, who holds out the hope of a great discovery and riches. Weildan exercises an almost hypnotic influence on the narrator. Similarly, Rice gives us her creation, Raglan James—a thief, a trickster, a sorcerer, a vampire hunter. (And surely we recall from Goethe's *Faust* Mephistopheles, a thief of the soul.)

Third, the mummy's eyes are jewels; but these stones aren't natural. They have a "mind" or "will" that effects a switch with the living person who looks at them too long. Then the person becomes blind when in the rotting body of the mummy. To be sure, Lestat is, in a sense, blinded to the truth of the situation by his pride and his feeling of indestructibility.

Fourth, Rice's own style seems influenced by Bloch's. Here are but two examples. First, in Bloch we read: "Good God! *I'm in the mummy's body!*" (295); in Rice we read: "—but it hit me, I was in! I was in the body! . . . Dear God, I'm in it" (165). Later, in Bloch we read: "Now, then, the tale is told" (296); in Rice we read: "The tale is told" (430).

Finally, both the narrator of Bloch's story and Lestat in Rice's novel struggle to get back their rightful bodies. Bloch's narrator fails and perishes. Rice's narrator, Lestat, eventually succeeds and lives again as an all-powerful vampire.

Still, although Rice borrows much from Bloch's fifteen-page short story, she goes beyond that tale's vagueness about how astral projection takes place, to detail a plan or cosmology that fits in with her purposes in writing this novel.

Other Astral Projection Fiction

Next, we review briefly just six representative short pieces from the extensive astral projection literary tradition. We know that Rice has "haunted" the stacks of both public and university libraries (Donovan 104). She also has a large personal library. On occasion, she even tells us directly about her reading interests. For example, she dedicates her 1989 novel, *The Mummy,* to, among others, Sir Arthur Conan Doyle for "Lot No. 249," a mummy story, and to H. Rider Haggard for *She,* an adventure novel. (Although interesting as background sources for *The Mummy*, these two works of fiction will not be treated here because they do not specifically deal with astral projection.) Indeed, she may or may not have read some of the following short fictional pieces. But her use of Lovecraft and Bloch indicates that these are the kinds of works she is trying to surpass in *The Tale of the Body Thief.*

1. Robert Barr, "The Vengeance of the Dead," in *Revenge!* (1896). Bernard Heaton has been experimenting with soul travel. On the astral plane, he meets the dead David Allen, a former enemy. David gets into Bernard's body, commits murder, then vacates Bernard's body so that Bernard will be blamed for the crime.

Barr contrasts having a frail body with having a strong, healthy body. We might recall the Body Thief's original (older) body and his stolen (younger) mechanic's body. But Rice depicts the specific sensations of being in a new body much more graphically, whereas Barr is unclear about the facets of body switching.

2. Arthur J. Burks, "When the Graves Were Opened," in *Black Medicine* (1925). Harvey invents a machine that permits soul travel. Jess, his friend, travels back to the Crucifixion and to the side of Pontius Pilate. But later the machine breaks down, stranding Jess with Pilate and putting Harvey in jail for Jess's body's death.

This story shows the soul traveling and observing, but not in a body. Of course, it has a disastrous ending. We might recall that Rice's Body

Thief can travel as a soul or spirit without a body: "I can leave my body for short periods, and during those periods I can search for you [Lestat] over vast distances. But I don't like that sort of bodiless travel at all" (128).

3. Marjorie Bowen, "The Avenging of Ann Leete," in *The Omnibus of Crime* (1929). Years earlier, Ann was killed by a young doctor. Her lover, now an older jeweler, had used psychic force to make the astral body of the murderer reveal the corpse's location. Just before he dies, he—and the narrator—can see her ghost.

Unlike Rice's novel, this story shows astral projection in a positive light. However, it is true that in Rice's work David does get a new, younger body at the end, through the Body Thief's forced switch.

4. L. Adams Beck, "The Mystery of Iniquity," in *The Openers of the Gate: Stories of the Occult* (1930). Dr. Livingstone, an occult detective, faces a difficult case. After taking a drug, Joyselle can project her astral body (detachable spirit) to lead men to suicide. Eventually, the doctor helps her to be cured.

Unlike Rice's more complex work, this story ends quite happily. Also, Rice's characters need no drugs to travel astrally.

5. C. Daly King, "The Episode of the Final Bargain," in *The Curious Mr. Tarrant* (1935). Special photographs show the etheric body and the physical body of Mary, who has been psychically atacked. One character releases his own astral body to help rescue Mary. Vagueness abounds!

For her novel, Rice saw the need for the soul to have *two* parts. One part, the higher soul, could leave the body. The primitive or "residual" (122) soul stayed in the body, but was incomplete without a higher soul.

6. Davis Grubb, "The Horsehair Trunk," in *Twelve Tales of Suspense and the Supernatural* (1964). Marius, the protagonist, finds he can project his astral body. He plans the perfect crime while in spirit form. But he enters the wrong cabin on the steamboat and slays his own physical body.

Grubb's ending is certainly surprising. Yet Rice's *The Tale of the Body Thief* ends with even more surprises. First, Raglan James takes over David's body. Second, Lestat makes the real David into a vampire (while David is in the young mechanic's body). Third, Lestat, Louis, and David end up as three vampire friends going off to Rio for the carnival.

Conclusions

On one level, *The Tale of the Body Thief* is a modern popular novel that appeals to both younger and older audiences through its major characters of Lestat and David Talbot. Its style is less florid, less ornate than that of Rice's *The Witching Hour* and *Lasher*. Yet its subject matter still fits into the supernatural realm.

Moreover, Rice's constant allusiveness—especially to the astral projection literary tradition as represented by Lovecraft and Bloch—is challenging and enriches *The Tale of the Body Thief*. Like other noted authors, she cannot be fully understood without some knowledge of the literary materials that influenced her.

The many apt allusions in *The Tale of the Body Thief* may be explored as keys to meaning that are worth following up. The focus on body-soul relationships in Lovecraft, Bloch, and similar writers connects with Rice's emphasis on Lestat's desire to be mortal again, to be redeemed, to be *not* just a devil, and to change. Rice's allusions to her sources and inspirations in film, art, and literature (only some of which were discussed in this chapter) can broaden the understanding and insight of those who will pursue them.

And finally, her fleshing out of a coherent plan in *The Tale of the Body Thief* for how astral projection works is a special contribution that goes beyond her sources and any analogues. Her theory of the two-part soul and her concrete descriptions of what it is like to inhabit a new body make her well-plotted thirteenth novel stand out for its special creativity and intensity.

Works Consulted

Ansen, David. "A Feast of Rats, Blood and Wild Rice." *Newsweek* 21 Nov. 1995: 93.

Barr, Robert. "The Vengeance of the Dead." *Revenge!* New York: Stokes, 1896. 44-60.

Beck, L. Adams. "The Mystery of Iniquity." *The Openers of the Gate: Stories of the Occult.* New York: Cosmopolitan, 1930. 138-89.

Bloch, Robert. "The Eyes of the Mummy." *The Opener of the Way.* 1938. Sauk City: Arkham, 1945. 284-98.

Bowen, Marjorie. "The Avenging of Ann Leete." *The Omnibus of Crime.* Ed. Dorothy L. Sayers. Garden City: Garden City Publishing, 1929. 825-37.

Burks, Arthur J. "When the Graves Were Opened." 1925. *Black Medicine.* Sauk City: Arkham, 1966. 90-110.

Conant, Jennet. "Lestat, C'est Moi." *Esquire* Mar. 1994: 70-75.

Donovan, Sharon. "Haunting the Stacks with Anne Rice." *Library Journal* 15 Oct. 1990: 104.

Ferraro, Susan. "Novels You Can Sink Your Teeth Into." *New York Times Magazine* 14 Oct. 1990: 27+.

Gates, David. "Queen of the Spellbinders." *Newsweek* 5 Nov. 1990: 76-77.

Grubb, Davis. "The Horsehair Trunk." *Twelve Tales of Suspense and the Supernatural*. Greenwich: Fawcett, 1964. 88-99.

King, C. Daly. "The Episode of the Final Bargain." 1935. *The Curious Mr. Tarrant*. New York: Dover, 1977. 244-84.

Lovecraft, H.P. "The Thing on the Doorstep." 1936. *3 Tales of Horror*. Sauk City: Arkham, 1967. 100-34.

Moritz, Charles, ed. "Rice, Anne." *Current Biography Yearbook*. New York: Wilson, 1991. 464-68.

Ramsland, Katherine. *The Vampire Companion*. New York: Ballantine, 1993.

Rice, Anne. *The Tale of the Body Thief*. New York: Knopf, 1992.

"We're talking science, man, not voodoo": Genetic Disaster in Anne Rice's *Mayfair Witch Chronicles*

Ann Larabee

Horror writers have traditionally used the language of contemporary science to give materiality and verisimilitude to their fantastic creatures. While science often fails to control nature in these stories, the truth of enlightenment science itself—its ability to objectively explain the forces of nature—is not questioned. But in the novels of Anne Rice, the scientific project is playfully exploded, exposed as another language in a postmodern pastiche of cultural references. In the Mayfair Witch cycle, Rice picks up the cultural discourse on genetic disaster, represented most spectacularly in *Jurassic Park* and in mass media discussions of the Human Genome Project. As science historian Evelyn Fox Keller has observed, the recent rise of molecular biology has been accompanied by a new faith in the "malleability" of nature, with a consequent goal of directing evolution along a strict path, set against a base-line norm of the "healthy" subject ("Nature" 294-95). Popular representations of genetic disease and genetic disaster provide a counter-narrative against the "new eugenics" ("Nature" 289), defying the systemic logic of the "norm" and opening up an horizon of possibilities. Anne Rice's Taltos, Ur beings who rise like Jurassic dinosaurs, are fabricated not only from an imaginary, ancient DNA, but from a collage of competing knowledge claims. The result is an apocalyptic narrative that, like the Taltos, is a postmodern hybrid of popular themes and genres, a grotesque double helix of science and voodoo.

Lasher, the second book of the Mayfair Witch cycle, introduces the mutant Taltos monster as a riddle, subject to various interpretations by institutional experts. Various physical samples from Lasher and his mother, doctor and witch Rowan Mayfair, are analyzed by "mad" scientist Mitchell Flanagan of the Keplinger Institute, a secretive organization engaged in genetic research and fetal tissue transplants. On the wall in Flanagan's office, looming over the scene like the Taltos monster himself, hangs a painting "full of cobalt and burning orange and neon green—as if painted by a Haitian artist who, having stumbled upon a

173

drawing of sperm and egg in a scientific journal, had chosen it for a model, never guessing or caring what it was" (*Lasher* 48). Thus, the focal secret, sexual reproduction, around which the Mayfair Witch cycle revolves, is given two representations by the voodoo artist and the geneticist, unwittingly locked together in a new aesthetic.

Both voodoo and genetics are, in themselves, hybrid, contingent discourses without purely linear traditions of metaphysical truth claims, as in Catholicism or physics. The word *voodoo* is an Americanized popularization of the Haitian belief system, more properly known as *vodoun*, which is much more complex and localized than Rice suggests. Her use of *voodoo* evokes sweeping popular themes of body possession and ritual magic, and is decontextualized from its political and social meaning. However, *voodoo* still contains the sense of pastiche, continually reconstructed from Roman Catholicism, African spiritualism, and popular iconography. *Voudon* has recently been even further hybridized in cyberpunk fiction, where it provides a metaphor for electronic "possession" of bodies by artificially intelligent, godlike programming codes. Here, distinctions collapse between technology and myth, machine and body, rational and counter-rational systems. Echoed in the spirit Lasher's colonizing of fetal cellular structure, the voodoo possession theme deconstructs traditional humanist modes of identity based on linear experience and memory, biosocial connection, and body integrity.

In the interdisciplinary Human Genome Project, the denaturing of identity occurs in the body's reduction to a genetic code that biotechnical engineers might control and manipulate for both public good and private gain. Once again, the body's deepest structures are subject to technological possession and rearrangement. The idea of the "human" fragments into codes, marked by good and bad genes, and individual identity transforms into a DNA fingerprint, seemingly wrested from social context. Donna Haraway writes that despite its claim to scientific objectivity, biomedical language constructs the body as an iconic postmodern object, a semiotic system, where sex and reproduction are theorized in military, strategic terms: "The body ceases to be a stable spatial map of normalized functions and instead emerges as a highly mobile field of strategic differences" (Haraway 211).

In the Mayfair Witch cycle, Rice presents voodoo and genetics as similar, intersecting, competing ways of explaining possession, disintegration of identity, and technological manipulation. Discussions of the Taltos collapse rational and counter-rational interpretations of the "secret buried in a forest of secrets" (*Lasher* 59). As Rowan Mayfair argues, "The witch and the doctor know the same thing" (*Taltos* 116). Her niece, Mona Mayfair, pregnant with another Taltos, explains that witchcraft is science, an impossible blend of "alchemy," "chemistry," "brain science," and "magic" (*Taltos* 240). Neither of these interpretations carries the weight of truth, since one continually undermines the other. Mitchell Flanagan dismisses "voodoo" psychic phenomenon as "crap" (*Lasher* 57), and the authoritative psychic researcher Aaron Lightner insists, "We're talking science, man, not voodoo" (*Lasher* 176). However, while genetic discourse lends an authority to the Taltos's believability, science itself is frequently critiqued. Haunted by her bargains with Lasher that allowed him into the world, Rowan Mayfair admits that her "judgment calls" were wrong: "We have such a terrible, terrible misconception of science. We think it involves the definite, the precise, the known; it is a horrid series of gates to an unknown as vast as the universe" (*Lasher* 203). Furthermore, the scientific project is subtly undermined by alternatives within the same sentence: "How can we get this scientific data, or whatever it is, from the Keplinger Institute?" (*Lasher* 177). Whatever it is—the bodily scrapings and samples from Lasher—resists representation or reduction to decontextualized information: voodoo is embedded in the scientific project.

Lasher is a thoroughly postmodern, biomedical, voodoo monster, whose "nature" is ultimately deconstructive and unlocatable. Like the cyberpunk lizard brain impulse erupting into sterile modern consciousness, the "Precambrian" Lasher brings horror and panic (*Lasher* 886). Coalescing from a chaotic state, he is a looping, self-organizing entity, or what David Porush might call an "autopoetic alien" (Porush 332). Without a central consciousness, cannibalizing the traits of the witches, Lasher is a representation without an original, like the souls of the Mayfair dead: "They are like unto the grooves of a phonograph record. Put the needle into the groove and the voice sings. But the singer is not there" (*Witching Hour* 909). The consciously manipulated cellular generation of Lasher evokes the anxieties surrounding the twentieth century's technological systems: extreme complexity, unstoppable acceleration and proliferation, and infinite repeatability. At Lasher's birth, Rowan finds that Lasher is an uncontrollable autonomous technology: "the cells were too strong; the osteoblasts swarming at their accelerated rate, just as everything within him worked at that rate, defensively and aggressively" (*Lasher* 206). In *Normal Accidents*, Charles Perrow suggests that disaster is inevitable in any complex, "tightly coupled" technological system (3). Complexity brings catastrophe, just as Lasher's invasion of Rowan Mayfair's mutant giant helix, comprised of ninety-six chromosomes, results in potential apocalypse for humankind.

But according to systems theory—the logic of the postindustrial age—disaster is also productive. Systems theorists in evolutionary biol-

176 The Gothic World of Anne Rice

ogy and sociology have proposed that the world is comprised of systems with interactive technological and biological components, allowing flows of information and energy. Thermodynamic, evolutionary processes in systems are sometimes accelerated by catastrophe. According to Vilmos Csanyi in *Evolutionary Systems and Society*, a large-scale catastrophe changes a system's identity, stimulating "new cyclic processes" and "new replicative chains": "*Catastrophes* caused by outside factors probably increase complexity more rapidly—but unpredictably" (112). Lasher's story is a similar narrative of invasion, mutation, and accelerated growth that alters the normative processes of human reproduction and social organization.

As Lasher prepares to incarnate himself in the body of Rowan's fetus, he explains to her that he "mutates matter," piercing and reorganizing cellular structure: "We are talking of fusion; of chemical change; the structural reinvention of cells, of matter and energy in a new relationship" (*Witching Hour* 868). With "tiny cells" that once knew "exactly where to go" (*Witching Hour* 850), the fetus has already been named "little Chris," given a stable identity from the Mayfairs, described as a highly inbred group like the Amish or the Mormons. The inbreeding of the Mayfairs, leading to the possibility of a Lasher, is not represented as a weakness or a defect, but a doorway to other modes of being. Lasher cleaves the traditional domestic order based on serialization and inheritance,[1] replacing this structure with a field of riddles, secrets, misnamings, and hybrid discourses. With his fragmented memory and love of nursery rhymes, Lasher is that which has no name, "no understanding even of a name" (*Witching Hour* 861), a "confluence of syllables never intended to be" (*Lasher* 211). He was named in a case of mistaken identity and disordered consonants, a confusion of Lasher with Ashlar. Comprised of a disarray of language and genes, Lasher emerges as a viable cultural mutation appropriate to the age of postatomic disaster. Thus, the monster carries the logic of Ground Zero, the void, the cypher, where origin is problematic and structure collapses, resulting in "a fission and fusion of ideas, substitution and supplementation, infinite extension in infinite process" (Schwenger 30).

Indeed, Lasher is spun from the Cold War's nuclear nightmares. His birth is a "fusion" and a "transmutation," a new, fearsome technology unleashed upon the world. Like the mutant ants of *Them*, Lasher is said to be "as alien from us as a giant insect" (*Witching Hour* 888). Rowan lets the metaphorical "bacillus out of the tube" (*Witching Hour* 888), a linguistic twist on the well-worn comparison between nuclear energy and the genie let out of the bottle. More overtly, psychic historian Aaron Lightner calls Lasher "a laser beam with ambition . . . a bomb that can think for itself" (*Witching Hour* 889), again evoking the specter of autonomous technology. The monster is born in a "great lurid blast of red light," his cells transforming "like a nuclear explosion" (*Witching Hour* 932, 933). Lasher, like the mutant Godzilla from the height of Cold War hysteria, comes to wreak havoc on an unsuspecting humanity, a being who will uncontrollably fission himself into a new species. Lasher explains, "As with fission, if it is achieved once, it can be achieved again" (*Witching Hour* 868).

Rice's frequent references to an impending doomsday, resulting from violations of secrets and Faustian bargains, resonate with nuclear images and themes. In his discussion of popular representations of nuclear energy, Spencer Weart discusses early associations between atomic physics and alchemy. Atomic scientists publicly used alchemical imagery in discussing their work, comparing the atom to a mystic life force that contained the secrets of evolution and immortality (Weart 38-40). Thus, atomic science was given an occult flavor in a cultural discourse comprised of physical experimentation and medieval spiritualism: science and voodoo. These images of the atom as an alchemical elixir of life, discovered through rational experimentation, persisted through most of the Cold War, even as the atomic bomb loomed over the world. Ironically, the bomb was popularly associated not only with omnicidal disaster, but with a highly eroticized rejuvenation of humankind through social and genetic reordering, made possible through the mediation of a nuclear priesthood, a select group of scientists with power over the atom's essential life force. Inheriting the narrative of the nuclear project, Lasher is described as "a meeting . . . of mystery and science, of something spiritual and a genetic irregularity of which that spiritual force took advantage" (*Lasher* 405). Furthermore, Lasher is an erotic life force that offers his maker, Rowan, immortality, power, and knowledge, the traditional terms of the Faustian bargain.

The metaphorical connections between nuclear and genetic engineering also have roots in early twentieth-century scientific projects. Evelyn Fox Keller observes that the discovery of DNA structure and the making of the atomic bomb shared a stereotypical narrative of "secrets, understood as the illumination of the female interior, or the tearing of nature's veil" ("Secrets" 178). Both molecular biologists and physicists described their projects in terms of birth, a cooption of maternal procreation.[2] The Mayfair Witch cycle borrows from these rather gothic conventions. The secret of Taltos reproduction—the double double helix carried in the Mayfair witches' cells—is pursued by psychic researchers and zealots who "consecrate" themselves to the "penetration" of "the horror and the beauty at the core" (*Taltos* 124). And from this central mystery, secrets expand and proliferate like a narrative fission: psychic research institution records, genetic records, Mona Mayfair's gynecological visits, psychic weapons, various plots, arcane witch knowledge, hierarchical institutional structures, private computer files, other monsters, hidden places, smells and auras, old attics, sexual desires, ethnic histories, identities, illicit experiments.

The overproduction of secrets creates a double world that reflects and distorts a normative one: for example, the Mayfair project to build a public medical research institute mirrors the Keplinger Institute, whose mad scientists are engaged in hidden experimentation. Thus, the Mayfair Witch cycle presents a funhouse of mirrors where images are doubled and redoubled. Even the essential Taltos mystery is double, for the race can reproduce itself either through inbreeding with each other or through cross-fertilizing with humans. The Taltos genes have been distorted enough through this cross-fertilization that they can never eugenically return to a pure racial strain, or base-line norm. The riddling and unriddling of the Taltos distorts the very idea of a formal, conventionalized secret at the heart of the interpretive, or scientific, project. The double secret, like an escalating crisis, ultimately escapes objective control and manipulation.

Furthermore, the pursuit of the reproductive holy of holies is given a twist that destabilizes the gendered scientific narrative. The occult scientist is a woman who willingly volunteers her womb for her own experiment, birthing a giant, autistic baby. Thus, maternal reproduction is not simply a metaphor coopted and emulated in a masculinized technological project; rather, maternity itself is denatured. Early on in the story, Rowan kills her superior at a research hospital, Karl Lemle, because of his work in fetal tissue transplantation. Lemle keeps an aborted fetus alive, wired up in an incubator, an artificial womb, ready to be harvested for a Parkinson's patient. He explains that "technically it is a nonperson, a non-human being" (*Witching Hour* 120). Once again, the subtext is that identity has been deconstructed in a denatured world of hybrids and transplants—the artificial womb holds a nonhuman. Lemle's secret fetal tissue experimentation obviously mirrors Rowan Mayfair's birthing of Lasher during which she deploys her own womb in a bargain with aberration, so that the maternal body itself becomes a sophisticated instrument for production of artificial beings. The involuntary process of fetal growth becomes a consciouslessly understood and manipulated project. Rowan Mayfair sees the possessed fetus rapidly evolving, "the DNA merging, and the tiny chains of chromosomes whipping and swimming as the nuclei merged, and all guided by her" (*Witching Hour* 933). But like her Frankensteinian counterpart, the witch geneticist falls under the domination of her abusive creature, unable to stop him from fissioning through the possession of other decontextualized, instrumental wombs.

What finally does stop Lasher is a simple artifact. His father, Michael Curry, kills him with a hammer driven into the soft part of the brain, a tool that had been used to renovate the Mayfair's ancestral home. Curry explain, "I used my strength as a man, and the simple tools" (*Taltos* 141). Thus, Lasher's story ends with a return to what Albert Borgmann has called "focal things and practices" (196), the technologies that are fully integrated into, and embued with meaning by, a community:

Focal things . . . are concrete, tangible, and deep, admitting of no functional equivalents; they have a tradition, structure, and rhythm of their own. They are unprocurable and finally beyond our control. They engage us in the fullness of our capacities. And they thrive in a technological setting. A focal practice, generally, is the resolute and regular dedication to a focal thing. It sponsors discipline and skill which are exercised in a unity of achievement and enjoyment, of mind, body, and the world, of myself and others, and in a social union. (219)

An opponent of the postmodern cultural absorption in advanced modern instruments, which he considers frivolous and vacuous, Borgmann calls for a restoration of *focus*, Latin for "hearth," where simple artifacts and traditional practices sustained a spiritualized family life within a coherent social context. Examples of focal practices include running, fly-fishing, or cooking and eating a family meal: each requires intimate, embodied knowledge and technique. Thus, deep engagement through focal things and practices stands against the postmodern device, like television, that "has step by step stripped the household of substance and dignity" (Borgmann 123).

Michael Curry represents this highly conservative emphasis on a Heideggerian authenticity in his happy job of Victorian restoration: "no amount of academic pleasure could ever satisfy his need to work with his hands, to get out in the air, to climb ladders, swing a hammer, and feel at the end of the day that great sublime physical exhaustion" (*Witching Hour* 54). Academic work—objective observation and interpretation—is remote from the authentic masculine work of hands, extended in simple tools. Curry's hands hold the psychic power of reading histories embedded in bodies and artifacts, reading the contexts of objects that give them meaning. His restoration of the Mayfair house allows its "classical plan" (*Witching Hour* 790) to reemerge, as it becomes the focal place for a great Mayfair reunion and a white wedding celebration. Thus, Curry's bloody murder of Lasher with the simple hammer, invested with its role as rebuilder and authenticator, strikes a blow against postmodern invasion and dissolution of traditional meaning structures, including gender.

While this might provide a neat end, governed by appropriate technologies, the Taltos invasion continues. After Lasher meets his demise, another Taltos—the original Ashlar—appears to retell the tale. Once again, apocalyptic images accompany him—he imagines himself as the last man "alone in the ruins" (*Taltos* 6) of the white city, both survivor and producer of ultimate destruction. Parented by Michael Curry and Mona Mayfair, Ashlar's future mate, Morrigan, is described as a "nuclear explosion" going on in her mother's womb (*Taltos* 274). And Mona Mayfair has such a powerful condensation of witch genes that she can "blow the top of the graph" (*Taltos* 31). The mating of male and female Taltos might take place "so fast and so successfully that its kind would quickly overtake the world" (*Taltos* 71), resulting in the extermination of the human species and a new Taltos millennium. However, the Taltos's relentless Terminator-like drive toward sexual union is finally peacefully accepted in a romantic denouement.

Ashlar is spun from different threads than Lasher. First of all, since he is an original being, extant over all human time, he does not coalesce from the void to take technological possession of a body. Nor does his mate, Morrigan. Taltos birth is now explained as a natural process, the "switching on" of dormant genes, "purely an expression of genetic potential" in the creation of hybrids (*Taltos* 273). While Lasher comes from a postmodern virtual hell, Morrigan comes "from God," since she "is born this way of two human beings, both of whom contain a mysterious genome" (*Taltos* 174). Thus, she embodies cultural meaning structures like religious faith and ordinary human-like reproduction, just as Ashlar restores a chain of historical meanings linked to an originary world, an Edenic utopia where the logos resides in the maternal body, representing plenitude and sensuality: "All Taltos are born knowing things—facts of history, whole legends, certain songs—the necessity for certain rituals, the language of the mother, and the languages spoken around her, the basic knowledge of the mother, and probably the mother's finer knowledge as well" (*Taltos* 321). Fusing nature and culture, maternal reproduction is the spiritual center of the Taltos community from which all action, meaning, and interpretation unfolds. While Lemle's artificial womb holds a nonhuman, a Taltos womb also holds a nonhuman, but in this case social context is restored, even deeply engrained, in reproductive activity.

The Taltos are also secretive genetic engineers, who reflect and redefine the scientific project of manipulating maternal reproduction.

Rather than a fragmented, denatured set of codes, the genome becomes a flexible, open narrative, resilient in the face of colonization. In exile, driven from their world by volcanic apocalypse, the Taltos encounter humans who invade them with their genes and memories. In order to survive, the Taltos consciously manipulate their own genome, embedding in their offspring focal practices like weapon-making, geography, and mapping, and "the Art of the Tongue":

They must look at the stars and never forget the various patterns that could guide them home. And this became part of innate knowledge very rapidly because we deliberately cultivated it, and this cultivation worked. . . . We could program into the innate knowledge all manner of practical things. (*Taltos* 353)

Thus, focal practices and technologies emerge as more than traditions that link the social body to a singular history: they are maps that reconfigure worldviews. Like the permeable genome, culture flexes, shifts, absorbs patterns, and becomes newly marked by close encounters with the Other. While such change might evoke the metanarratives of nuclear holocaust, it is not necessarily apocalyptic, nor does it call for a return to an essential Nature. There is no returning to the nontechnological Garden, or to a eugenic norm in a purified genome. As archives for both human and Taltos knowledge, the Taltos easily adapt even computers, with genetic datafiles, into their cultural reproductive processes.

The success of the Ashlar-Morrigan merger and the demise of Lasher suggest two possible paths through the inevitable catastrophes of social and biological change. Both herald the end of "humans," defined as the baseline norm to which the aberrations of aliens and witches are held. The fluid dynamics of narrative and genetic cross-fertilizations inevitably lead to the disintegration of that ever-elusive norm, which can only be represented in its relation to the apocalyptic deviation. The choice is between Lasher and Ashlar, the postmodern incubus for whom the scientific project is denatured, violent, and antisocial, and the atavistic primogenitor who is the channel for new modes of being that merge nature and culture, human and nonhuman, in intimate ways, through a fully socialized scientific practice. Thus, the *Mayfair Witch Chronicles* play with popular debates on evolution and scientific progress, concluding that neither can be fully rational or controlled.

Notes

1. Gillian Brown identifies sequence, serialization, and accumulation as fundamental to the American ideal of the domestic, including its representation in Cold War fallout shelters.

2. Associations among masculinity, eroticism, reproduction, and technology, particularly in terms of nuclear energy, have been identified by several authors, including Evelyn Fox Keller, Brian Easlea, Carol Cohn, and Sally Hacker.

Works Cited

Borgmann, Albert. *Technology and the Character of Contemporary Life.* Chicago: U of Chicago P, 1984.

Brown, Gillian. "Nuclear Domesticity: Sequence and Survival." *Arms and the Woman: War, Gender, and Literary Representation.* Ed. Helen M. Cooper, Adrienne Auslander Munich, and Susan Merrill Squier. Chapel Hill: U of North Carolina P, 1989. 283-302.

Cohn, Carol. "Sex and Death in the Rational World of Defense Intellectuals." *Signs* 12.4 (1987): 687-718.

Csanyi, Vilmos. *Evolutionary Systems and Society: A General Theory of Life, Mind, and Culture.* Durham: Duke UP, 1989.

Easlea, Brian. *Fathering the Unthinkable: Masculinity, Scientists, and the Nuclear Arms Race.* London: Pluto, 1983.

Hacker, Sally. *Doing It the Hard Way: Investigations of Gender and Technology.* Boston: Unwin, 1990.

Haraway, Donna. "The Biopolitics of Postmodern Bodies." *Simians, Cyborgs, and Women: The Reinvention of Nature.* New York: Routledge, 1991.

Keller, Evelyn Fox. "From Secrets of Life to Secrets of Death." *Body/Politics: Women and the Discourse of Science.* New York: Routledge, 1990. 177-91.

——. "Nature, Nurture, and the Humane Genome Project." *The Code of Codes: Scientific and Social Issues in the Human Genome Project.* Ed. Daniel J. Kevles and Leroy Hood. Cambridge, MA: Harvard UP, 1993. 281-99.

Perrow, Charles. *Normal Accidents: Living with High-Risk Technologies.* New York: Basic Books, 1984.

Porush, David. "Frothing the Synaptic Bath." *Storming the Reality Studio: A Casebook of Cyberpunk and Postmodern Fiction.* Ed. Larry McCaffery. Durham: Duke UP, 1991. 330-32.

Rice, Anne. *Lasher.* New York: Knopf, 1993.

——. *Taltos.* New York: Knopf, 1994.

——. *The Witching Hour*. New York: Ballantine, 1990.

Schwenger, Peter. *Letter Bomb: Nuclear Holocaust and the Exploding Word.* Baltimore: Johns Hopkins UP, 1992.

Weart, Spencer. *Nuclear Fear: A History of Images.* Cambridge, MA: Harvard UP, 1988.

"He's not one of them":
Michael Curry and the Interpellation of the Self
in Anne Rice's *The Witching Hour*

Ellen M. Tsagaris

To stare into the blank, flat face is to look into a world where your
actual presence is unnecessary . . . where you live to be alive . . .
because flatness is the friend of death and death is the great leveller.
—Dick Hebdige

In *Lenin and Philosophy*, Louis Althusser argues that the ideology
of any given society "interpellates" an individual living in that society
into subjection. In other words, the individual is "hailed" or called into
accepting the social mores of the ideology (173). Moreover, reader
response theory requires that the text is an understood vision or point of
view shared by a defined group of readers. The reader is encouraged to
look for signs that the protagonist is "one of us," or part of a community
with which the reader can relate. For example, Dick Hebdige writes in
his essay on postmodernism "The Bottom Line on Planet One" that
readers wander through the environment of a book picking up whatever
they find appealing. In other words, the reader "cruises" the text for
something interesting (267).

In her novel *The Witching Hour*, American author Anne Rice draws
the character of her protagonist Michael Curry in such a way that the
reader is invited to cruise the text in search for clues that will allow the
reader to form a bond with him. The reader feels a sense of community
with Michael who, we are repeatedly told, is a "nice guy" put in a very
bad situation. He is an Everyman who becomes the victim of tragedy
while going about his everyday affairs. Considering the recent terrorist
bombing in Oklahoma City where nearly two hundred people were anni-
hilated while going to work and minding their own business, Michael's
plight becomes even easier to understand.

In *The Witching Hour*, Rice deals with the theme of modern individuals caught in circumstances beyond their control. The modern
person is isolated; s/he no longer can enjoy the community of others that
is based on common belief in ritual and custom. Instead, Michael Curry

185

and others like him must reinvent themselves constantly to adapt to the serendipitous situations in which they find themselves. A failure to adapt could be and usually is fatal for a person like Michael. Rather, like the famous petals scattered along a wet bough in Ezra Pound's poem "In a Station at the Metro," Michael and those like him are fragmented, lonely individuals looking for a bond with someone else. Most of Michael's family has died; his friends no longer understand him, and his romantic relationships are usually failures. He feels he has bonded with one woman, but when she becomes pregnant with their child, she aborts it. When he forms a bond with the heroine of the novel, Dr. Rowan Mayfair, she, too, miscarries their child under supernatural circumstances. In contradiction to John Donne's famous words, Michael is, indeed, left floating alone as a forsaken island in the sea of humanity. What is ironic about Rice's novel is that the community Michael is offered at the end of the novel is an evil community of witches, who invite him to join them in hell. Positive, nurturing connections with others seem to elude him, so that his kind, gentle nature is constantly tried. In many ways, he is roaming the streets of San Francisco, trying to fit into an affluent, fast-paced lifestyle his financial success affords him, but longing for the older, simpler, family-based lifestyle he had in New Orleans as a child. When he achieves those family-based connections, they nearly kill him.

The reader connects with Michael, and is able to establish intimacy with him, because he appeals to all "good" people who have bad things happen to them. Wolfgang Iser calls this ability to realize the text in such a way that allows bonding with Michael *konkretization* (77). One reason *konkretization* is possible is that tough, wealthy, Michael is not arrogant or pretentious, two stereotypical characteristis often linked with money. The reader can bring to the text a history similar to Michael's, so that s/he is able to sympathize with him and interpret the text according to his or her own life. Michael, the hero of *The Witching Hour*, is forty-eight years old. Though born in New Orleans, he has lived a good part of his adult life in San Francisco. There, Michael has founded a construction business restoring old Victorian houses. His business has made him a millionaire, but he continues to work on the construction site himself to maintain ties with his employees and with the people who are his clients. He does not want the class distinctions and isolation that money creates. After a windy day of walking on San Francisco's North Beach, Michael becomes involved in an accident and "drowns." Dr. Rowan Mayfair, a surgeon from Tiburon with extraordinary healing powers, saves Michael by hauling him onto her boat. She administers first aid to the unconscious man, then calls an ambulance. She wants to remain anonymous. Upon awakening, Michael tells of images he has seen while "dead," and he discovers a disconcerting power his hands have developed. Whenever he touches anything, images from the life of the person who has just touched the object flash thorough his mind. One by one his friends leave him, and Michael thinks that they are right; he is becoming delusional. He hides in his room watching the old film *Great Expectations* and looking for meaning in his life. Thinking he will go mad from the images, he contacts Rowan in an effort to discover what the power means. The two ultimately fall in love and marry. When the novel climaxes, they are awaiting the birth of their child.

Dr. Rowan Mayfair is adopted, but she learns that, like Michael, she is originally from New Orleans. She, too, has disconcerting powers; her anger can cause people to die on the spot. She discovers her family is a group of powerful witches and that they came from Scotland some three centuries ago. A group called the Talamasca that studies paranormal events has compiled a huge file on the Mayfair family, which Rowan and Michael later read. The Mayfair legacy, symbolized by a large emerald, has been passed down for twelve generations, and the power has been strengthened through a system of inbreeding and through intervention of a spirit named Lasher. Lasher was first conjured by Suzanne Mayfair, the first Mayfair witch. For her efforts at conjuring the spirit, Suzanne is burned at the stake. (The spirit's own story is told in Rice's novel *Lasher*.) Suzanne's daughter, Deborah, is saved by Petyr van Able, a member of the Talamasca. Eventually, the Mayfairs move to Martinique, then to New Orleans.

Rowan's mother, Deirdre, is not a very powerful witch. As a result, her aunt, Carlotta Mayfair, an elderly attorney with an iron will, has kept Deirdre either drugged or institutionalized for most of her adult life. It is Carlotta who arranges for Deirdre's child, Rowan, to be adopted by Ellie Mayfair, a California cousin. When Deirdre dies, Carlotta notifies Rowan. She and Michael meet in New Orleans to try to solve the mystery of his hands and near-death experience. By the end of the novel, Lasher invades Rowan's body, so that she gives birth to him in physical form on Christmas Eve, the witching hour. In the process, Lasher kills her own unborn child. Rowan leaves with Lasher, but not before Michael discovers them and Lasher attempts to murder him as well. By the end of the novel, Michael is recovering, but very ill. The following two novels, *Lasher* and *Taltos*, continue the story of Michael and Rowan against the history of the Mayfair witches.

At one point in *The Witching Hour*, Dr. Morris, who treats Michael at the hospital after Rowan Mayfair saves him from drowning, phones Rowan to request an interview for Michael. After Rowan agrees, Dr.

Morris says, "And Dr. Mayfair, let me tell you right now, this guy is just one very nice guy." Rowan answers, "I know," and Dr. Morris continues, "He really is suffering, this guy" (132). Implicit is the idea that the reader, too, is a "nice, moral person" who wants the good guy to triumph. Moreover, the reader's pity is stirred, here is a nice guy, one of us, who is really suffering. Of course, we want someone to help him and sympathize in his plight. As Iser writes in "The Reading Process," "The manner in which the reader experiences the text will reflect his own disposition" (80). While, as Iser notes, the factual outcome of the text will be different, the reader will be able to identify with the characters by noting similarities with her or his own experience. Furthermore, H.R. Jauss notes that a literary text "awakens memories of the familiar, stirs particular emotions in the reader" (84). Rice, a great admirer of Dickens and other Victorian novelists, is doing nothing more than establishing intimacy with the reader, just as her Victorian counterparts did through the use of epithets like "Gentle Reader." Annette Kolodny writes in "A Map for Rereading" "[T]here is an intimate interaction between readers and writers in and through which each defines for the other what s/he is about" (48).

Michael, the "nice" Everyman, appeals to the twentieth-century reader's sense of tradition. Because of the intimacy established with the reader, Michael's tradition becomes the reader's. The latter effect is crucial if the reader is to gain any meaning from the book at all. Once again, Kolodny discusses in "A Map for Rereading," the importance of tradition in reader response theory. According to her, many women writers in the nineteenth and early twentieth century were alienated from male-authored serious literature contemporary with them because they had no tradition to look to (Kolodny 47). Kolodny aptly quotes another critic, Harold Bloom, for the proposition that without tradition, a reader cannot understand a particular text. As Bloom says, "What happens if one tries to write, or to teach, or to think or even to read without the sense of a tradition?" (qtd. in Kolodny 47). Later on, Bloom says, "That which you are, that only can you read" (qtd. in Kolodny 55). If one substitutes the world "code" for "tradition," one can apply this quote to Michael's viewpoint in *The Witching Hour*. As a result, the reader realizes that she is being asked to identify with Michael's traditions. H.R. Jauss seems to agree with Bloom because he says that the "frame of reference for each work develops in the historical moment of its appearance from a previous understanding of the genre, from the form and themes of already familiar works, and from the contrast between poetic and practical language" (83).

Of course, what Bloom ignores and Kolodny identifies is that it is gender that alienated certain nineteenth-century female readers who had, for example, no tradition of whaling, and thus had great difficulty relating to *Moby Dick*. As Kolodny indicates, as women's literacy increased, novels about the sewing circle, and not the whaling boat, began to be written and read by women (49).

Rice, however, does not ignore the problem of gender. She gives Michael androgynous qualities, as well as traits attributable to women, so that he becomes universal and appeals to female as well as male readers, as Katherine Ramsland notes (*Prism* 328). For one thing, Michael collects Christmas ornaments as many other people do, particularly women. For him, Christmas is not important because it is a religious holiday but because he senses behind it "a great, shimmering history that went back and back through the millennia to dark forests where fire blazed and pagans danced" (*Witching Hour* 63). For him, Christmas is another way to fulfill the need for ritual in his life. Even when he has spent Christmas alone, Michael has felt the need to maintain connections with memories of family-filled Christmases by decorating the tree with his ornaments. The narrator says, "He had formed himself to go through with the old rituals, and long after Aunt Viv had gone to bed, he'd sat by the tree, a glass of wine in his hand, wondering where his life was going and why" (*Witching Hour* 893). Michael has made adding to his collection an annual tradition and lovingly repacks the ornaments for a journey to New Orleans. He ponders the history of Christmas as he wraps in tissue tiny houses, carousel horses, tiny birds made of feathers, china, candy canes and silver-plated stars (*Witching Hour* 893). He is looking forward to starting a new tradition of decorating the tree on Christmas Eve with Rowan. He hopes it is a custom they will begin for their unborn child.

Anne Rice enjoys giving Michael some of her own hobbies, just as she will later have Ash of *Taltos* collect the same antique dolls she herself enjoys. For Ash, the dolls, made of various materials, help him to love different types of human beings (*Taltos* 434). For Rice, the doll obsession has turned into a museum, just as it has for Ash, her character (Ramsland, *Witches' Companion* 91). Rice also admits that she shares Ash's view on capitalism and art, and that "manufacture makes possible beauty for the masses" (Rice qtd. in Ramsland, *Witches' Companion* 91).

Rice finds homage to androgyny fitting. She might agree with Carolyn Heilbrun, who argues in *Toward a Recognition of Androgyny*, "Androgyny suggests a spirit of reconciliation between the sexes . . . a full range of experience open to individuals who may, as women, be aggressive, as men tender (*x-xi*). In other words, Rice's powerfully built male characters like Michael typically have androgynous qualities. In her biography of Rice, *Prism of the Night*, Katherine Ramsland calls this mixing of genders in Rice's books "gender busting" (205). For example, while Rowan Mayfair, Michael's wife, prefers sailing and the outdoors, Michael prefers to read Dickens and to collect delicate antique Christmas ornaments (Rice, *Witching Hour* 893). In high school, Michael was a football star, but he enjoyed sentimental movies, too (*Witching Hour* 65). He is gentle and loves young children and is not afraid to cry when one of his former lovers aborts his unborn child (*Witching Hour* 64). Also, Michael shares many traits in common with Deirdre Mayfair, Rowan's mother. Both have dark hair and coloring, grew up in New Orleans and are forty-eight years old. By the end of the book, the ill and weakened Michael takes over the invalid Deirdre's old room and even takes over the rocking chair on the porch (964). Also, Rice has stated that Michael Curry represents her imagination, which she considers to be male, as well as her own alter ego (Ramsland, *Prism* 342). Like Michael, Rice grew up in New Orleans, moved to San Francisco, had dark hair, drank Miller tall cans, and was forty-eight when she wrote the book.

For all her invitations to the reader to embrace Michael and his point of view, Rice employs reader response theory a little differently. While Iser, Kolodny, and other reader-response theorists emphasize that the character's desire to belong to a community motivates his actions, the community Michael represents encompasses the reader, not the characters that make up the Mayfair family. In fact, in order to contrast his goodness with their "badness," the reader is constantly told that Michael "is not one of them" (*Witching Hour* 727). Here, Rice puts a twist on the technique Conrad uses in *Lord Jim* when Marlowe and the other characters identify with Jim by repeatedly stating "He's one of us." In fact, Michael constantly questions his role in the Mayfair legacy and the mystery of Lasher because he realizes he is different from the Mayfair witches.

Rowan, the designée of the witches' legacy, also dissociates herself from the "evil" Mayfair witches. Understandably, it is harder for her to do so because she is an orphan raised away from the witches' home base of New Orleans. She is so hungry for knowledge of her family and of her own identity that she is actually seduced by the legacy. Still, Rowan differentiates between herself and the former designées. At one point, after Michael uses telepathic power in his hands to touch Mayfair artifacts in order to learn Lasher's origins, Michael becomes terrified and physically sick. Rowan ministers to him and says reassuringly, "It's their house, Michael, I'm not one of them" (*Witching Hour* 726).

Michael also wonders if he has been chosen in some way to continue the legacy saying, "I don't know why I'm involved, any more than I did before" (*Witching Hour* 727). He acknowledges he acts according to Free Will, but in the fashion of Althusser, questions if Lasher and the Mayfair Witches have only deluded him into believing he has Free Will. He says "But how the hell do I fit in with my Free Will intact. I mean, what is 'all planned'" (*Witching Hour* 629). Michael ponders the various communities he could have belonged to that related him to the Mayfairs, including his New Orleans heritage, his early sightings of Lasher, and his similarities with Deirdre (*Witching Hour* 629). The reader learns in *Taltos*, that what links him with the Mayfairs is that he carries a gene that allows him to mate with a witch and produce a Taltos, a creature like Lasher in physical form, that is nearly immortal. In typical reader-response style, Michael reads the text of the Mayfair history and responds by looking for connections with himself, concluding, "God, there is no way to interpret this" (*Witching Hour* 630). As Aaron Lightner, his friend later tells him, "What's important is that you interpret" (*Witching Hour* 730). Aaron's advice is really the main premise behind reader response theory. Michael is also an architect who is trained to see patterns in everything; he sees his own life as part of a great pattern, too (*Witching Hour* 195). This belief that he is part of a pattern influences his point of view about the other characters and their history.

By the novel's end, the reader experiences the story almost entirely through Michael's point of view. In keeping with the general premises of reader response theory, Michael's interpretation of the events that befall the Mayfair family become central. His viewpoint takes over, and his interpretation is critical to interpretation of the plot. Michael's point of view is important because the reader has by now identified with his "nice guy" image completely. For example, chapter 54 is written entirely in quotes; it is a subtext/journal Michael writes as a coda to the other subtext of the novel, the Talamasca's *File on the Mayfair Witches*.

There is no doubt that Michael's point of view defines and dominates the meaning of the book. For example, many of the short, declarative paragraphs of the journal begin, "I believe," as if St. Michael himself were giving testimony before God (*Witching Hour* 964).

At times, Michael's discourse is almost religious, as when he states "For ours is the power and the glory, because we are capable of visions and ideas which are stronger and more enduring than we are" (*Witching Hour* 964). The opening words of the quote emulate the last words of "The Lord's Prayer," "for thine is the kingdom and the power and the glory forever." Since Althusser defines religion as one of the institutions that establishes codes people follow (143), the reader is "hailed" as a novice into the code Michael establishes. Yet Michael still retains a discourse that is recognizable to the ordinary person. It would be easy to turn him into a literal St. Michael, an allegorical figure battling evil for the sake of good. Such a dualistic reading of Michael's character would limit the story of the Mayfair witches completely. It is the "gray areas," the faults and eccentricities making up Michael's character that make him interesting. We need to be assured that he is one of us, that he is a nice guy. Yet we also need to know that, like us, he is human and therefore imperfect. In this way, we can understand that he is doing what so many others must do, trying to understand and make the best of a bad situation.

Even Rice's not-so-nice protagonists are understandably human. For example Lestat, Rice's vampire hero, is not purely evil. Lestat is interesting, partly because he believes that God created him just as he created all other creatures. Lestat comes to see himself as an avenging angel and only preys on murderers. In *The Queen of the Damned*, the third book of *The Vampire Chronicles,* Lestat saves humanity. In *The Tale of the Body Thief*, he falls in love with a nun and leaves the Church a generous monetary contribution. Like Michael, he is a complex personality with both admirable and not so admirable traits.

By the end of *The Witching Hour*, Michael's code has been implemented for he says that faith in change is what sustains a person through the horrors like those he has suffered at the hands of the evil Lasher. He writes, "That is my credo. That is why I believe in my interpretation of the story of the Mayfair witches" (*Witching Hour* 964). Because we as readers identify with Michael, his credo becomes our credo or code as well. Furthermore, Michael uses second person throughout his discourse. Someone is clearly meant to be an audience for his work. His account at the end of *The Witching Hour* is not personal and private. He attempts to give meaning to the vision he has at the end of the novel where all the Mayfair witches gather to seduce him into hell by reasoning that Lasher caused it. Still, he is adamant in his rejection of their invitation. While the gruesome specters of Stella, Deborah, Suzanne and the others beckon and cajole, Michael refuses to join them. For them, he is an "anti-saint" who will bring them back to human form, unlike St. Michael, who saved redeemed souls and cleared their way to enter heaven. Antha Mayfair says to him, "We're all saved now, Michael" (*Witching Hour* 945) while Marguerite Mayfair assures him, "We're all on the same side, *mon cher*" (*Witching Hour* 945). Yet Michael refuses to be one of the witches and cries out "I don't believe it. I don't accept it" (*Witching Hour* 947).

Not only does Michael not accept the ideology of the witches, he changes ideologies during his entire life. Michael Curry reinvents himself throughout the story depending on the ideologies of the various societies he inhabits. For example, the narrator states that Michael is a "self-made man," born into a working class background yet well-educated and at the same time interested in working with his hands. Though he has become a wealthy businessman and sophisticated traveler comfortable in almost any environment, Michael never forgets his Irish American/New Orleans roots. As the narrator again aptly says, "Though Michael had invented himself as many a person has done in California, creating a style perfectly in tune with the style of so many other self-invented people, he was always partly that tough kid from the Irish Channel who had grown-up using a piece of bread to push his peas onto his fork" (*Witching Hour* 57). In the same spirit of thought, Rice has said in an article by Sophia Diamantis for *Propaganda* magazine that she sees Lasher as an incarnate being who cannot be defined; Lasher himself says he is not yet defined but "definable" (11).

One way Michael breaks what Althusser called ideological state apparatuses like religious systems is to either ignore them or deal with them abstractly. For example, Michael "gets along" with his "liberal friends principally because he did not bother to argue with them, and while they were shouting at each other over pitchers of beer about foreign counties where they had never been and would never go, he was drawing pictures of houses on napkins" (Rice, *Witching Hour* 57). Michael shares his ideas, political and otherwise, in abstract ways that could have several interpretations. His detachment makes him feel like an outsider, "an outsider in the American twentieth century" (57), and he is happy no one pays attention to his opinions to the point of trying to convert him.

Even supernatural forces cannot convert Michael. At the opening of *The Witching Hour*, we meet Michael after Rowan saves him from drowning in the freezing waters off San Francisco Bay. Michael has had a near-death experience where a group of figures implore him to do something, but he cannot remember what his task is, nor who the figures are (29). Michael can touch things and get impressions of the people who touched them before he did. He can also read minds. Though seriously injured, Michael will not give in to the discourse of the hospital; we are told he "got violent" in the ambulance on the way to the hospital, and he refuses to follow a traditional course of treatment for his condition. He leaves the hospital and refuses a mental-health evaluation, preferring instead to seek his own course of treatment. Later, Lasher, the spirit who haunts the Mayfair family and who serves them as both mentor and tormentor, appears to Michael through his life in an effort to draw him into his schemes for the family. Yet Michael continually resists Lasher. He becomes an allegorical figure and, like his namesake St.

Michael, the Prince of the Archangels, he fights the spirit Lasher and wins. During the novel's end and climax, Lasher attempts to seduce Michael into committing suicide so that he will no longer interfere with Lasher's plans for Rowan.

The idea of being part of a defined community is a compelling one for Rice. The four novels that make up *The Vampire Chronicles* focus on the vampires as beings who band together and form their own communities because their monstrousness has alienated them from humanity. Lestat, Louis, Armand and the others establish their own culture, with its own rules and "Ideological State Apparatuses" that "hail" or "interpellate" the members of the culture. Rice's novels *Cry to Heaven* and *The Feast of All Saints* deal with the real people who were alienated historically because of birth, alienage or race. *Cry to Heaven* deals with the community of castrati singers in Renaissance Italy and with the combination of admiration and ostracism they had to contend with. The castrato protagonist, Tonio, voices his despair at this inability to feel as a man or woman (Ramsland, *Prism* 203). He says, "Oh, if only I understood either of you, either of you feels . . . if I were part of one or the other, or even part of both" (qtd. in Ramsland, *Prism* 203). *The Feast of All Saints* has for its subject the free people of color who lived within the confines of the city of New Orleans during the Civil War and who ruled their own community, but who had no place in the white world.

If Michael Curry is not one of the Mayfair witches, he is certainly intended to be "one of us." The reader is encouraged to identify with his goodness, his "niceness," and his compassion. In *Lasher*, the sequel the *The Witching Hour*, Michael becomes an even more important part of the "good" Mayfair family as they join as family members and psychic healers to save Rowan and themselves from the evil Lasher. Rice is careful not to make Michael an allegorical saint who sees only in black and white. He would be two-dimensional and basically uninteresting if all he could do was slay devils. In fact, according Ramsland in *The Witches' Companion*, St. Michael the Archangel was the protector of redeemed souls against Satan's assault (390). The connection with Michael Curry is obvious; Michael has twice been redeemed from death. He does not die at the end of *The Witching Hour* because he must live to kill Lasher, the "spirit" in Lasher. Like his namesake the saint, Michael casts Lasher back into hell.

For Michael Curry, innate goodness is not defined the same for each individual. Therefore, no code or ideology can ever "hail" him with complete success. He is a universal man, comfortable in any situation because he is capable of adapting. Because of his ordinariness, Michael is familiar to the average reader. The reader then wants to *konkretize* the text by identifying with Michael, and by interpreting Michael's experiences with his or her own.

Furthermore, the reader is able to relate to Michael because, like the saint for whom he is named, he chooses to rescue people. He does not judge, but will fight "evil" as he defines it, even at great cost to himself. Michael feels goodness and morality are subjective and not defined by society. He will support his community, but not be condemned by it. So, he says he does not believe in a hell comprised of horror and chaos. He claims, "If any revelation awaits us at all, it must be as good as our ideals and our best philosophy. . . . If that isn't so, then we are in the grip of a staggering irony. And all the spooks of hell might as well dance in the parlor" (*Witching Hour* 965).

While he is somewhat set apart from mere mortals because of his allegorical associations with St. Michael, who fought the devil, this connection in many ways only strengthens the reader's compassion for him. This touch of sainthood makes him into a sort of Christian martyr, one of us who "went the extra mile" and sacrificed himself to save his fellow humans. What stronger sense of responsibility to a community is there?

Works Cited

Althusser, Louis. "Ideology and the State." *Lenin and Philosophy*. Trans. Ben Brewster. London: New Left Books, 1977. 127-74.

Diamantis, Sophia. "The Gothic Rice." *Propaganda* (Spring 1994): 10-11.

Hebdige, Dick. "The Bottom Line on Planet One." Rice and Waugh 260-82.

Heilbrun, Carolyn. *Toward a Recognition of Androgyny*. New York: Knopf, 1973.

Iser, Wolfgang. "The Reading Process." 1974. Rice and Waugh 77-82.

Jauss, H.R. "Literary History as a Challenge to Literary Theory." 1967. Rice and Waugh 83-91.

Kolodny, Annette. "A Map for Rereading: Gender and the Interpretation of Literary Texts." *The New Feminist Criticism: Essays on Women, Literature and Theory*. Ed. Elaine Showalter. New York: Knopf, 1992. 46-62.

Ramsland, Katherine. *Prism of the Night: A Biography of Anne Rice*. New York: Plume, 1992.

——. *The Witches' Companion: The Official Guide to Anne Rice's* Lives of the Mayfair Witches. New York: Ballantine, 1994.

Rice, Anne. *Taltos*. New York: Knopf, 1994.

——. *The Witching Hour.* New York: Knopf, 1990.
Rice, Philip, and Patricia Waugh, eds. *Modern Literary Theory: A Reader.* New York: Arnold, 1989.

The Historical Novels of Anne Rice

Bette B. Roberts

Anne Rice is best known for her gothic novels, especially those in *The Vampire Chronicles* and *The Witching Hour* series, but readers who enjoy her fiction are beginning to explore her historical novels, in particular *The Feast of All Saints* (1979) and *Cry to Heaven* (1982). In an interview with Susan Ferraro, Rice said that she decided to try a different genre in the late 1970s because she was stung by some of the negative responses to her first novel, *Interview with the Vampire* (Ferraro 76). It is not surprising that Rice would turn from the gothic to the historical novel, since the two genres are closely aligned. Critics who like to categorize different types of gothic fiction, in fact, label books that are predominantly gothic, that is those sustaining a prevalent sense of fear and doom, as historical-gothic if they are set in a historical past and include actual events and historical figures, such as Sophia Lee's *The Recess*.

While Rice does not bring actual historicism to her gothic novels, she easily moves her vampires and witches from present to past and evokes different time periods and settings for her globally traveled gothic protagonists. In her innovative adaptations of gothic conventions, she also tends to humanize gothic characters, to create villain-hero types whom we see from the inside, and to place them in families, groups, and communities that appear to have a social context. Central to her vampires' and witches' experiences is the journey toward awareness and renewal through apparent destruction as these characters learn how to survive in an existential reality.

In analyzing her two historical novels, we find that many of the same traits that make her gothic novels powerful and appealing carry over into her efforts with the historical genre: the variety of narrative strategies to recapture a convincing sense of the past, the focus upon characters to convey the inner, deep impact of historical events, the importance of family relationships, and the movement toward liberation of self as protagonists mature through their interplay with social conflicts and values. Within these larger common denominators between her gothic and historical novels are other recurrent issues that continue to be important in the renewal process, such as growing beyond the oppressive

197

impact of Catholicism and discarding conservative attitudes toward sexuality. As in the gothics, where the forces that threaten survival involve obstacles to self-development and awareness, here the sources of evil reside not in the megalomaniacal Akasha or Lasher but in the historical realities of racism or inhumane custom.

The blending of historical fact and fiction has traditionally been a risky venture. As George Dekker argues, to call a novel "a 'historical romance' is . . . to direct attention to its extraordinarily rich, mixed, and even contradictory or oxymoronic character" (26). Dekker later defines the tension in this genre that is pulled "towards the contrary poles of romance and realism, myth and history" (306). Technically beginning with Sir Walter Scott's *Waverley* novels, the historical novel fictionalizes actual characters and events. The effective historical novel gives the impression of recreating the actual past while also engaging the reader in a fictional experience. There is always the difficulty of maintaining a fidelity to the facts while not allowing these facts to stifle creativity. As Harry B. Henderson explains, the central problems of the aesthetics of historical fiction are how to convey "the immediacy of experience of the past," or how to reorder materials in an attempt to recreate this experience (8). The past may end up as a theatrical backdrop that does not seriously pervade the characters or provide causation (as sometimes happens in Scott), or the vitality and complexity of the characters may be sacrificed by a slavish attention to historical accuracy. In order to avoid either of these extremes with characterization, critics argue that the most sensible approach is not to center upon famous personages as protagonists but rather to portray fictional characters whose lives are caught up in and influenced by history and culture.

Scott set the standard in *Ivanhoe*, his story of warring Saxons and Normans in medieval England. He sought to portray, as C. Hugh Holman and William Harmon point out, "an age when two cultures are in conflict; into this cultural conflict are introduced fictional personages who participate in actual events and move among actual personages" (229). Elizabeth Gaskell's *Mary Barton*, Dickens's *A Tale of Two Cities*, and Boris Pasternak's *Dr. Zhivago* are examples of this tradition, whereby large numbers of carefully delineated characters on both sides of a conflict exemplify the impact of historical events. Yet, as Holman and Harmon state, in one major variation of the Scott paradigm, a historical novel may focus instead on a few characters who loom larger than the cultural conflicts that motivate them, as in Hawthorne's *The Scarlet Letter* (230). Sustained by an informed social vision throughout the action, the characters undergo struggles that carry the weight of historical values and ideas.

Just as Rice's gothic fiction demonstrates tremendous variety in her approaches to gothic materials, such as the first-person that concentrates on Louis in the *Interview* or the multiple narrators that convey the large cast of opposing forces in *The Queen of the Damned*, her two historical novels represent well-established but different traditions of the genre. In *The Feast of All Saints* she follows Scott's example of a culture in conflict and poised on the edge of change, specifically the racial tensions and social caste system in Louisiana during the 1840s that lead up to the Civil War. In *Cry to Heaven* she writes a Hawthornian historical novel, in which the lives of the Italian castrati in the early-eighteenth century are represented by only two characters, Marco Antonio Treschi and his opera mentor Guido Maffeo. Discussing her approach to *The Feast* with her biographer, Katherine Ramsland, Rice stated that she wanted the novel to be "translated from the interior of a culture," and to "feed information slowly and naturally" (192). Painted on an epic canvas, *The Feast* depicts characters from different generations and families illustrating all sides of the racial conflict—the whites, the *gens de couleur*, the freed slaves, and the slaves—whose lives are intricately connected and affected by their position in the caste system. In contrast, perhaps from her response to the originally poor reception of *The Feast* (Ramsland 192) as well as from her desire to experiment, *Cry to Heaven* relies on a single, concentrated plot of revenge to intensify the enormous impact of castration. In both novels the protagonists mature from innocence to experience as disastrous events force them to come to terms with themselves and find ways of achieving independence within their social milieus. Given her approach to recreate the impact of a culture rather than actual events, it is not the intent here to research historical fact in order to separate historical fact from fiction. In afterwords to both of her historical novels, Rice cites the sources she researched and the names of real people, events, and places she included in rendering the worlds of her subject matter. She is also careful to explain that all of her main characters are fictional.

The oppressive structures and values of these milieus provide cause-and-effect plots in both works, but in *The Feast* the causes are demonstrated through many climactic actions that affect large numbers of minor characters as well, as their experiences parallel the maturation process of the protagonists. In *Cry to Heaven*, however, the plot depends more upon psychological reaction than actual events since Tonio must come to terms with his forced castration, which occurs toward the beginning of the novel. While in *The Feast* the Dickensian authorial point of view oversees all of the characters, provides many different perspectives on events and traditions, and creates a dense narrative style, in *Cry to*

Heaven the reader sees the world primarily through Tonio's eyes and secondarily through Guido within the omniscient voice, so that the prose seems lighter and lyrical in its closeness to character. Rice's use of her native New Orleans not only connects *The Feast* to her gothics but also provides an atmosphere rich in symbolism that enables her to intensify the external conflicts, foreshadow events, and establish connections in a complicated plot. In *Cry to Heaven,* Rice uses the climatic conditions and historical reputations of Naples, Venice, and Rome to create effects sometimes similar to those of New Orleans, while she relies upon recurrent specific symbols such as the erupting Vesuvius to intensify the psychological torment of Tonio. In both novels, the atmosphere is dark, violent, and ominous, as in the gothics. Here, however, the mood supports the idea of social injustice and the need for change.

In *The Feast of All Saints* this gothic atmosphere emanates from racial prejudice. Rice focuses on the *gens de couleur,* who are below the whites in social class and above the freed and unfreed slaves. The Ste. Maries, a family of color, experience the impact of the caste system. The adolescent Marcel and Marie suffer and then recover from losses: Marcel is deprived of his lifelong goal of going to Paris and educating himself; the lovely Marie is raped by five white men. The destruction and self-renewal process in their lives is previewed by the excerpt from John Donne's sonnet at the beginning of the book:

> Batter my heart, three-person'd God; for, you
> As yet but knocke, breathe, shine, and seeke to mend;
> That I may rise, and stand, o'erthrow mee', and bend
> Your force, to breake, blowe, burn and make me new.

Marcel's renewal means achieving financial independence from his white father, Philippe Ferronaire, who has withdrawn his support; intellectual confidence from his teacher, Christophe Mercier, who has taught him how to become an excellent scholar; and emotional maturity from his own experiences with Anna Bella and Aunt Josette, who have helped him gain respect for his own race. Given the standard that an historical character's "deeds, values, and psychological problems" should have a representative historical significance" (Dekker 305-06), the portrait of Marcel's growth is effective in recapturing the American past leading up to the Civil War. Like Hawthorne's Robin Molineux, his throwing off his father to achieve personal independence is carefully intertwined with his understanding the constructive role he may play in an unjust racial culture.

While the novel is primarily Marcel's story, it is also that of his sister Marie. Like Marcel, Marie experiences violence by the hands of whites that forces her to realize truths about herself and thereby become independent. Marie is prevented from marrying the *gens de couleur* man whom she loves because her mother and aunts intend for her to become the kept mistress of a wealthy white man so that she can support her family. After she becomes the victim of the vengeful Lisette, who takes her to Lola Dede's brothel where Marie is raped, her slow recovery depends upon her regaining her self-esteem. Through the patience, kindness, and substance of women of her own race, especially Dolly Rose, she accepts her own sensuality and discovers her strength as a woman. Her maturation, like Marcel's, is explicitly delineated. When Richard Lermontant finally gets to see her after her ordeal, he notes her change; some "new fire radiated from within. It was as if the young girl he'd known had been an unstamped coin, and here was the woman" (*Feast* 538). Richard's determination to marry her in defiance of the oppressive caste system ensures a reward for her suffering and promises hope for social change.

In demonstrating the pervasiveness of racial discrimination, Rice not only traces the maturation of Marcel and Marie, but similar to Scott's narratives, sets up counterpoint patterns of families and individuals representing different racial groups (whites, *gens de couleur*, freed and unfreed slaves) within the larger conflict. As indicated above with the Ste. Maries and Lermontants, many comparisons are invited among family members, especially parents and children, older and younger generations, men and women in alliances and marriages who experience the effects of the caste system. While Grandpere Lermontant and Richard's parents applaud his bravery in challenging the status quo, Celeste and the Ste. Marie aunts cling to their traditional ways of coping with white male supremacy and remain incapable of understanding the young people's needs. The loving, respectful relationship between Rudolphe and Madame Suzette Lermontant contrasts not only with the destructive alliance between Celeste Ste. Marie and Philippe Ferronaire but also with the loveless and hostile marriage of Philippe and his wife Aglae.

Vincent Dazincourt offers further diversity within the white side of the racial conflict. At first his behavior does not distinguish him, though he is clearly more sensitive and humane than his brother-in-law Philippe in handling slaves and running *Bontemps*. Yet he is not unwilling to involve himself in mixed racial alliances, first with Dolly Rose, with whom he fathered the unfortunate Lisa, and then with Anna Bella. Unlike his brother, however, Vincent comes to realize the destructive nature of these relationships and shows the same capacity for self-sacrifice as Richard—in this case by giving up the woman he deeply loves.

Vincent enters into the alliance with Anna Bella because he assumes that his emotions are not at risk; his upbringing and ignorance have taught him that "all Negroes were fools" (*Feast* 335). Yet unexpectedly he falls in love. After treating Anna Bella and their child badly at first, after the fashion of Philippe, Vincent has a change of heart. In the same nobility of spirit that prompts him to defend Marie's honor and hunt down her white rapists, he makes permanent legal provisions for Anna Bella and their child. His growth and awareness point toward the possibility of change in the attitudes of the ruling class.

The worthy Anna Bella illustrates the interconnectedness of the characters and their impact on one another. The daughter of a freed slave who rises in status because she attracts a white man's love, Anna Bella was earlier looked down on by an immature, prejudiced Richard because of her African features and neglected by Marcel, who saw a relationship with her as an obstacle to his going to Paris. By the end of the novel with Vincent now out of Anna Bella's life, Marcel's appreciation of her shows the growth of his character. Even Christophe benefits from her generosity, as she nurses his friend and lover Michael through a bout with yellow fever.

The complexity of devices that Rice uses to unify this large group of characters and plots and to underscore her themes is apparent in the *secretaire* that Marie gives to Anna Bella upon her alliance with Vincent, an occasion celebrated like a wedding. Marie, having received the gift from her white father, Philippe, does not realize that he had stolen it from his own wife, whose grandmother had left it to her. Seeing the little treasure now housed at Anna Bella's and knowing that his sister misses it, Vincent figures out that Philippe stole it from his own white family to give it to Marie. Vincent's disrespect for his brother-in-law's corruption and his awareness of the pain it causes to loved ones force him to understand his own part in the system that revolts him.

The *secretaire* is just one example of Rice's keen attention to detail in establishing the intricacy of racial attitudes that permeate the novel. Through other conflicts within the main plots, she further illustrates the complexities of the historical background and social hierarchies. The respectable Rudolphe Lermontant gets Christophe Mercier out of Dolly Rose's house when the white Captain Hamilton is expected, since Hamilton would have the right to kill Christophe in finding him there. Furious with Christophe for putting him in this position, however, Rudolphe tells him, "I have never never . . . cowered before any white man in my life!" (*Feast* 233). Vincent goes to calm Captain Hamilton by reminding him that "a man of color cannot defend himself against a white man at all." He explains further that "in some circles it is judged an act of cowardice to quarrel with a man who cannot defend himself" (*Feast* 233).

Not surprisingly, Rudolphe defends his daughter Giselle's honor later when a white man named Bridgeman from Virginia insults her on the street. Unable to attack a white man physically, Rudolphe insults him, but since this action, too, is "a crime in itself," Bridgeman takes Rudolphe to court. When the testimony of witnesses and Rudolphe's own status in the community vindicate him, the out-of-towner is flabbergasted: in Virginia, Bridgeman says, "they would have strung that 'negra' from the nearest tree branch and lit a fire beneath him to send him on his way. What was this place, New Orleans, what with the abolitionists in the north and 'negras' attacking white men on the street?" (*Feast* 317). While Rudolphe's experience shows his strength, it also brings home to Marcel the reality that they are "people of color living in a white man's world" (*Feast* 320).

Christophe, too, experiences these social realities when he tries to bring the slave Bubbles into the classroom with the other students of color. As the parents withdraw their students from the school, Christophe realizes that he must either remove Bubbles or give up the idea of educating his own race. Rudolphe tells Christophe that he has taught many of his own black apprentices to read and write, but in private. He explains that they are living in a caste system, where people of color have won their

precarious place in this corrupt quagmire by asserting over and over that it is composed of men who are better than and different from the slaves! We get respect in one way, Christophe, and that is by insisting ourselves on what we are. Men of property, men of breeding, men of education, and men of family. But if we drink with slaves, marry slaves, sit down in our parlors with slaves . . . then men will treat us as if we were no better! (*Feast* 248)

Indeed, the lot of the slaves who hover in the background is far worse, as illustrated by Lisette and Bubbles and by the horrifying glimpses Rice provides: slaves displayed on the auction block, slaves loaded onto ships, and slaves abused on the plantations, such as the beating of a pregnant slave at *Bontemps* by the cruel overseer. In educating Marcel on the history of his race, however, Tante Josette explains why she believes that American slaves, unlike the Haitians, will not revolt:

Slaves have been bred for generation upon generation, domesticated and not by blatant atrocity, but by some system far more subtle and efficient, something akin to the cotton gin and the refining mill in its precision and its relentlessness.

No, it would not happen here, because we've beaten them, cowed them, and ground them utterly *and completely into the dust. (Feast* 460)

While Rice does not depict any change in the slaves' conditions in her focus upon the *gens de couleur,* the maturations of her main characters Marcel and Marie, the strength and independence they achieve from suffering and loss, and the commitment of the Lermontants and Christophe to assist and educate people of their own race suggest the larger direction of their culture in moving away from injustice and oppression based on race toward equality. Indeed, the action of the novel carries out Rice's intention to pay tribute to the people of color in New Orleans. According to her biographer, she chose the novel's title to commemorate them as the "forgotten saints" celebrated on "The Feast of All Saints" (Ramsland 183).

The same theme of regeneration through destructive violence announced by Donne's plea at the beginning of *The Feast* is conveyed by the personal transcendence of Tonio Treschi in *Cry to Heaven,* but in a very different historical and social context. Set in early-eighteenth-century Italy, the novel takes its Blakean title from the pleas of the castrated male singers who sing in the churches and opera houses: "Children mutilated to make a choir of seraphim, their song a cry to heaven that heaven did not hear" (*Cry* 47). Instead of depicting opposing forces in a social conflict through multi-plots and many characters, however, Rice relies this time upon the painful experience of one main character to expose the injustice and inhumanity of the culture in which he lives.

Tonio Treschi, at fifteen, becomes the victim of his grasping brother Carlo, who will stop at nothing to remove Tonio as the rightful heir and assume the Treschi fortune and rank in Venetian society. Taking advantage of the reputation of Tonio's fine voice and his love of singing, Carlo hatches a Jacobean plot of gothic revenge and horror. Tonio is forcibly castrated and reputed by Carlo's lackeys to have done the deed himself in order to preserve his voice. Unlike the brutal split between Marcel and his father and Marie's rape in *The Feast of All Saints,* Tonio's castration occurs early in the novel so that the rest of the action emphasizes his psychological conflict in response to this major injury. The music teacher Guido, also duped by Carlo, takes the mutilated and devasted Tonio to the conservatorio in Naples, where Tonio's constructive development as an operatic singer is interconnected with his difficulty in accepting the loss of his manliness and his destructive desire for revenge. Marked by many omens of impending doom, the action moves relentlessly toward Tonio's confrontation with Carlo in Venice, where Carlo's villainy causes his own death. Freed of his revenge, confident of his own sexuality, and successful as an operatic singer, Tonio comes to terms with the limitations of his life and finds his fulfillment in a love relationship with the liberated Christina Grimaldi and his career.

The concentration of this plot indicates how different *Cry to Heaven* is from *The Feast of All Saints* as a historical novel. While both works depend on the maturation of the protagonists to dramatize historical realities, in *Cry to Heaven* the focus is entirely on Tonio and his maestro Guido. Other castrati are part of Tonio's life at the conservatorio and in the opera, such as Domenico and Paulo, but in comparison with the more fully developed cast in *The Feast*, they remain shadowy characters. Rice also places the forced castration at the beginning of the novel to establish the gothic plot of revenge that sustains suspense until the final confrontation with Carlo. In a technique similar to her creation of vampires to aggrandize human responses to inescapable conditions, she gives Tonio wealth and aristocratic heritage, which exaggerates the plight of the castrati. Rice acknowledged to Ramsland that "no Venetian aristocrat had ever been made into a castrato" (198). In fact, Guido has the more typical experience that suggests larger sources of social injustice. Knowing "only routine hunger and cruelty among the large peasant brood to which he was born the eleventh child," he was "sold outright" by his parents and castrated when he was six. "And all of his life, Guido remembered he was given his first good meal and soft bed by those who made him a eunuch" (*Cry* 3). While the cross Guido must bear is the tragic loss of his voice during adolescence, Tonio has been cheated out of his inheritance, expelled from his family, and denied his role as a husband and father: "Nor would the Church ever receive him, save for the lowest Orders, and even then only by special dispensation" (*Cry* 183).

While in *The Feast* Catholicism provides a rich source of imagery (especially the Virgin Mary associations with Marie) but no spiritual comfort for characters like Marie and Anna Bella, in *Cry to Heaven* the culture of the church permeates the whole musical aura of the novel. Rice is remarkably restrained in her treatment of the church's role in the castration of male singers, particularly in light of her criticism of Catholicism and the ironic Christian images in her gothic fiction. Yet as in the passage above, the ironic understatement is extremely effective in condemning the church's underlying complicity. To perform the church's music and satisfy the audience's pleasure, castrati are common. The unfortunate young Guido is proud to become one of them: "it was the soprano singer whom the world worshiped. It was for him that kings vied and audiences held their breath; it was the singer who brought to life the very essence of the opera" (*Cry* 5). Later in Rome, it dawns on Tonio that "eunuchs had come into fashion and necessity" because of the church's "ban on performing women." As Ramsland explains, "Since the perfect soprano of a young boy could only be preserved by castration, men were mutilated for the sake of social conventions" (203). The blind church that refuses to receive them lies behind this barbarism. Startling in its simplicity, one scene shows Tonio in a carriage on the way to the Vatican, when he notices a sign in a small shop: "SINGERS FOR THE POPE'S CHAPEL CASTRATED HERE."

As the major cause for the boys' cries to a heaven that does not hear, the Church is shown to be more ignorant than cruel in the rather neutral portrait of Cardinal Calvino. Tonio realizes that the cardinal mistakenly believes that Tonio was probably an urchin saved from poverty by being castrated to sing in the holy choirs. The cardinal also fails to appreciate the worth of aesthetic and physical pleasures. Tonio "could sense that in some way all of these pleasures—poetry, art, music, and their feverish coupling—were bound up with the Cardinal's notion of those enemies of the soul: the world and the flesh" (*Cry* 381). Though Tonio tries to explain the sheer ecstasy and joy of singing and hearing music, the cardinal, who manages to conquer what he sees as his depravity, fails to understand why Tonio feels no guilt over their sexual pleasures and remains unable to overcome his conviction that they are evil. Although the aesthetic truths of Rice's "savage garden" are not included in this novel, the narrowness of the cardinal's perspective compared with Tonio's liberating acceptance of physical pleasure underscores the limitations of the Church and the prevailing existential philosophy of Rice's fiction.

Just as Marcel and Marie had to transcend an oppressive racial culture, Tonio must come to terms with his sexual debility and its implications on his family. Within this process, however, the issues are developed more psychologically through Tonio's internal struggles. Still a cause-and-effect plot, the structure of the action is based on two main devices that convey the complexity of his character: first his positive and negative sides, the love and revenge that move him toward maturity yet hold him back, and second the narrative counterpoint or parallel between his gradual sexual maturity and his attitudes toward singing female roles in the opera. The Maestro Cavalla tells Guido that Tonio "is a pair of twins in the same body, one loving music more than anything in this life, the other hungering for revenge" (*Cry* 337). Even after Tonio has fallen deeply in love with Christina, Guido realizes that he is "being slowly torn apart. It was the battle of those twins he was witnessing: the one who craved life, and the one who could not live without the hope of revenge" (*Cry* 461). Ramsland points out that the central metaphor for Tonio's dual personality is Vesuvius, the dormant volcano representing both sexual tension and the illusion of surface appearance. It becomes Tonio's symbol of restrained power . . . Carlo represents his dark side—the victim, Guido, his good side—heroic transcendence. When one side gains strength in Tonio's life, the other recedes. (Ramsland 201)

Occasionally the repressed, violent, destructive side of Tonio erupts when he is with Guido and when he is overly defensive to criticism. His great successes on the stage and his love of Christina fortify his positive side, so that by the time he meets with Carlo, he has conquered the darkness. He tells Carlo: "I am done hating you. . . . Done fearing you. It seems that you are nothing to me now but some ugly storm that drove my undefended bark off course. . . . I want no more quarrel with you, no more hatred, nor spite" (*Cry* 524).

Within this central pattern is the parallel development of Tonio's gradual evolution as a performer and his acceptance of himself as a man, castrated yet capable of deeply passionate love—an intricate connection between his life and art. When he first arrives at the conservatorio, he refuses to sing at all: "The thought of it was too much; it was like giving in to them, and it was entering into the very nightmare role they had written for him as if this life were an opera, and they had given him this hideous part" (*Cry* 170). As he progresses from singing for Guido in the conservatorio to singing at the contessa's chapel and then performing at the opera, he also moves from shallow to deeply satisfying sexual relationships with Domenico to Guido to the Cardinal Calvino—and finally to Christina. He conquers at last his aversion to playing female parts, the final step in becoming a true castrato.

In keeping with the androgyny that gives Rice's vampires a liberating transcendence from gender roles, Tonio feels a "sense of illimitable power," an "exhilarating strength" when he puts on the costume that transforms him into a woman for his performance. Shortly before his great triumph in Rome with Bettichino, he tells the costume designer, Signora Bianchi, "Make me so beautiful and so much the woman that I could fool my own father should I climb on his knee" (*Cry* 410). Confident of his manliness in giving Christina sexual pleasure, he exploits his eunuch traits to the fullest off stage when he poses as a prostitute in black mourning to attract Carlo. This confrontation scene is not only delicious in meting out Jacobean justice to Carlo but conclusive in symbolizing the maturity of Tonio, who has given over revenge and found freedom in his adversity. It also demonstrates Rice's success in a complete intermingling of character motivation with the impact of cultural or historical truths.

As Marcel's and Marie's conflicts are echoed in other characters, so Tonio's inner divisiveness is reflected in the fewer minor characters here, who may also be interpreted as projections of the opposing sides within Tonio. Ramsland believes that all of the characters mirror Tonio's repression and

seem to be wearing masks. Christina, a contessa who attracts him, wants the freedom of a man; the Cardinal, a man of religious purity, exhibits brutally carnal desires; Marianna is both cruel and caring, with beauty that hides her ugliness; Carlo appears innocent of malice; Guido seems to hate Tonio when he actually longs for him; men dress as women, women as men. Even Venice, at times glorious and mysterious, has a whorish and seedy interior. (202)

Going further with a "symbolic layering" of doubles, Ramsland cites the "double imagery in the background: two recurring nightmares, two contessas, two men killed by Tonio, a duet between two castrati, and repeated attention to mirror images," among other examples.

We see further variation of the dual imagery that emphasizes Tonio's internal conflict with his dual nature when we compare the two women Tonio loves, his mother Marianna and his lover Christina. Both women were pressured into marrying older men, though for different reasons. Becoming Andrea's wife and hiding the truth that Tonio is in fact Carlo's son, Marianna remains childlike herself and resorts to alcohol to cope with her secret conflicts. Upon Carlo's return she remains dependent on him, despite her anguish at losing Tonio. As Carlo explains later, "Do you know what she said to me, that I had ruined her, destroyed her, driven her to madness and drink and taken from her her only comfort, our son" (*Cry* 515). Christina, however, the "butterfly struggling from the cocoon," manages to rise above her dependence upon men after her husband's death and find her freedom. A skilled painter, she tells Tonio that she is not interested in remarrying: "I've been married. I was obedient. I did what I was told" (*Cry* 449). Tonio, tormented that he is unable to marry her and give her a child, is slow to be convinced that she is truly committed to her art: "Why is it difficult for you to understand that I want to be free and to paint, to have my studio, to have my life as I please?" (*Cry* 449). One of Rice's liberated females, in this culture Christina is the rare but perfect soulmate for Tonio. Her hair spilling down "a shower of corn yellow over him," her love lightens his darkness.

Rice uses light and dark imagery in both of her historical novels, where darkness dominates as an appropriate mood for social cruelty. Yet the effects she creates differ. In *The Feast*, the wetness and darkness of

New Orleans add to the general bleakness of conditions for the *gens de couleur* and, similar to London scenes in Dickens's *Bleak House,* suggest pervasive corruption and disease. In July the

rain had inundated the cemeteries so that one burial for the parish had to be made in a veritable pool of muddy water; and the bodies of the yellow fever victims were beginning to pile up at the gates, giving off a stench sufficient to sicken the oldest citizen who had seen it summer after summer. (*Feast* 129)

Before Christophe returns from Paris, the rain beats "through the rotted shutters" of his mother's home, where the wallpaper hangs "in yellowed strips from the damp ceilings." Marie is led to Madame Lola's during a thunder storm foreshadowed by Richard's imagining a menacing darkness surrounding her. Yet on their wedding day, he sees only an "uncommon radiance."

In *Cry to Heaven* the lights of both love and music appear more often, as the shifts back and forth dramatize Tonio's conflict and culminate in his going north to the colder climate of Venice to seek out Carlo, then arriving finally in the sunny warmth of Florence, where he rejoins Christina, Guido, and his music. Before he loves Christina, Tonio's desire for Guido radiates "out into the darkness." After the consummation of their love, the imagery suggests love and hate coexistent in Tonio. As they walk out into the streets of Naples, "the windows looming at every turn out of the dark were filled with lovely yellow light and then there was the blackness" (*Cry* 249). Tonio looks over to Guido in the warm tavern and sees the flame in his eyes: "you are my love, and I am not alone, no, not alone, for this little while" (*Cry* 250). The brilliance of stage lights and music also counter the darkness of revenge; Paulo's voice, for instance, fills "the room like a bright golden bell."

Toward the end of the novel, shortly before Tonio leaves to meet Carlo, Rice uses the *moccoli* in Rome, the "great closing ceremony of these last few hours before the beginning of Lent," to create suspense and reinforce the meaning of light and darkness. Climactic group scenes used to educate main characters and intensify emotional states are a familiar device in her other novels, such as the Parisian performance of the vampires in the *Interview,* the rock concert in *Lestat,* the pagan orgies in *The Queen of the Damned,* and the Mardi Gras in *The Witching Hour.* Lighted candles appear everywhere; "The entire street below was a sea of dimly lit faces, each protecting its own flame while trying to extinguish another: Death to you, death to you, death to you" (*Cry* 479). While the religious origin behind the folklore ritual is apparent, that is, those without lights (of faith in God) are cursed, so is the meaning of

Tonio's love for Christina as the source of his renewal. The symbolic suddenly becomes real, however, when Tonio must actually defend himself against Carlo's men, who attempt to stab and strangle him but are subdued by the cardinal's guards.

This scene stands out because this novel relies less upon actual violent episodes than a pervasive atmosphere of doom. Tonio feels anxious from the beginning when he is ignorant of the true Treschi family relationships; he has an "eerie feeling" about the "things unspoken in this house," and Guido and Christina share Tonio's dread of looming disaster when they observe him in Rome. This gothic anxiety is all the greater because of the horror in the beginning, the scene of Tonio's castration. Both Tonio's mutilation and the later confrontation with the villainous Carlo are carried out in darkness, in the shabby rooms of centuries-old buildings along winding canals, which resemble the labyrinthine streets of New Orleans in *The Feast of All Saints* in their appropriateness for crime and murder.

While these streets are threatening places, they may also be filled with crowds of people engaging in religious ceremonies or going to the theater. Tonio's experiences take him into the cozy small taverns among the common people, as well as into the elegant ballrooms and salons of the grand palazzos. As Rice contrasts the claustrophic, narrow streets of New Orleans with the wide vistas of *Bontemps* and *Sans Souci* in *The Feast* to emphasize the great gulf between the countryside and the city, here she makes careful distinctions among Venice, Naples, and Rome that are relevant to the historical subject at hand. In Naples, for instance,

Her singers, her composers, her music had fully superseded those of Venice. And they had long ago eclipsed those of Rome. Rome, however, was still the place for a castratro's debut, as far as Guido was concerned. Rome might not be producing singers and composers, but Rome was Rome. (*Cry* 287)

The climb up Vesuvius outside of Naples provides a psychological passage for Tonio similar to Marcel's crossing the Mississippi River in *The Feast*. Venice is the city to which Tonio returns and fulfills his father's dying wishes, though in a way different from what his father intended. Believing that the independence of Venice would be preserved by protecting its noble aristocratic families and referring to the present dissipation of great fortune in the corruption of "gambling, pomp, and spectacle," his father Andrea charged Tonio to "keep our enemies beyond the gates of the Veneto" (*Cry* 59). Andrea had therefore banished Carlo beyond the gates, but when Carlo returns, it is up to Tonio to assume the true responsibility of a Treschi, a role that confirms his maturity in the same way that Marcel's remaining in New Orleans does. The decisions of both men who have cast off their corrupt fathers (Carlo and Philippe) demonstrate their growth and resolve personal and cultural crises.

While Rice supports transcendence and liberation through light and warmth, she also works with religious associations. Tonio arrives in Florence shortly before Easter, a time of renewal, of the spirit conquering death. Also, Florence seems "as beautiful to him as the sleeping Bethlehem of Christmas paintings" (*Cry* 529), a comparison suggesting birth rather than death. Interestingly, the love of the liberated Christina has been important in leading Tonio toward fulfillment, just as the influence of Christophe Mercier as a teacher has helped to lead Marcel out of darkness in *The Feast*. As the cosmopolitan outsider who leaves Paris and returns to the racial tensions of New Orleans to improve the lot of his own people, the bisexual Christophe is a role model for Marcel and the epitome of someone who rises above an inhumane social morality to assume the personal responsibility his freedom allows. In addition to his teaching, Christophe edits *L'Album litteraire*, published entirely by men of color. However hopeless it may appear at this time, Marcel defends the journal to his Tante Josette and respects Christophe's commitment to his race. According to Ramsland, there is likely significance in the name Christophe, which, as a form of Christopher, the name of Rice's son, suggests a "new beginning" (203). Ramsland's observation would apply as well to Christina, who provides a fresh start for Tonio.

In both of these historical novels as in her gothic fiction, Rice includes sexual liberation as a way of demonstrating personal transcendence. Although they are treated more conservatively in *The Feast of All Saints* than elsewhere, descriptions of sensual awareness and varieties of sexual activity are pertinent to a novel based on alliances between white men and women of color. The origins of white men becoming attracted to black women are traced to the upbringing of white children tended by female slaves. Recalling his own childhood, Vincent reasons: "though he would never truly have given in to the desire to force himself upon one of his slave women, he had known that desire in some place a little less obscure to him than his dreams" (*Feast* 296). It is significant that when Vincent and Anna Bella end their alliance, she consummates her love for Marcel and experiences for the first time the freedom of loving a man of her own race:

For her it had been a surrender of the body and the heart. She had devoured him utterly, his honey-brown skin, his clumsy passion, his feline grace, and it had cast into dim light forever those many nights with Michie Vince when, so eager to please, she had never once thought of herself. (*Feast* 564)

Like other women of color—Celeste, Juliet, Dolly, and finally even Marie—Anna Bella expresses her passionate nature openly. Sexual freedom signifies the importance of greater tolerance, social responsibility, and freedom of personal choice, as it does in *Cry to Heaven*, where Rice describes sexual encounters more graphically.

Indeed, Tonio's experiences with Domenico, Guido, the cardinal, the Count di Stefano, and finally Christina anticipate the explicit sexual erotica that Rice would soon write. These passages also answer questions concerning the capacities left to the castrati, as well as characterizing transcendence through a blending of gender roles. Given the social norm that eunuchs would engage in homosexual relationships, Tonio's heterosexual attachment to Christina violates the status quo. An experienced lover equally comfortable playing female and male roles with his male lovers, he achieves confidence and a fulfilled sexual life through Christina's unconventional attitudes. His sense of renewal is enhanced when he discovers that she is a virgin: "She belonged to him. The sight of the blood on the sheets pushed every other rational thought out of his mind. She was his and she had been no other man's before, and he felt madness, he felt lust" (*Cry* 447). The extent to which the confidence in their relationship gives them both freedom is apparent in the scene where he invites Christina (who is dressed in a soldier's uniform) to get close to him backstage when he is wearing his female costume. In their inverted, carefree roles, they display a rare example of humor in this otherwise dark novel: "Her little hand gathered up his skirt, it felt for the nakedness underneath, and finding the hard organ, grasped it cruelly, so that he whispered under his breath, 'Careful, my darling, let's not ruin what's left' " (*Cry* 473).

Erotic passages and gender issues are central to the larger conflict of forced castration here, as they are in describing the racially mixed unions in *The Feast*. When still unwilling to sing female parts, Tonio believes that he will always "be divided. Always there would be pain. Pain and pleasure, intermingling and working him this way and that, and shaping him, but one never really vanquishing the other; there would never be peace" (*Cry* 275). While he refers to his psychological torment, his vacillation between the pleasure of singing and the burden of revenge, the pain-pleasure principle elsewhere derives from the ecstasy of homosexual encounters and points toward the sadomasochism of Rice's sexual fantasies and erotica.

While she later follows up on sexual exploration as the major catalyst for liberation, here the sexual crises are part of the characters' larger confrontations with inhumane historical realities. In both novels, the protagonists do not seek out affliction in order to be reborn, as John

Donne's persona does in the religious sonnet, but the battering that they undergo is a ravishing of the severest kind. Their suffering at the hands of unfeeling social institutions and cultures and the personal victories they achieve expose social injustice and inhumanity and forecast imminent change. Her two historical novels in relation to the gothics thus reveal the continuity of her existential vision and the variety of her artistic innovations with established literary traditions. The persistent darkness and violence of these fictional worlds challenge the resilience of the human spirit and affirm its capacity for survival.

Works Cited

Dekker, George. *The American Historical Romance*. New York: Cambridge UP, 1987.

Ferraro, Susan. "Novels You Can Sink Your Teeth Into." *New York Times Book Review* 14 Oct. 1990: 27+.

Henderson, Harry B., III. *Versions of the Past: The Historical Imagination in American Fiction*. New York: Oxford UP, 1974.

Holman, C. Hugh, and William Harmon. *A Handbook to Literature*. 6th ed. New York: Macmillan, 1992.

Ramsland, Katherine. *Prism of the Night: A Biography of Anne Rice*. New York: Dutton, 1991.

Rice, Anne. *Cry to Heaven*. New York: Knopf, 1982.

——. *The Feast of All Saints*. New York: Simon & Schuster, 1979.

Degrees of Darkness:
Gens de Couleur Libre Ethnic Identity
in *The Feast of All Saints*

Marte Kinlaw and Cynthia Kasee

Anne Rice seems to have carved out a comfortable niche in contemporary fiction. Writing tales of the supernatural, inhabited by vampires, ghosts, and witches, she builds on a tradition as old as Edgar Allan Poe and as modern as Stephen King. But there is also another group of writers from whom she has drawn inspiration. In an interview she stated

I was always a Southern writer. . . . Books that I have cherished and loved are books like Faulkner's *The Sound and the Fury*. Reading over and over the language in that book and loving it. I feel my writing has always been very much influenced by those lush Southern writers. (Diehl 63)

Faulkner, Welty, O'Connor, McCullers, and others have been described as belonging to a genre known as "Southern gothic." Characteristic of this style is a sense of decay and dissolution, a tension caused by unrevealed secrets and taboos broken, as well as a sense of topicality.

From its very beginning, Anne Rice's writing has been evocative of New Orleans. Although she left the city at the age of fifteen, only to return as an already best-selling novelist, a regional atmosphere has always been present in her work, sometimes obviously, at other times more subtly.

Gens de Couleur Libre

It was while researching for her first book, *Interview with the Vampire* (1977), with many scenes set in antebellum New Orleans that Anne Rice first became aware of a subculture intrinsic to the development of the city of her birth (Ramsland 1991)—the *gens de couleur libre*, or "free people of color."

She was to base her second novel on them, a novel in which she began to develop themes that would echo in later books. From the vampire, the ultimate "outsider," an animated corpse disguised among the living, she moved to the free people of color. Created from both black and white cultures, but belonging to neither and in fact, often despised by and cast out from both, they too were outsiders. Alienated on both sides, they were transfixed in an amorphous middle ground, creating a fragile society with the trappings of tradition that denied and transformed the past.

Their lives were often dictated by random physical manifestations of their genetic makeup, a "lottery" that focused them wholly on complexion and facial features. They equated dark skin and "African features" with primitiveness, evil, ignorance, and shame; conversely, they saw light skin and "white features" as signs of purity, goodness, intelligence, and social mobility. Rather than the symbolic "darkness" of the soul that would color her later work, in this novel—*The Feast of All Saints* (1979)—Rice's characters face a quite literal darkness, a perception of themselves *as* a people based upon skin color and racial purity. Their entire world was defined by degrees of darkness.

In this chapter, some terms should be noted. For purposes of aligning Rice's characters' self-awareness of shade with their cultural affiliation, we have assigned the terms "black" and "colored" to correspond to "African," and *"gens de couleur libre"* or "free people of color," respectively. This is not meant as the authors' endorsement of such division. However, we recognize the historic authenticity of these terms and that these characters dwelt in a world defined by them.

The Feast of All Saints examines this society and its historic context in a two-year period in the lives of four main characters and several minor characters. It is set primarily in New Orleans in the early 1840s, a time when French culture was the daily reality of most Louisianans, but a time also when the fear of growing "American" influence was causing sharp lines of loyalty to be drawn. Essential to Rice's examination of the lives of the colored people is an understanding of the events that lead up to their "creation" and the insidious role that "placage" played in it. Placage was the semirespectable system by which white male planters set up colored women as their mistresses, engendering families of mulatto children acknowledged by the colored but not the white branches on their family trees.

History

As early as 1719, African slaves were being sold in New Orleans (Elfenbein 1989). Africans in this era were coming from the Senegambia region, and as a relatively homogeneous group, they were able to retain a great deal of their culture. Under French rule, slave families were kept intact, African languages were not forbidden, nor were African religions banned. All these elements served to create a very "African" slave population culturally (Hall 1992). While coercive sexual relations were likely already occurring at the white master's prerogative, the cultural "otherness" of these slaves made them seem too "foreign" for planters to want to create the quasi-family structure of placage with them.

The first official mention of free coloreds in New Orleans comes in 1722, just two years after the first two legally sanctioned interracial marriages (Hall 1992; McCants in Desdunes). The nature of the relations that gave rise to this group is not noted, but it is mentioned that free coloreds in early-eighteenth-century New Orleans looked down on black Africans (Shuffleton 1993). This openness about distancing themselves from the African portion of their ancestry may have been the source of some of their acceptability to whites. In fact, the 1725 marriage of Jean Raphael (a Martiniquan *gen de couleur libre*) to Marie Gaspart (a white woman from Flanders), a direct violation of the French Code Noir and the social sanction against colored men having sexual access to white women, appears to have caused little furor (McCants in Desdunes). This is possible evidence of this tolerance of free coloreds due to likemindedness with whites. The shared ancestry and attitudes made them decidedly less "other" than the Africans in the eyes of the French.

"Miscegenation" (interracial sexual congress with or without marriage) in the first decades of the eighteenth century was already a fact of life. It had begun when the French explorers and traders intermarried (or "interbred") with Native American women. The practice carried on when African and mulatto slaves came to Louisiana. This black-and-white miscegenation was less acceptable to French administrators than the red-and-white sort had been.

Toward the ends of reversing this trend, the French Crown sent eighty-eight white women prisoners to New Orleans in 1721. The prisoners were "delinquent women," thought to be more willing to accept the hardiness of New Orleans life than their more genteel counterparts. Although their presumed sexual license was intended to subvert miscegenation, not a single one gave birth to an illegitimate child in this era of scant, unreliable contraception. However, a large number of mulatto babies continued to be born to black or colored women, indicating that behavior was not changing. Even the importation in 1728 of numerous "casket girls"[1] of higher moral expectations failed to stop the practice called "sleeping black." In fact, some casket girls reputedly were co-founders of free colored families (Davis 1991; Dominguez 1986; Elfenbein 1989).

Contrastingly, French policy in Saint-Domingue (the entire island of Hispaniola) did not keep slave families intact, and gave *gens de couleur libre* a large measure of social mobility. The dismantling of

African slave families undermined the passing on of much of their cultures, with the notable exception of religious elements which underpinned voodoo. The "otherness" of the African diminished and French men and African women became the progenitors of a large mixed populace. Initially, this was the result of rape or coercion, but as free coloreds became more aware of the relative freedom they possessed, they actively allied with their white fathers, while clearly distancing themselves from their African mothers.

The children of these unions, acknowledged by their white fathers, born free or freed young, educated and to some extent monied, prospered in a niche that served as a buffer between black and white. These free colored were strongly Francophile and sought complete identification with their French kin by very publicly dissociating from Africans. This did not merely refer to social relations; sexual relations with blacks were cast in the light of disgust, and many free colored took the ultimate step of owning slaves (Davis 1991; Dominguez 1986; Hall 1992).

The active rejection of what would later be termed "negritude" was a double betrayal of an African identity. Not only did blacks view the voluntary social distance of the coloreds as a personal rejection. The refusal to recognize an African cultural background meant the free coloreds were also rejecting their ancestors, and ancestor reverence was an intrinsic element of most traditional African faiths (Hall 1992).

The revolutionary efforts of such as Dessalines and L'Ouverture brought violent change to Saint-Domingue. Whites and coloreds were killed in the uprisings, with many others fleeing to New Orleans for refuge. This second group of free coloreds, those spawned in the social ferment of the West Indies, were the ancestors of the characters in Rice's *Feast*. A bloody insurgency had made them even more contemptuous of Africans than the free coloreds "native" to New Orleans (Davis 1991; Sterkx 1972). Thus, the stage is set for those characters who people *The Feast of All Saints*.

Marcel

The free people of color were faced with a difficult choice, one common to many multiracial/ethnic people, in particular those descended from radically different social and economic strata. They could either conceal part of their heritage or be subject to prejudice and racial animosity. In many cases, the denial of the ancestor in the lower-ranking group was so strong that, after several generations, they were unsure themselves from whom they descended.

In the case of the *gens de couleur libre*, there was little doubt that, traced back far enough, their ancestors would have included slaves.

Anne Rice portrays this in a scene where Marcel Ste. Marie learns that his mother, Cecile, who was taken from Saint-Domingue during the revolution, was the child of a white, French plantation owner and an African slave. This discovery changes his entire perspective, causing him to question for the first time the entrenched institution of slavery that surrounds him. His own birth is the result of a liaison between his mother and another French planter (Philippe Ferronaire), forcing him to examine the effect that this intermingling of blood has had on his life.

"That he was part African . . . anyone could figure, and the white and black blood in him had combined in an unusual way that was extremely handsome and clearly undesirable" (Rice, *Feast* 11). This description of Marcel intimates that his appearance is undesirable in the sense that he could not "pass" for white. It was possible for people of color who bore no obvious African physical traits to marry into white families who were unaware of their heritage. These unions were often successful, although at the expense of contact with members of the family who could not "pass." There was often though the latent fear of children who would bear hereditary evidence of their black forebears.

The "black baby syndrome" is a peculiar malady, centered in the American South. It has long been held (in contradiction of genetic fact) that, even after generations of intermarriage have produced very light-skinned offspring, a very dark-complected baby will be born to one of them (Berry 1963). This myth has been a mainstay of Southern literature[2] and folklore. It has been portrayed as the sad consequence of true, but morally wrong, love. In fact, this cautionary tale was told to keep the color bar intact. Whites feared the ability of "bright mulattoes" (a colloquial term for light-skinned mixed-race people) to "pass" and marry into their families (Woods 1972). Fear of a "black baby" kept whites from marrying people whose family trees were not known. It also forced free coloreds to continue to self-identify, lest they suffer the possibly fatal consequences of being "discovered."

Marcel's revelatory experience brings him up short with respect to his attitude toward blacks, but it also makes him even more aware that, at least in New Orleans, he must stay "in his place." His further revelation that he cannot imagine himself settling down with Anna Bella (his closest friend and lover-for-a-night) for fear a family will tie him forever to this ethnic hierarchy unsettles him. "All his life he had known that he was not white, but snug in the tender advantages of his special world, he had never for a moment dreamed that he was black" (*Feast* 97).

During the time in which *Feast* is set (1842), the pressure was very strong on young "gens" like Marcel to leave New Orleans. As the colored caste grew in number, Irish immigrants and freed slaves swelled the population of the city and opportunities dwindled. Anti-immigrant and antiblack hostilities grew, egged on by the belief that these conditions were worsened by the American presence. It was clearly not a good time to be a well-educated, handsome, ambitious young free colored man, a person whose very existence was evidence that the color hierarchy is not truly sacrosanct.

Spanish rule in Louisiana (1768-1803) had been culturally nominal. French customs continued, including Spanish confirmation of the prevailing racial order. However, the Spanish had made manumission easier, a fact that frightened French whites observing the *gens de couleur libre* ranks swell (Hall 1992; Mencke 1979; Root 1992; Williamson 1980). Their fear was growing that free coloreds would eventually ally with blacks, either inciting rebellion or joining them in insurrection (McCants in Desdunes).

This fear had been fanned in the 1750s when Mackandal, a *gen de couleur* in Saint-Domingue, had rallied blacks and coloreds to poison all whites on the island. Executed in 1758, he became the national martyr the rebels needed, his image fomenting the successes of Dessalines and L'Ouverture. As those refugees mentioned earlier fled to New Orleans, whites panicked at the thought of blood-thirsty blacks making their way to the mainland. Louisiana thus banned importation of Saint-Domingue blacks in 1763, but those free coloreds who were Marcel's ancestors were suspect, and all those decades later, so was he (Hall 1992; Dominguez 1986).

Marcel's progenitors reaped the harvest of black rage in Saint-Domingue and white fear in French New Orleans. By his era, the public presence of the free coloreds made them seem a looming enemy to the white power structure. For one thing, *gens de couleur libre* constituted almost one in four people in New Orleans at this time. For another, interracial unions were no longer discreet. The 1805 census indicated that nearly nine percent of all households in New Orleans were headed by a white man and a black or colored woman (Dominguez 1986). Finally, investigation of the 1795 Point Coupee Conspiracy (a planned slave uprising) had shown several *gens de couleur libre* instigators (Hall 1986).[3]

These powerful forces intent upon curbing the free coloreds' social mobility acted upon Marcel Ste. Marie. So did the long family tradition of the Ferronaires to send their (secret) mixed-raced sons to Paris for higher education. Marcel becomes obsessed with the idea of going to Paris, where he will "become a man" without the legal and social constraints he is becoming all too aware of as he grows older. Secure in the belief that his father, Philippe, will send him abroad when he comes of age, Marcel devotes himself to his studies at the school of Christophe Mercier, whom he greatly admires. Marcel sees Christophe as a role model, a young man of mixed blood who escaped to Paris and published his writing there. Marcel and Christophe share philosophical ideals; Marcel desires above all things to learn, to become an educated man who truly understands things. It is as if, unable to overcome the stigma placed on him by his physical appearance, he will compensate for it by a superior intellect. He is envious of his white half-brothers, thinking that they must have finer books, better tutors. Like most planters' children in that era, Philippe's legitimate sons received as much education as necessary for them to be able to read a few verses in the Bible and keep the accounts of the plantation.

Philippe is content to condescend to Marcel's dreams from afar, calling him "my little scholar" (*Feast* 301) and being indifferently amused by his demonstrations of intelligence, as if they were tricks performed by a trained pet. He is more concerned that Marcel is not being taught to put on airs, acting above his (unfortunate) station in life. When Philippe ultimately refuses to follow through on his promises, Marcel goes to his father's plantation for a face-to-face confrontation that is a pivotal scene in the novel. Typical of the vivid imagery and symbolism Anne Rice is noted for, the building tension of revelation of long-kept secrets is palpable.

Enraged by the appearance of his personified indiscretion on his property, Philippe attacks Marcel with a riding crop in one of the slave cabins. It is Felix, Philippe's slave-footman, who protects Marcel, trying to take the crop's blows for him, keeping Marcel from being beaten to the floor. After this violent rite of passage, Marcel is better able to come to terms with his ancestral past and his African blood. From the "aunt" who took his mother from Saint-Domingue (Tante Josette), he obtains and reads books that give him a sense of pride in what his people were able to accomplish on their own.

Much has been written about the "third generation" principle with respect to immigrants. Recently, it has been applied to the ethnogenesis of contemporary biracial identity (Sollors 1986). In brief, this theory holds that the first generation of a cultural group encountering prolonged contact with another cultural group will strongly maintain their own traditions, often as a defense against acculturation. The second generation will reject the parental traditions, embracing the cultural "other," in an attempt to assimilate and survive. The third generation will view the second as rootless betrayers of their ancestors. Not only will the third generation identify with the customs of the first, they may over-identify to give themselves credibility. This often follows an epiphany of some sort. This is precisely the situation in which Marcel finds himself at his aunt's Cane River plantation library.

While most first-generation African slaves were not permitted to maintain their traditions, those in the French New World often were. Even the Saint-Domingue Africans were able to keep a spiritual identity and tie to the past by syncretizing their beliefs to Roman Catholicism (Hall 1992; Root 1992). Therefore, when Marcel sees the emptiness of Cecile's facade (as a result of this revelation of his African past), he begins the third generation process. Visiting the grounds of a neighboring plantation, he is struck by the architecture of an outbuilding. It reminds him of buildings he has seen in a book on Africa. He finds the house beautiful; that he observes its use as the site of a generative African custom is a telling symbol. This house is the only thing of an African nature defined as beautiful by, and of, the *gens de couleur* in the novel.

Tante Josette is the link between Marcel and his heritage. She is the repository of history, a function that is usually relegated to at least one character in most of Rice's work. Although she herself is the one who "rescued" Marcel's mother from her Africanness, she helps him to understand the chain of events that made him into the person he is. She introduces him to an alternate lifestyle, a world of landowning colored planters who have only tangential relations with their white neighbors. Distanced from both white and black, nevertheless, they live in a world culturally permeated by whiteness, and do not see themselves as having anything in common with their black contemporaries (this whole interlude is based on the life of a real free colored family, the Metoyers, pseudonymically referred to as the "Letoyants" in Woods's *Marginality and Identity: A Colored Creole Family Through Ten Generations* [1972]).

Ultimately, Marcel realizes that the promise of this life free from oppression and prejudice is empty, and that the planters' existence is held together as much by blind will as anything else. But Tante Josette holds out little hope for their future as the Anglo-Saxon mindset takes over from the French and Spanish. Marcel sees for the first time the possible fate of the *gens de couleur.* No longer able to exist in between, they will be forced to move in one direction or the other, either assimilated into the white race or subjugated by it. Still, he decides to return to New Orleans. his newly found sense of self enabling him to face a difficult future.

Anna Bella

The worldview of the *gens de couleur libre* in antebellum New Orleans was essentially Eurocentric, and was shaped by the successive codes of the French and Spanish. The Americans were an encroaching reality that could not be ignored, and their attitude toward mixed-blood people clashed dramatically with Creole society's. To be an American was to be an outsider, tolerated, but never accepted.

The most fully developed character who is presented as an American in *Feast* is that of Anna Bella Monroe. At times in the novel, she functions as a quiet center. As dramatic events and emotional scenes unfold around her, she displays an almost serene self-awareness. While those around her struggle for identity, Anna Bella knows who she is, and it is not what anyone around her thinks her to be.

The orphaned child of freed American slaves, she is described as having "broad African features" (*Feast* 211). Although her skin is white, she is pitied for her African mouth and nose. Throughout the book, there are references to "good hair" and "good noses" (i.e., "white features"). Anna Bella appears unaware of those who snub her behind her back, only hurt by the withdrawal of Marcel Ste. Marie, whom she had grown to love. She realizes that marriage to Marcel is unlikely, because of their age difference and social standing, but she is frightened of the idea of marrying one of the free blacks around her. She is one of the few characters who is troubled by thoughts that she might he displaying prejudice.

The situation is quite different for Anna Bella's counterpoint, Marcel's sister, Marie. While Marcel is becoming aware of all the limitations and obstacles inherent in his inability to "pass," while Anna Bella is being ridiculed for her African features, Marie is constantly being mistaken for white. This fact does not go unnoticed by her mother, Cecile. Described as "a petite white woman carved in dark stone" (*Feast* 322), she is protective of Marcel and jealously resentful of Marie and her Caucasian appearance, although she herself is partly responsible for it. So determined is she to hide all traces of her African ancestry, Richard Lermontant, childhood friend of Marcel and Marie, realizes that he has never heard the mention of color at Cecile's table. Further, he recognizes that he would be unsettled at the thought of mentioning it in her presence. While Anna Bella remains unconcerned with her Africanness, all around her are focused on denying theirs.

Richard becomes involved with Marie, for which his father (Rudolphe) warns him that Cecile Ste. Marie will not approve of her daughter marrying a "colored" man. He cautions that the daughters of placage always follow their mothers' tradition. The tradition involved taking a white "protector," often a man encountered at the Quadroon Balls. By this, mulatto and quadroon women were set up in small houses in the Vieux Carre, where they remained as mistresses until their benefactors married or tired of them. Occasionally, the unions lasted longer, creating quasi-families, unrecognized in the formal sense by the father, but informally seen as more material evidence of the father's prosperity and virility. In such a long-term union, Cecile and Philippe, and many others like them, bore children, diluting the undesirable African blood more with each successive generation.

It is not the sort of willfully racist structure in which we would expect to find Anna Bella, with her racial equanimity, but eventually, she too falls prey to placage.

It is possible to draw an analogy between the characters of Anna Bella and Cecile. Anna Bella is, for all intents and purposes, a black woman with white skin. Cecile is a white woman with black skin. Anna Bella, raised in a familial and cultural environment in which she was not taught to despise her heritage, is able to maintain her personal integrity and will not allow herself to be debased and degraded, even in placage. Cecile on the other hand, although considered by all to be incomparably beautiful and proper in manner, is consumed by a self-loathing that manifests itself in barely-controlled hysteria. She lashes out at all around her, her slaves, her children, her friends—all except for her white lover, whom she treats with an obsequious devotion.

Race and ethnicity are not the same thing. While anthropologists point out that race is not a biological reality, social scientists are well aware of its social reality. Gene frequencies and groupings of phenotypes (observable physical traits) are the stuff of the biological study of human variation. However, the tendency for people to seek easily definable categories of information has lead to the social units called "race."

While many nations categorize mixed-race people into their own groups, the Anglo-dominated United States has never done this (Mencke 1979; Root 1992). The rule of "hypodescent" has been the law of the land; literally, hypodescent means that one drop of blood from a minority group made you a member of that minority group. This was most assiduously applied with black/white mixtures. (Shuffleton 1993; Williamson 1980). The level of paranoia regarding identification of varying degrees of admixtures can be seen in the nine official terms used in French Louisiana to define mixed-bloods[4] (Dominguez 1986; Davis 1991; Root 1992).

Ethnicity is quite another matter. It is the combination of beliefs and behaviors that a group uses to enact their identity. Ethnicity is always changing in response to a group's ideas about itself being changeable. The interplay between the emic (the group's view of itself) and etic (outsiders' views of the group) is what sociologists call "negotiating ethnicity." In order for *gens de couleur libre* to constitute a group separate from blacks/Africans/slaves, and to receive social concessions from the white hegemony, they had to negotiate an ethnicity acceptable to the whites. This was based almost exclusively on a belief that race was the same as ethnicity, and its most essential feature was the rejection of all things black/African (Shuffleton 1993).

As colored preference for light complexion and Caucasian features intensified, more phenotypically white people were born. Continued infusion of white genes with the colored gene pool (through placage, rape, and intermarriage specifically sanctioned by court case) made for a group whose ethnicity was often at odds with genetic reality. As more coloreds were able to "pass," whites forced coloreds to more obviously identify themselves. As early as the 1788 Tignon Law (which forbade free women of color from publicly wearing any headcovering fancier than a bandanna), whites were legally codifying their growing racism (Berzon 1978; Sollors 1986 and 1989).

In this atmosphere, the idea that a person who was phenotypically white and French in culture was actually white, although the result of racial mixing, was anathema. In this structure of predicating ethnicity on race, Cecile and most of the other free coloreds were obsessively focused on racial purity; however, it is apparent that Anna Bella stands as an example of a person who understood that identity and perception were not bound by facial features and skin tone.

La Famille Lermontant

On the wall of the house of the Famille Lermontant there hung a portrait of Jean Baptiste, a mulatto slave who was freed before the Spanish acquisition. Taking the surname of his master, he founded the family that, by 1842, was a bastion of bourgeois respectability. "We're talking about a caste . . . that has won its precarious place in this corrupt quagmire by asserting . . . that it is composed of men who are better than and different from slaves" (*Feast* 279). Rudolphe Lermontant heads this family, an undertaker who counted both white and black among his clientele. He is intelligent, a discerning man who understands the tenuousness of his people's position.

Families like his were in contrast to the households of placage. They married other free coloreds, their skin color or lighter, generally. Rice points out that Richard Lermontant would consider marriage to Marie Ste. Marie, who appeared Caucasian, even though she is illegitimate, whereas he would never marry someone like Anna Bella, light skinned, but African featured. Anna Bella would taint the Lermontant lineage. They believed themselves to be the responsible factor that allowed the *gens de couleur libre* to exist as a class. Mrs. Lermontant (Suzette) was even a member of the Benevolent Society, whose function was to provide for poor colored children.

The house of the Lermontants is based upon the Hermann-Grima House in the French Quarter (Ramsland 1991). It is referred to in the novel as a citadel-like, imposing façade. It presents a face of dignity and conformity to the outside world, while within, it allowed the family to be proud of an ancestor representing their humble beginnings with roots in the subculture that became the demimondaine.

When the teacher, Christophe, brings his young slave, Bubbles, into the classroom with the children of the prosperous free coloreds, he is given a lesson in how sharp the lines of division are drawn between free colored and slave. In a matter of days, the wealthy coloreds withdraw their children from the school. It is Rudolphe who must remind the idealistic Christophe of the realities of the world in which they live. Whatever their actions in private, in public they could not ally with slaves against a white society that feared their combined strength. In defense of their submissive position, the slaves rarely revealed knowledge about themselves, protecting what little individuality they possessed. They hoarded information about their masters as currency, passing it along a secretive grapevine. This knowledge could be revealed for remuneration, or presented as one might bestow a gift or favor.

The society of the slave thus remained a mystery to their owners, and their customs were looked upon as superstitious and barbarian. In particular, whites had a fear of voodoo, as shown by the vilification of Lola Dede, the voodooienne. When it becomes obvious that Lisette, Cecile's slave, is having dealings with the mambo (voodoo priestess), she is reprimanded and warned that she will be punished if the behavior continues. It was by such stringent rejection of African elements that *gens de couleur libre* kept their fine homes, professions, and family reputations.

Lisette grew to maturity with the promise of her eventual manumission held in front of her like the proverbial carrot on a stick. Told by her father (and master), Phillipe, that she would be freed when she came of age, provided she was compliant, she is installed in Cecile's household, slave to a woman who has supplanted her mother in Philippe's bed. As Lisette watches her half-siblings reap the benefits of their mother's sexual barter, she and her mother are wholly dependent upon Philippe's whims, a man whose tendency is to do whatever is the most convenient thing for him.

As Philippe's two acknowledged and one unacknowledged bastards move toward adulthood under the same roof, tensions escalate. Lisette becomes involved in voodoo as a means of asserting some control, in much the same way she trades on the slaves' secret grapevine of information. She will never be accepted into a society that reveres European values, whether it be peopled by whites or free coloreds, so she becomes more and more "African" in response. This also provides her with a means to dominate her free siblings, as most *gens de couleur* regarded voodoo with a mixture of fear and awe.

Lola Dede embodies voodoo and thus, all things African. Voodoo, Shango, Candomble, Obea—words that struck fear in Euro-Americans. That all these faiths derived from aboriginal traditions of Nago (Yoruba), Ibo, Dahomey (Fon), and other nations made them no more palatable to whites. In rigidly Catholic Louisiana, voodoo was simply demonic. People (usually adherents) died from voodoo curses, and whites and free coloreds feared they could be next. They forbade slaves from attending services, except the Congo Square dances they (wrongly) believed innocuous. Even rationalists who discounted the African beliefs' mystical power justly respected its repertoire of poisons (harkening back to Mackandal's call) (Hall 1992).

Therefore, the voodoo priestess and her religion exemplified the dangerous "otherness" of the African. That slaves managed to attend services anyway, and used the events to pass information, made voodoo a formidable tool. Throughout this novel, and many other works on this locale, this powerful secret sect is portrayed as the one totally African thing that slavery could not strip away. As such, it is the cultural enemy of the fragile gentility of La Famille Lermontant *and* the Ste. Maries, themselves the faces of respectability (and semi-respectability) in *gens de couleur libre* society.

Lisette's involvement with Lola Dede is not just based on faith; there are allusions to possible prostitution at the mambo's home. In this way, Lisette could enact rebellion by selling herself, in essence "stealing," since she is the property of another. A respectable union for Lisette with another slave is clearly not in the cards, as Philippe would not want his bloodline sullied by mixture with a black man's.

When Philippe dies without freeing Lisette, and a desperate Cecile takes out her anger and fear by threatening to sell Lisette into the fields, Lisette takes her revenge on the whole free colored stratum. She has vicariously enjoyed watching Marie's introduction to polite society, knowing that her white skin will buy her a comfortable protector. Now she turns on Marie, fooling her into trust, then taking her to Lola Dede's, where Marie is drugged and gang-raped by white men. Marie is now "ruined" for a decent man, brought low in accord with her slave half-sister's station in life. Lisette's purpose is derailing Marie's ability to settle into a comfortable placage; Marie had designs to marry Richard Lermontant, though, and this incident makes her an unacceptable choice for the Lermontant family. No daughter-in-law of Rudolphe Lermontant would be caught in a voodoo den, where she was virtually inviting the sexual assault that occurred.

Rice makes it apparent that Rudolphe understands his own hypocrisy. He is made painfully aware of his people's dangerous social position between white and black when his daughter, Giselle, is accosted by a white man from Virginia. He believes her to be fair game for his sexual advances, as it is inconceivable to him that "nigger women got up like Southern belles" (*Feast* 354) could have another purpose besides pandering to a white man's desires.

When Rudolphe impulsively attacks the man in the street, he is arrested, jailed, and charged with assault and with verbally insulting a white man. Historically, the latter crime alone could have resulted in Rudolphe's exile from Louisiana, or five years of forced labor and expulsion (Davis 1991; Dominguez 1986).

In the ensuing trial, charges against Rudolphe are dismissed, but only after a patronizing address from the bench, in which he is forced to accept that his good luck is the result of a presumption that he is naturally inferior to a white man. Rudolphe should have known better, but in light of the circumstances, he would not be held to account. In another situation, the judge implies, involving a person with less standing in the community, the outcome might have been drastically different.

It is also implicit that, in this case, the Virginian is viewed as the outsider. The judge and Rudolphe are both aware of the ways in which he is expected to keep his place. The citizens of New Orleans considered themselves to be urbane and sophisticated, whereas the uneducated stranger, with his tirade about lynching "negras" is clearly not. The underlying sensibility of the judge seems to be, we will take care of our own problems with the coloreds in our own way, implying that the free coloreds are theirs to do with as they wish.

Conclusion

Primary to Anne Rice's work is the concept that good and evil are perceived in a relative fashion, dependent upon each individual's system of belief. Each community establishes within itself the parameters of acceptable behavior, but how are the boundaries derived? Morality is defined by group consensus, but that consensus can be changeable and inconsistent. In *The Feast of All Saints*, good and evil are equated by the in-group as being literally allied with lightness and darkness. Even here though, their parameters are inconsistent within a generation and changeable across generations.

The Feast of All Saints was one of Anne Rice's least successful novels. When it was originally released in 1979, it sold fewer than twenty thousand copies. It is a novel that is difficult to characterize, and received mixed reviews, some decidedly hostile (Ramsland 1991). It has been said that the novel might have been better received had the author been African American or the work a more direct social commentary.

Anne Rice was to write only one other historical novel, *Cry to Heaven* (1982), which was also not well received before she decided she was not suited to the genre. Her later novels often involved historical settings, but never with the same detail or emphasis. In *The Feast of All Saints*, a unique social comment *is* made, but it may not be the most obvious one. Whatever its success or failure on a literary level, it is an honest and painstaking attempt at the portrayal of a people who might not otherwise come to the attention of the general reader. In the years since its publication, the field of research on the story of the free people of color has expanded dramatically. It is these stories—stories of real people whose lives were paralleled by the characters in Anne Rice's novel—that must be preserved and cherished.

Notes

1. "Casket girls" were so called because they brought their few possessions with them to Louisiana in small wooden boxes shaped somewhat like caskets.

2. Notably, DuBose Heyward's 1931 *Brass Ankle, A Play in Three Acts*.

3. More famous slave uprisings, such as those lead by Nat Turner (1831) and Denmark Vesey (1845), also included mixed-race and/or free colored people among the abettors. However, it should be noted that the Point Coupee Conspiracy germane to this article included white and Native American co-conspirators, the revelation of which did not discernably increase fear of these groups.

4. Terms are as follows, with admixtures noted in "blood quanta": "Mango" or "Sacatra" (7/8B, 1/8W), "Sambo" or "Griffe" (3/4B, 1/4W), "Quadroon" (1/4B, 3/4W), "Octoroon" (1/8B, 7/8W), "Mustee" (any mix of black and American Indian), "Meamelouc" (1/16B, 15/16W), "Sang-mele" (1/64 B, 63/64W).

References

Berry, Brewton. *Almost White*. Toronto: Macmillan, 1963.

Berzon, Judith R. *Neither White Nor Black: The Mulatto Character in American Fiction*. New York: New York UP, 1978.

Davis, F. James. *Who Is Black? One Nation's Definition*. University Park: Pennsylvania State UP, 1991.

Desdunes, Rodolphe L. *Our People and Our History: A Tribute to the Creole People of Color in Memory of the Great Men They Have Given Us and of the Good Works They Have Accomplished*. Ed. and trans. Sr. Dorothea Olga McCants. 1911. Baton Rouge: Louisiana State UP, 1973.

Diehl, Digby. "Playboy Interview: Anne Rice." *Playboy* Mar. 1993: 53-64.

Dominguez, Virginia R. *White by Definition: Social Classification in Creole Louisiana*. New Brunswick: Rutgers UP, 1986.

Elfenbein, Anna S. *Women on the Color Line: Evolving Stereotypes and the Writings of George Washington Cable, Grace King, Kate Chopin*. Charlottesville: UP of Virginia, 1989.

Hall, Gwendolyn M. *Africans in Colonial Louisiana: The Development of Afro-Creole Culture in the Eighteenth Century*. Baton Rouge: Louisiana State UP, 1992.

Heyward, DuBose. *Brass Ankle, A Play in Three Acts*. New York: Farrar, 1931.

Mencke, John G. *Mulattoes and Race Mixture: American Attitudes and Images, 1865-1918*. N.p.: UMI Research, 1979.

Ramsland, Katherine. *Prism of the Night: A Biography of Anne Rice*. New York: Dutton, 1991.

Rice, Anne. *The Feast of All Saints*. 1979. New York: Ballantine, 1986.

——. *Interview with the Vampire*. 1976. New York: Ballantine, 1977.

Root, Maria P.P. *Racially Mixed People in America*. Newbury Park: Sage, 1992.

Shuffleton, Frank, ed. *A Mixed Race: Ethnicity in Early America*. New York: Oxford UP, 1993.

Sollors, Werner. *Beyond Ethnicity: Consent and Descent in American Culture*. New York: Oxford UP, 1986.

——. *The Invention of Ethnicity*. New York: Oxford UP, 1989.

Sterkx, H.E. *The Free Negro in Ante-Bellum Louisiana*. Rutherford: Fairleigh Dickinson UP, 1972.

Williamson, Joel. *New People: Miscegenation and Mulattoes in the United States*. New York: Free, 1980.

Woods, Frances Jerome. *Marginality and Identity: A Colored Creole Family Through Ten Generations*. Baton Rouge: Louisiana State UP, 1972.

The World of *Forever Knight*:
A Television Tribute to Anne Rice's New Age Vampire

James F. Iaccino

Before we see how Anne Rice's first novel in *The Vampire Chronicles, Interview with the Vampire* (1976), has impacted on the television medium, let us briefly examine how the image of the vampire has changed in horror films over the last seven decades. This should give us the proper historical perspective to make any later correlations between the Rice novel and one vampire teleseries in particular, *Forever Knight*, which has attained a cult status since its premiere in 1992.

Vampire Film History

The screen's very first vampire film, *Nosferatu* (1922), presented Count Orlock as a "walking skeleton" of horror. His domed hairless scalp, pointed ears, and long tapering fingers contributed to the "living corpse" appearance. As the film proceeded, Orlock's looks became progressively more repellent; this, no doubt, was due to the vampire's surroundings of the trappings of death—"funerals, disease, pestilence, even hordes of crawling rats following in his wake" (Everson, *Classics* 192; Skal 53-54).

Tod Browning's 1931 version of *Dracula* was the next significant film to cast the vampire in a totally different image. Now we have an "impeccably groomed Bela Lugosi" as the Lord of the Undead, who possesses all the charms and social graces of the Stoker, Old World nobleman (Everson, *More Classics* 32). His eastern European accent allowed Lugosi to emphasize every word with a theatrical abandon. He also invested a good deal of energy in the count's role, most notably in the assorted hand gestures (which have become the vampire's trademark) and the penetrating eyes upon the victim's neck.

It was not until the late 1950s that the vampire would resurface in another interpretation, this time from the London Hammer Studios. Actor Christopher Lee made a conscious effort not to recreate the Lugosi characterization in his *Horror of Dracula* (1958). Rather, he gave his version a more restrained type of sophistication, coupled with an almost superhuman strength when confronting his enemies. Perhaps the most interesting feature of the Lee portrayal was his sex appeal: women found him strangely attractive and even desirable. Later films in the Hammer series (*Dracula Prince of Darkness*, 1965; *Dracula Has Risen from the Grave*, 1969) would capitalize on this theme, emphasizing the victim's erotic addiction to the kiss of the vampire. What was only implied in the Stoker novel became much more sexually explicit in these Dracula cinematic incarnations (Preiss 270). Unfortunately, after fifteen years of playing the part of the infamous count, a much older (and far less sensual) Lee decided to end his vampiric career with *The Satanic Rites of Dracula* (1973). Even though the production values deteriorated in the later Dracula entries (especially *Taste the Blood of Dracula,* 1970, and *The Scars of Dracula*, 1971), the Hammer Studios should still be credited for giving the vampire a real sexual potency and vitality that most definitely affected later portrayals such as Frank Langella's *Dracula* of 1979 (McCarty 26).

Television was also able to offer up a compelling image of the cursed wanderer in the mid-1960s with the daytime gothic soap, *Dark Shadows*. When 175-year-old vampire, Barnabas Collins (characterized brilliantly by Jonathan Frid), came to Collinwood, audiences immediately were drawn to the suave, middle-aged man with the mysterious past. In the course of the series, it was revealed that Barnabas was not always a creature of the night. The curse of immortality was placed upon him by a spurned lover, Angelique, who just so happened to dabble in the deadly arts of sorcery and witchcraft. The vampire's sole desire was to free himself from the "undead" state so that he could live a normal existence and marry his reincarnated love, Josette duPres (Leigh-Scott 121-28). A temporary cure to Barnabas's condition was found when Dr. Julia Hoffman was able to isolate the destructive vampiric cell in his bloodstream. But the treatments proved to be so potent that they nearly destroyed the vampire in the process of healing him; thus, it became clear to Barnabas he could never change what he was fated to be. *Dark Shadows* became so popular that a film treatment of this vampire story line was made in 1970, entitled *House of Dark Shadows*.

What distinguishes *House* from other films is its concentration on the more human qualities of the vampire, not the least of which is the loathing of his (no longer "its") own shadow nature and an almost fanatical desire to change the circumstances, if possible (Iaccino 68). Vampires like *Count Yorga* (1970), the interracial *Blacula* (1972) and even *Bram Stoker's Dracula* (both the 1974 television movie and the 1992 Coppola production) owe a good deal to Barnabas Collins; he became the prototype of what the bloodsucker is today: fair of face and very sensual, yet deeply angst-ridden over his condition. One need only see Ben Cross in the 1990s television remake of *Dark Shadows* to determine the extent to which the vampire has acquired his own unique film personality (Pierson 12-14). We have left behind the one-dimensional, repulsive Nosferatu character and have given the undead an assortment of very human, three-dimensional attributes, which will, no doubt, continue to grow in the horror genre in the decades to come.

Interview's Further Development of the Cinematic Vampire

Previous to Rice's *Interview with the Vampire*, there were few films that emphasized the homosexual (or for that matter, lesbian) nature of vampires. The ones that did came from Hammer and were variations of Le Fanu's *Carmilla* (1872) or the Countess Bathory story (Eyles, Adkinson, and Fry 51-52, 55-56). Polish emigree Ingrid Pitt was able to exude the necessary sensuality in her role as the vampire stalking her female victims and drinking (or bathing in) their blood. Memorable titles as *Lust for a Vampire* (1970), *The Vampire Lovers* (1971) and *Countess Dracula* (1972) gave Hammer the boost it needed to stay afloat a few more years in the movie industry; however, as Pirie observes, the lesbian-type of vampire never became the acceptable image since it was a drastic move away from the cinematic tradition of an immortal with strong heterosexual urges (123). Luckily, Anne Rice resuscitated this fascinating archetype at a time when studios were not being especially creative or innovative.

The homosexual tone of *Interview* is manifested in the earliest pages when the recently converted Louis sleeps face-down in Lestat's coffin. Though there is a certain distaste for being so close to the one who made him a vampire, Louis is nevertheless attracted to the handsome creature. Louis's first kill also happens to be a male slave—not the typical female who swoons at the vampire's touch. While he is drinking from the neck of the victim, Louis becomes so hypnotized by the feeding ritual that he does not realize he is still draining the man's blood until well after his death. This act is comparable to a communal ecstasy, of two same-sexed lives becoming unified through the spilling of blood. Furthermore, Louis's relationship with the vampire Armand is most explicit in its sensuality. Louis describes his longing for Armand in such strong terms that he can barely contain himself. All he can do is stare at the beautiful creature, basking in his glow, wishing his mentor Lestat could be as loving towards him (Rice, *Interview* 24, 29, 256).

Another change can be observed in the Rice text, namely, the vampire's apparent invulnerability to religious objects. Louis tells the interviewer that he is not repelled by crosses; in fact, he loves to look upon crucifixes whenever the opportunity presents itself. As far as the traditional means of disposing a vampire with a wooden shaft through the heart, it is pure "bull-shit . . . [and has] no magical power whatsoever" (*Interview* 23). One can infer that a good deal of the vampire myth is utter superstition, passed down from one generation to the next in order to make the creature more heathenish and completely without redemption.

We can trace the roots of Rice's areligious conception to the Hammer Films once more. In *Dracula Has Risen from the Grave*, Christopher Lee is staked in his coffin, yet is able to remove the shaft from his heart and throw it at his attackers before fleeing the violated premises. Though Lee protested against the insertion of this sequence, the groundwork had been established for a major reformulation of the vampire myth (Eyles, Adkinson, and Fry 99). (The earlier *Horror of Dracula* was already toying with the idea of having the vampire limited to the human form, unable to change into such creatures of the night as the bat or wolf.) The 1970s continued to depict some significant alterations, the most notable being presented in *The Night Stalker* (1972) and *Dracula A.D. 1972*. Here we have two films in which the vampire shows absolutely no fear of the cross. The *Night Stalker* vampire, Janos Skorzeny, advances upon the contemporary version of Dr. Van Helsing, eccentric reporter Carl Kolchak, with little hesitation even though Kolchak brandishes a huge metal cross directly in Janos's face (Kaminsky and Mahan 127). Likewise, in Hammer's 1972 updated version of Dracula, the count is able to grab the crucifix around Jessica Van Helsing's neck and fling it aside without too much trouble, apart from some minor burns around the hand that held the object. The cinema had set the stage for Rice, allowing her to go one step further by eliminating the need to have any religious articles whatsoever in her vampire stories.

Finally, up until *Interview,* the vampire was usually cast as a middle-aged to older type of immortal, with experienced actors like Lee or Frid playing the major roles. Of course, there were the exceptions such as the David Peel portrayal of Count Meinster in Hammer's 1960 *Brides of Dracula* (Iaccino 28; Pirie 81). Upon reading *Interview*, one immediately detects how young *all* the vampires look. Louis is in his mid-twenties (and Lestat is not that much his senior), while Claudia is only a child of five. Interestingly, films after *Interview*'s publication assimilated the youthful archetype into their creatures. Frank Langella, Ben Cross, and Geraint Wyn Davies (of *Forever Knight* fame) became the popular culture icon, possessing all the right characteristics including the appropriate maturity to complement the "pretty boy" appearance (Guiley 68).

Correlations Between Forever Knight *and* Interview

One would think that after the failure of the prime-time television version of *Dark Shadows* (1991) and the syndicated *Dracula: The Series* (1990–91), another vampire show would not be able to capture the attention of most viewers. However, there were reasons for the demise of the former programs. The *New Dark Shadows* was preempted several times by an "untimely international incident . . . the Gulf War had begun" (Pierson 20). And *Dracula*'s episodes had only thirty minutes in which to tell their stories, a period far too brief to sufficiently focus on the contemporary image of the count, one Alexander Lucard (that's "Dracul" spelled backward), whose identity had been discovered by the descendants of Van Helsing.

All this changed with the premiere of the late-night CBS teleseries, *Forever Knight* (1992), which was loosely based on an unsold television pilot, *Nick Knight* (1989). By airing the one-hour program in this block of time, the network realized *Forever Knight* would not have to contend with many other competitive shows, thus allowing it to acquire a cult following very early on in its run. When CBS bought the rights to *David Letterman,* it was forced to eliminate all its "After Prime Time" programming, including its most popular entry, *Forever Knight.* Fortunately, the loyal fans were able to convince many syndicated markets to continue the *Knight* show in a second season of episodes. The timing could not have been better. Interest in the vampire genre, according to a *Forever Knight* press kit, was "extremely high . . . [given] Columbia Pictures financially successful *Bram Stoker's Dracula* . . . the upcoming movie based on Anne Rice's bestseller, *Interview with the Vampire*; and Rice's fourth volume of the popular Vampire Chronicles, *The Tale of the Body Thief*" (Press Release, *Forever Knight*). *Forever Knight* was able to survive another season because of the aforementioned factors, and the hopes were that it would move beyond cult-show status with its prime-time premiere on the USA Cable Network in fall of 1995.

When *Forever Knight* was being conceived, it was no surprise that Canadian actor Geraint Wyn Davies was selected as the lead vampire, Nicolas Knight. He had played the role of Jonathan Harker in a stage production of *Dracula* and was also a semi-regular on *Dracula: The Series*, playing Van Helsing's overly neurotic vampire son, Klaus (Bloch-Hansen, "Forever" 51). Rounding out the cast of vampires were Nick's mentor, LaCroix (Nigel Bennett) and his former vampire mate, Janette (Deborah Duchene). Bennett had an extensive history of horror series credits before joining the *Forever Knight* team, including diabolical parts on *Friday the 13th* (1988) and *Beyond Reality* (1991). He also studied the Bram Stoker novel before doing a stage version of *Dracula*, and finally had an opportunity to read Anne Rice's *Interview* before the second season of *Knight* got underway (Bloch-Hansen "Unlife" 55). Duchene herself was involved with such horror teleseries as *Beyond Reality* and played the character of Lucy Seward in *Dracula* on stage. Since all three actors had some knowledge of the vampire genre, they were able to bring fascinating interpretations to their *Knight* roles and quickly developed the proper chemistry for the series' successful triad.

Let us now note some of the more striking similarities between *Forever Knight* and Rice's *Interview with the Vampire*, beginning with a plot analysis and then a consideration of some of the major themes to both the series and novel.

Plot Comparisons Between Knight *and* Interview

Upon first glance, it would appear that *Forever Knight* and *Interview with the Vampire* have nothing in common. While both have youngish-looking vampires, Nicolas Knight and Louis Pointe du Lac, *Forever Knight* inserts its creature more within a modern setting than *Interview*. Nick is a vampire cop working the graveyard shift who uses his special powers to battle crime in the streets of Toronto, Canada. Like many contemporary superheroes, he can fly as well as see in the dark, plus he has the extra advantage of possessing the bat's supersensitive hearing. All these abilities make Nick an unstoppable force, and his human partner, Detective Don Schanke (John Kapelos), often wonders how he is able to solve cases so quickly without the typical police backup. Promotions for the show continued to emphasize the crime-fighting aspects of *Knight* well into its second season ("See a vampire take a bite out of crime" [Press Release, *Forever Knight*]); yet, there is a more significant component to the program that should not be over-looked. *Knight* is about a cursed wanderer who wants to regain his mor-tality and live a normal existence, rather than being continually consumed by the savage bloodlust. (In fact, Nick hopes that by protect-ing and serving humanity in his role as a policeman, he can come that much closer to redemption for all the sins he committed over the past centuries.) The vampire's angst-ridden nature is the major element that holds the teleseries together and is what ultimately links the Rice novel to its very core (Johnson 78).

In the two-part opener, entitled "Dark Knight," flashbacks are used very effectively by series creator and producer, James Parriott, to show viewers how Nicolas was brought over to vampirism in the year 1228. After being bitten by LaCroix (Nigel Bennett), Nick is initiated in a satanic ceremony in which he completely drains a human female of her blood (Melton 225). Nick enjoys hearing the heartbeat of the victim get progressively weaker as he removes the life essence from her. The parallels to the Anne Rice text are hardly coincidental. Similar to LaCroix, Lestat has made sure to secure a human in order to train his sweet Louis in performing his first kills back in 1791. When Louis plants his teeth in the neck of the captured servant, he too is mesmerized by the sucking noise and the beat of the man's heart growing slower and slower seemingly without end (Rice, *Interview* 29). Both LaCroix and Lestat monitor these proceedings, making sure that their vampire "sons" perform the feeding ritual properly. Their respective statements, "You can't deny what you are," and "You can't turn back now," reflect the strong power these vampire mentors exert over their students. One might almost say LaCroix and Lestat are personifications of the Jungian shadow, the dark side of the vampire's nature (Iaccino 189-90). They play a vital role in reminding Nicolas and Louis what they really are (i.e., immortal and amoral creatures of the night) as well as what they can never be again (i.e., the frail humans of a past life).

Janette (Deborah Duchene) is also introduced in the pilot movie. Although her part is brief, we learn that she and Nick lived with LaCroix for many years; moreover, Janette has had a sensual relationship with Nicolas for at least a century's duration and understands his aversion to taking human lives though she herself has no such pangs of conscience (Melton 225; Show Description, *Forever Knight*). It is her love for Nicolas that allows her to be his important confidante throughout the ages. Later episodes expand upon these personality characteristics of Janette. Apart from her "demon child" appearance, *Interview*'s Claudia bears a remarkable resemblance to Janette in attitude and disposition. Both enjoy preying on the humans, taking great satisfaction in each kill they make (*Interview* 102). Yet they are still drawn to their tortured vampire mate (Nicolas and Louis), hoping their love will be the effective cure for the frenzied state each experiences. Janette and Claudia, moreover, are instrumental in freeing their companion from the head vampire's clutches, thereby dissolving the long-established vampiric trinity. While the young Claudia employs a more drastic means of ridding herself from Lestat (first poisoning him, then stabbing him multiple times, and finally drowning him), the older and wiser Janette is much more subtle in her approach. She helps Nicolas assume new identities and book passage on various vessels; she even uses her abilities as a vampire to keep LaCroix from doing permanent harm to her former lover. The vampiric triad of the series and Rice novel will be examined in greater detail in the next section of this chapter.

Pertaining to the death of the vampire mentor, the "Dark Knight" opener has Nick liquidating LaCroix in a fashion highly reminiscent of

Mademoiselle Claudia's own bloodthirsty techniques used on Lestat. Nick first spears LaCroix with a meat hook and then sends a flaming wooden spear directly into his chest. (It should be mentioned that the movements of the vampires occur at faster than normal speeds as they struggle to the death. Credit should be given to Anne Rice as the first to imbue the vampires with this fascinating ability to supplement their incredible strength and hypnotic powers [*Interview* 25].) Naturally, Nick believes that LaCroix is consumed in the resulting blaze. However, the master returns in the final episode of *Knight*'s first season, appropriately entitled "Love You to Death." Similar to Lestat's reappearance at the end of *Interview*, LaCroix is whole and still a mighty force to be reckoned with as the *Knight* series progressed into its second year of episodes. One comes away from the teleseries and novel wondering whether anything could ultimately kill such powerful creatures as LaCroix and Lestat. Perhaps Lestat best sums it up by communicating to the reader that sunlight, fire, even a stake through the heart, might have little effect on those who have learned to accept (and live with) their immortal condition (Rice, *Lestat* 3).

Thematic Comparisons Between Knight and Interview

Given this brief plot analysis, we will now deal with the dominant themes of the *Forever Knight* show and attempt to correlate them with the *Interview* text. The ones most salient to this reviewer are the vampiric trinity's father, the "love-hate" mentor-student relationship, and the macro-vampiric groups of the given period.

The vampiric trinity's father. LaCroix and Lestat are the vampire fathers of the respective series and chronicles. Both Nicolas and Janette refer to themselves as LaCroix's children for he has made them "flesh of his flesh, blood of his blood, kin of his kin" (Stoker 293). In Lestat's opinion, Louis and Claudia are also beholden to him since he has decided to share the gift of immortality with them. In fact, Lestat makes Claudia a vampire so that he can continue to keep Louis as his eternal companion as well as assist him in the rearing of their new daughter (*Interview* 92-95). LaCroix uses Janette in pretty much the same manner, only in this case it is her attraction as a sexual mate (not a helpless child who requires the proper adult supervision) that bonds Nicolas to his master. And so each vampire family, consisting of two males and one female, is held together by its most powerful member, the vampiric father.

Noted psychoanalyst Carl Jung describes the father image as one of the strongest archetypes in human history because it can affect the entire psychological development of those placed under the parent's charge.

Jung attributes an almost supernatural, even vampiric quality, to this mythical father: "He is possessed of a quite extraordinary power . . . he is held fast and fascinated by it and uses this magical influence on his children . . . making them into slavish puppets [doing his will for the remainder of their lives]" (*Freud* 315-16). This is a good depiction of how Lestat and Lacroix treat the members of their triad, as dependents who cannot grow or develop without their influence and continual presence. Unfortunately, it is this very inability of the vampire fathers to recognize their "children" as individuals with their own unique destinies to fulfill that leads to an outright family rebellion on the charges' part and an eventual disintegration of the vampiric trinity.

Forever Knight's LaCroix physically matches some of the more prominent characteristics of the father archetype, including his age and acquired wisdom (Hopcke 104). Lucian LaCroix is one of the more ancient vampires who survived the last days of Pompeii, as disclosed in the episode "A More Permanent Hell." Throughout his two thousand years of immortality, the elderly (yet very sophisticated) mentor has accumulated enough knowledge of human history to pass on to his vampire offspring, Nicolas and Janette. His career as a proconsul in the Roman legions before becoming a vampire has provided LaCroix with the proper training to be an effective leader among the mortals and has allowed him to maintain his vampire family for at least several centuries' duration (Johnson 81).

On the other hand, *Interview*'s vampiric father, Lestat de Lioncourt, is neither as old as LaCroix nor does he have the level of experience necessary to hold his nuclear family together for long. His physical features are described in the opening section of *The Vampire Lestat*. He is six feet tall, has thick blonde hair, and is a fairly young immortal who was approximately twenty years of age when the curse of the undead was placed upon him by a dying vampire named Magnus (*Lestat* 3, 79-97). Inheriting Magnus's fortune, he seeks out the ancient Marius who explains how the vampiric lineage began in ancient Egypt. Lestat then travels to New Orleans and there encounters Louis and Claudia (which is the start of the *Interview* tale). It is not surprising that after several decades of living together, his offspring attempt to kill him. It has only been half a century that Lestat has been in the vampiric state (from 1760 to the beginning of the 1800s), and like his very young children, he too requires further schooling from an elder such as Marius (Melton 366-67). While LaCroix and Lestat are both fathers, clearly the former can handle the parental responsibilities much better and keep his vampiric trinity intact throughout the ages. To a certain degree, *Forever Knight*'s LaCroix is a blend of the paternal Lestat and the omniscient Marius; this mix of "Ricean" features definitely creates a more intriguing image of the vampire mentor on the small screen.

The "love-hate" mentor-student relationship. According to Jung, a common characteristic of many archetypes, or "universal images which have existed since the remotest times" (*Archetypes* 5), is that they possess an ambivalence, having the potential for positivity as well as negativity, inspiration as well as destruction (Hopcke 16). The way the vampire copes with the "lost" human side is laden with a good deal of Jungian ambivalence. By embracing the new existence of an immortal, the supernatural creature must abandon *all* human wants and desires including love and companionship (Leigh-Scott 127). This dilemma may not be effectively resolved for every vampire novitiate, and so alternating feelings of attraction and repulsion are occasionally directed toward the masters who inducted them into the vampiric state.

Interview's Lestat is continually disappointed that Louis is unwilling to accept his vampire nature. He points out to Louis on several occasions the following facts:

Vampires are killers . . . whose all-seeing eyes were meant to give them detachment. . . . They are lone predators and seek for companionship no more than cats in the jungle . . . and if you find one or more of them together it will be for safety only, and one will be the slave of the other, the way you [Louis] are of me. (*Interview* 83-84)

More than anything else, Lestat wants Louis to enjoy killing humans as much as he does. Since the student does not follow his teachings, preferring to destroy animal life instead of human, Lestat begins to reject Louis and all of his moralistic principles.

Lestat especially despises Louis's yearning to return to the mortal state. He finds such a goal unfathomable and does not want Louis to entertain the possibility of going back to the human form. Yet, time and time again Louis considers what it would be like to be flesh and blood, much to the chagrin of the mentor. These are some of the comments delivered by Lestat to Louis when such tense situations arise:

Louis . . . you are in love with your mortal nature! You chase after the phantoms of your former self . . . and in your romance with mortal life, you're dead to your vampire nature! . . . You cannot, as a man, go back to the nursery and play with your toys, asking for the love and care to be showered on you again simply because now you know their worth. So it is with you and your mortal nature. You've given it up. You no longer look "through a glass darkly." But you cannot pass back to the world of human warmth with your new eyes. (*Interview* 81-82)

Though the words of Lestat are honest and truthful, Louis would rather pursue a dream of his making than live the more depressing, yet realistic, existence of his teacher.

As soon as Louis decides to leave Lestat and go his own way, the master turns the child, Claudia, into one of the undead so that Louis will feel some "human" obligation for her upbringing. This is the major turning point in the *Interview* mentor-student relationship. Any dislikes or resentments that Louis may have had for Lestat are now converted into strong feelings of hatred toward "the monster" who forever changed the life of a sweet innocent. These new emotions fester in Louis, yet he remains with Lestat fearing that his despicable master will kill the child if he should ever depart. In Louis's own words, "all this was meant for me, to draw me close [to Lestat] and keep me there [forever]" (*Interview* 97). Paradoxically, Louis experiences an intense psychological isolation from his father while the two share the same quarters, which, as Reep, Ceccio, and Francis state, contributes to a magnification of his already present orphan state. It is fascinating that the more helpless orphan, Claudia, is the one to turn on Lestat when she discovers he made her into a vampire child. Her "slaying of the dragon father" provides the opportunity for her and Louis to break the shackles of their slavery and gain their freedom.

The *Forever Knight* teleseries also focuses on the strained, often-times orphaned relationship the vampire son, Nicolas, shares with his father, LaCroix. Here, however, the emotions expressed by the vampires are much more extreme and at times quite destructive. When LaCroix initiates Nicolas into vampirism, he is pleased that his protégé accepts his gift of immortality. It is a love that binds the two together, so long as Nicolas does not question LaCroix's actions. Over the centuries, though, Nicolas realizes he has taken too many human lives, and the guilt forces him to kill no more (Show Description, *Forever Knight*). In the "Dark Knight" episode, LaCroix is not at all pleased that Nick Knight has become a law enforcer, protecting the very humans that were supposed to be the prey of all vampires. To paraphrase the father's remarks, he gave Nicolas a wonderful type of existence, and the "boy" repaid him with rejection, hostility, and eventual desertion. Rather than continuing to tolerate this embarrassment to his race (and himself), LaCroix decides to kill Nick. He almost succeeds in decapitating Nicolas with a shard of window glass, but right at the critical moment, the vampire son recovers and plunges a fiery stake into his father's chest in an effort to remove this parent from his life forever. The vampire struggle to the death is a reflection of an intense emotional change that has occurred between the mentor and his student. The strong love that initially attracted the two has been converted to an equally powerful hatred that now repels them, to the point where each wants to be rid of the other's presence permanently. What Louis and Lestat can only feel and think about in *Interview* gets acted out with a vengeance by Nicolas and LaCroix in the *Knight* pilot.

As the series progressed, LaCroix developed a major personality change in how he related to Nick, moving from an irrational destroyer to a more concerned, ever-watchful parent (Bloch-Hansen, "Forever" 51). In the episode "Killer Instinct," LaCroix decides to give his rebellious son a second chance, accepting the good as well as the bad within Nicolas. Actor Nigel Bennett indicates a possible reason for this sudden switch: "LaCroix started off by trying to beat it [the reality of Nick's vampiric existence] into him. That clearly failed, so he has resorted to a more persuasive means . . . by sitting back and waiting for him to come to terms, bit by bit [with who he really is]" (Bloch-Hansen "Unlife" 55). This more mellow, less antagonistic approach has added a new dimension to the vampire relationship. Both are able to endure each other's physical presence as well as seek each other out when the need arises. This makes it possible for LaCroix to be an effective advisor, helpmate, and even a loving father to a much more receptive Nick.

Of course, there are still things that infuriate LaCroix, one of which is the desire by Nicolas to search for a cure to his vampiric condition (done up in the fine *Dark Shadows* tradition) (Melton 225, 599). One should recall that Lestat was also repulsed by Louis's desire to be mortal again. In the memorable "Father's Day" episode of *Knight*'s second season, LaCroix reflects on why he is so opposed to Nicolas's pathetic quest. By changing his true image from vampire to human (with the help of friend and pathologist Dr. Natalie Lambert), Nick is rejecting his vampiric lineage. This is an overt slap in LaCroix's face. All fathers, including LaCroix, want their sons to return the love and loyalty they have been given. The attempt by Nicolas to go back to the mortal state is designed to erase this centuries-old familial relationship. Moreover, as depicted in the "Be My Valentine" episode, a new human bonding is beginning to form between Nicolas and his female "therapist-savior," Dr. Lambert (Bloch-Hansen, "Forever" 50; Episode Guide, *Forever Knight*). Naturally, LaCroix tries to sever the connection by planning to make the good doctor into one of his creatures, thereby insuring that Nicolas will return to the vampire fold (similar to Lestat's intentions with Claudia). But, at the last moment, LaCroix stops himself, knowing he cannot force the choice upon Nicolas. The mentor can only hope his student will not succeed in finding a cure and, in time, will return, a prodigal son.

The homoerotic elements of the vampire father-son relationship should not be ignored in either the *Interview* tale or the *Knight* teleseries. Both masters want the protégé to be a loving companion to reduce the loneliness and isolation of their supernatural existence. The aversion that each son shows to this lifestyle does not weaken the father's homosexual tendencies; if anything, it adds further fuel to these desires (Reep, Ceccio, Francis). While the Rice and Parriott vampires cannot engage in human sexuality, they can still entertain such thoughts and do everything up to the point of the physical penetration. The *Knight* series emphasizes the erotic elements to a far greater degree than *The Vampire Chronicles* do, owing, no doubt, to its weekly format, which provides for a more effective (as well as consistent) emotional development of the vampire characters. Still, without the influential works of Anne Rice, there probably would not be a *Forever Knight* show, certainly not one in which the ambivalent mentor-student relationship would occupy such a major place.

The macro-vampiric groups. We must also consider the larger vampiric communities from which these sons and fathers sprang. Many contemporary screen monsters, from the werewolves of *The Howling* series (1981-present) to the zombies of George Romero's *Living Dead* trilogy (1968-1985), are presented as "part of a much larger system of fellow creatures sharing the same curse" (Iaccino 79-80). So too with the vampires of the Rice *Chronicles* and Parriott series.

In *Interview with the Vampire*, Louis intends to seek out others of his kind, even if it means traveling the entire globe. He relates to Lestat,

I know they must exist. . . . And I'm confident I shall find vampires who have more in common with me than I with you. Vampires who understand knowledge as I do and have used their superior vampire nature to learn secrets of which you don't even dream. (*Interview* 81)

As he and Claudia travel throughout eastern Europe, they do discover other vampires, but they are more like mindless corpses wandering the countryside in search of anything to prey upon (including them). It is not until they reach Paris that they chance upon the more sophisticated creatures like themselves. These vampires, under the leadership of Armand, have formed a theatrical group and perform plays on a nightly basis for their human audiences. Each production ends with the slaying of a mortal virgin, thus sating the vampires' continual craving for blood as well as pleasing the attendees who are mesmerized by the realistic special effects (*Interview* 217-28).

Rice's Theatre des Vampires is a fascinating concept because it shows how vampires have adapted to their immortal condition. Using the theatre as a cover, the creatures are able to engage in their blood orgies without arousing the suspicions of their human prey. By combining their intellects, they have developed a very effective system of group survival. At the same time, the vampiric group is able to offer the humans their much needed entertainment, to the point where mortals will keep coming back again and again much to the pleasure of their stalkers.

Forever Knight's contemporary Canadian nightclub, the Raven, is modeled upon the Parisian Theatre des Vampires. Under the management of Janette, it is used by the vampires as a major feeding center much like the theatre. The human patrons are not aware they are being scoped as well as selected by the highly discerning predators; all they are interested in is finding compatible dates for the evening, little realizing they are the next item on the menu. At times, however, the vampires at the club are forced into revealing their true natures to the humans, usually when a major crisis is at hand. In the episode "Curiouser and Curiouser," they have to deal with a gang of hoodlums invading their territory, while in "A More Permanent Hell," they start to panic over the prediction that the entire mortal population will be destroyed in a meteor collision (Episode Guide, *Forever Knight*). Apart from these unusual circumstances, the Raven vampires are able to maintain a low profile, insuring them a continuous food supply for many years to come.

LaCroix provides a valuable service to the vampiric community as well with his nightly radio talk show. Transmitted to thousands of vampire ears, LaCroix's messages offer words of hope and encouragement to his kind. His voice is able to unite the various factions, making them a truly invincible force in the present-day world. There are times, though, when LaCroix communicates feelings of depression and sadness along the airwaves because Nicolas has decided to turn his back on the community (Bloch-Hansen, "Unlife" 56). He wants others to know how much he hurts and hopes that his "son" will hear his cries and return to him. (That Nicolas listens in on the talk show is an indication that LaCroix's dream might become a reality someday.) LaCroix is not afraid that humans might tune in to these rather intimate conversations and even participate in them, as long as they are able to perceive some relevance of the discussions to their constrained lives. While Lestat assumes the contemporary identity of a rock musician instead of a radio host, he also wants his voice to be heard by mortals and immortals alike (*Lestat* 15-17). By assuming such visible positions within society, the vampire fathers are able to grow in power until they are able to exercise their leadership skills in the respective human and vampiric communities.

Conclusion

As we have observed, there are some interesting connections between the *Forever Knight* series and the first novel in Anne Rice's *Vampire Chronicles, Interview with the Vampire*. As the *Knight* teleplays evolved over the course of the series' second season, more similarities have unfolded, especially with respect to the second book in the *Chronicles, The Vampire Lestat*. Both Lacroix and Lestat have now become more likeable, even personable, characters. This was chiefly due to the inclusion of the mentor's point of view, which supplanted the bigoted one each vampire son so tenaciously held. According to Lestat, he "hated him [Louis] for his dishonesty . . . for [all] the lies he told about me. But the love was far greater than the hate . . . [for] he was my companion as no other immortal had ever been" (*Lestat* 16). So too with the spurned LaCroix who will always regard his protégé, Nicolas, with a genuine fondness and deep affection. In the episode "Be My Valentine," LaCroix even finds himself acquiring such human feelings of love and desire when he is introduced to Nicolas's mortal sister, Fleur (Claire Rankin). Though Nick cannot believe the change that has come over LaCroix, the viewer is able to accept it because the perspective had shifted from the prejudicial student's to the more forlorn mentor's. Once Lestat and LaCroix are able to narrate their own accounts, they can attain an almost heroic stature in the eyes of their audience.

One other correlation should be noted. In *Knight*'s "A More Permanent Hell" teleplay, LaCroix's own daughter, Divia (Kathryn Long), places the vampire's curse upon him. While this scene is an inversion of Claudia's vampiric induction, it more closely resembles the parental initiation described in *The Vampire Lestat*. Here we have Lestat turning his dying mother, Gabrielle, into one of the undead (*Lestat* 151-59). This mother-son, Oedipal complex clearly provided the incestuous base for *Knight*'s corresponding father-daughter, Electra syndrome. As *Forever Knight* entered its third (and final) season of episodes, more striking parallels have been observed with the other novels in *The Vampire Chronicles* and they only await the proper analysis. There remains little doubt that the *Knight* show may have given Anne Rice the ultimate tribute as well as provided her with a new generation of fans eager to know more about the vampire mythos.

Works Cited

Bloch-Hansen, Peter. "Forever and a Knight." *Starlog* 212 (Mar. 1995): 50-53.
——. "Unlife to Live." *Starlog* 215 (June 1995): 54-57.
Everson, William K. *Classics of the Horror Film*. New York: Carol, 1990.
——. *More Classics of the Horror Film: Fifty Years of Great Chillers*. New York: Carol, 1990.
Eyles, Allen, Robert Adkinson, and Nicholas Fry, eds. *The House of Horror: The Complete Story of Horror Films*. London: Lorrimer, 1984.
Forever Knight Press Kit. Los Angeles, CA: SSA Public Relations, 1994.
Guiley, Rosemary Ellen. *Vampires Among Us*. New York: Pocket, 1991.
Hopcke, Robert H. *A Guided Tour of the Collected Works of C.G. Jung*. Boston, MA: Shambhala, 1992.
Iaccino, James F. *Psychological Reflections on Cinematic Terror: Jungian Archetypes in Horror Films*. Westport, CT: Praeger, 1994.
Johnson, Kim Howard. "Knight Shift." *Starlog* 214 (May 1995): 78-81.
Jung, Carl G. *The Archetypes and the Collected Unconscious: The Collected Works*. Vol. 9, Part 1. Trans. R.F.C. Hull. Princeton, NJ: Princeton UP, 1990.
——. *Freud and Psychoanalysis: The Collected Works*. Vol. 4. Trans. R.F.C. Hull. Princeton, NJ: Princeton UP, 1990.
Kaminsky, Stuart M., and Jeffrey H. Mahan. *American Television Genres*. Chicago: Nelson-Hall, 1988.
Leigh-Scott, Katherine, ed. *The Dark Shadows Companion: 25th Anniversary Collection*. Los Angeles: Pomegranate, 1990.
McCarty, John. *The Modern Horror Film: 50 Contemporary Classics*. New York: Carol, 1990.
Melton, J. Gordon. *The Vampire Book: The Encyclopedia of the Undead*. Detroit: Visible Ink, 1994.
Pierson, Jim. *Dark Shadows Resurrected*. Los Angeles: Pomegranate, 1992.
Pirie, David. *The Vampire Cinema*. New York: Crescent, 1977.
Preiss, Byron, ed. *The Ultimate Dracula*. New York: Dell, 1991.
Reep, Diana C., Joseph F. Ceccio, and William A. Francis. "Anne Rice's *Interview with the Vampire*: Novel vs. Film." Paper presented at the annual meeting of the Popular Culture Association. Philadelphia, PA, Apr. 1995.
Rice, Anne. *Interview with the Vampire*. 1976. New York: Ballantine, 1993.
——. *The Vampire Lestat*. 1985. New York: Ballantine, 1989.
Skal, David. *Hollywood Gothic: The Tangled Web of "Dracula" from Novel to Stage to Screen*. New York: Norton, 1990.
Stoker, Bram. *Dracula*. New York: Signet, 1992.

Contributors

Ray B. Browne is chairman emeritus of the Popular Culture Department at Bowling Green State University. With Marshall Fishwick, he founded the Popular Culture Association/American Culture Association, the *Journal of Popular Culture*, and the *Journal of American Culture*. He is the author and editor of more than fifty books on various aspects of American and world cultures.

Joseph F. Ceccio earned the Ph.D. in English at the University of Illinois at Urbana-Champaign. Currently he is professor of English at the University of Akron in Ohio. His publications include two textbooks and numerous articles on professional writing and literary topics. He teaches a variety of undergraduate and graduate courses on novels of Anne Rice and Joyce Carol Oates, Shakespeare and his world, legal writing, and writing for MBAs. He has presented papers on Anne Rice's works at the last three annual meetings of the Popular Culture Association.

William A. Francis is professor of English and associate dean of the Buchtel College of Arts and Sciences of the University of Akron. He has published an article on Vance Bourjaily in *Critique* and interviews with Bourjaily in *Names* and the *Literary Review*. His interviews with New Orleans novelists Sheila Bosworth, Nancy Lemann, and Christine Wiltz appear in *The Southern Quarterly*. His article on New Orleans novelist Mollie Davis was published in *Louisiana Literature*.

Gary Hoppenstand is an associate professor teaching in the Department of American Thought and Language at Michigan State University. He has written numerous books and articles on a variety of topics ranging from American literature to popular culture studies. His most recent book, *Clive Barker's Short Stories: Imagination as Metaphor in the Books of Blood and Other Works*, was published by McFarland in 1994. He is currently at work on two projects: an analysis of Sir Arthur Conan Doyle's "Professor Challenger" adventures and a textbook anthology for HarperCollins entitled *Popular Fiction*.

James F. Iaccino, professor in psychology at Benedictine University in Lisle, Illinois, has extensively examined the various movie genres, attempting to relate them to Carl Jung's psychoanalytic theory of archetypes. His first text, *Psychological Reflections on Cinematic Terror* (published by Praeger Press in 1994), has successfully correlated Jung's archetypes with films specifically in the horror genre while his upcoming work, entitled *Jungian Reflections within the Cinema*, relates the images to an even more diverse range of films within the sci-fi and fantasy genres. Jim has recently developed an original, undergraduate course at Benedictine University on the psychology of horror films based on his research, and hopes to eventually use the Jungian model to perform a content analysis of some of the great literary works in horror and science-fiction.

Edward J. Ingebretsen, S.J., associate professor of English at Georgetown University, is the author of many essays on American gothic fantasy; he has written two books of poetry as well as *Robert Frost's Star in a Stoneboat: A Grammar of Belief* (1995) and *Maps of Heaven, Maps of Hell: Religious Terror as Memory from the Puritans to Stephen King* (1996). A member of the National Board for the American Culture Association, Ingebretsen is currently working on "Creating Subjects: Making Monsters"—an examination of the intersection of gothic horror formula in current political representation.

Cynthia Kasee holds degrees in English, sociology, and American Indian studies and is an assistant professor at the University of South Florida in the Interdisciplinary Social Science Program. Her research specialties are Native women, Southeastern tribal ethnology, and the construction of ethnic identity. A member of the National Association of American Indian/Alaska Native Professors and the National Association for Ethnic Studies, she here uses her experience with the process of negotiating ethnic identity to analyze the society of Free People of Color. Her most recent publications include "Identity, Recovery and Religious Imperialism" in *Women and Therapy* and contributions in *Real Human Beings: An Anthology of Contemporary Cherokee Prose.*

Marte Kinlaw is a freelance writer and independent researcher. This piece is part of a longstanding collaboration with Cynthia Kasee, with projects including co-convening a Union Institute seminar, "The Mythic Image," and a descriptive study of Native American images in the Florida tourism industry. From 1990 through 1994, she was involved in the Bay Area Renaissance Festival of Largo as a member of the folk group "Faire Falderal," performing traditional and original songs.

Ann Larabee is an assistant professor in the Department of American Thought and Language at Michigan State University. Her work on technology and culture has appeared in *American Studies, The Canadian Reivew of American Studies*, and *Postmodern Culture*. She is currently at work on a study of social interpretations of twentieth century technological disasters.

Terri R. Liberman is a professor of English at Norwich University in Northfield, Vermont. In the past she has worked in the field of American literature, particularly on Henry James, but her recent interests have been in the field of popular culture. She has presented papers on Braun's Cat Who series, the television show *Roseanne,* the film *Fried Green Tomatoes,* animal rights, and women's studies subjects, as well as three papers on the *Vampire Chronicles* of Anne Rice.

Kathryn McGinley has a B.A. in English from Adelphi University. Born in New York City, where she currently resides, she has worked for publishing houses such as Putnam Berkley and Simon & Schuster and is attending a graduate program in creative writing. An aspiring novelist, she has written reviews, stories, and poetry for university publications and is currently working on her first novel.

Katherine Ramsland holds a Ph.D. in philosophy and a master's in clinical psychology, and teaches philosophy at Rutgers University in New Jersey. She has written ten books, most of which relate to Anne Rice, including a biography, *Prism of the Night.* Her three official guides to Rice's work are *The Vampire Companion, The Witches' Companion,* and *The Roquelaure Reader.* Her forthcoming *The Anne Rice Reader* features articles on all facets of Rice's career. She has also published short fiction and a cookbook and is currently at work on a biography of Dean Koontz.

Diana C. Reep is professor of English at the University of Akron, where she teaches courses in film, American literature, and professional writing. She is the author of two books of literary criticism, *The Rescue and Romance: Popular Novels before World War I* and *Margaret Deland*, as well as numerous articles on such topics as the portrayal of women on television, soap operas, and western films. In addition, she has published a textbook, *Technical Writing: Principles, Strategies, and Readings*, articles on professional writing topics, and a novel. She received her Ph.D. in English at the University of Wisconsin-Milwaukee.

250   Contributors

Bette B. Roberts returned to faculty ranks as professor in the fall of 1995, having completed six years as chair of the English Department at Westfield State College. She teaches composition, British literature, development of the novel, and gothic fiction. Her interest in the gothic goes back to her doctoral work at the University of Massachusetts in Amherst; her dissertation on *The Gothic Romance: Its Appeal to Female Writers and Readers in Late-Eighteenth Century England* was published by Arno Press in 1980. She has written many essays on gothic fiction, and most recently, the book *Anne Rice* for Twayne's United States Authors Series (1994).

Garyn G. Roberts is the author and editor of several books on popular culture. His most recent book, *Dick Tracy and American Culture: Morality and Mythology, Text and Context*, received a 1995 Edgar Award Nomination from the Mystery Writers of America. He received his Ph.D. in 1986 from Bowling Green State University and is a faculty member in the Communications/English Division of Northwestern Michigan College, Traverse City, Michigan.

Frank A. Salamone is professor of anthropology and sociology at Iona College, New Rochelle, N.Y. He has written *Gods and Goods in Africa*, edited *The Yanomami and Their Interpreters, The Fulbright Experience in Nigeria, Art and Culture in Nigeria and the Diaspora*, and other works, including many articles on religion, identity, and music. Fieldwork in Nigeria, Ghana, Kenya, the United Kingdom, and the United States has provided him with material on identity in various settings. The study of popular culture provides an excellent means for understanding the formation and presentation of self and identity.

Aileen Chris Shafer, an associate professor emerita at West Virginia University, has published essays about the works of Anne Tyler, T.S. Eliot, Samuel Clemens, and Walt Whitman in *Studies in Short Fiction, Yeats-Eliot Review, Southern Studies, The Long Islander*, and in *Anne Tyler as Novelist*, edited by Dale Salwak. Additionally, she has published book reviews and miscellaneous articles about topics as diverse as business writing and teacher education.

Ellen M. Tsagaris received her doctorate in English from Southern Illinois University at Carbondale in May 1996. She holds both an M.A. in English and a J.D. from the University of Iowa. She has taught at Southern and various other colleges and universities. Tsagaris has presented papers on Rice at the Annual Virginia Woolf Conference, the University of Missouri Graduate Student's Conference, Columbia, and the American Conference of Irish Studies. She has also published on Rice in *Emerging Perspectives: Selected Papers from the Third Annual Virginia Woolf Conference*. Tsagaris has written numerous fiction and nonfiction pieces for various periodicals and scholarly publications.

Index

253